JORDANS

HOLME MILLS, BIGGLESWADE

Family Cycling
guidebook

Jordans Family Cycling Guidebook

Published by Emap Active Create
Emap Active Ltd
Homenene House
Orton Centre
Peterborough
PE2 5UW

Telephone: 01733 237111; Fax: 01733 288129; Email: active.create@emap.com
© Emap Active Ltd

ISBN 0 9533087 6 6

Emap Active Create
Publisher: Phil Broughton
Editor-in-chief: Rob Carter
Routes editor: Nick Cotton
Creative editors: Keely Docherty-Lee, Sarah Flitcroft
Illustrator: Steve Hall
Research: Samantha Moon
Contributors: (words) Nicky Crowther, Nick Harper, Emma Kendell, Lindsey Smith (Sustrans);
(design) Phil Long, Richard Browne, Ed Knowles

Jordans Cereals Ltd
Ed Olphin
Gordon Harrison
Emily Turner

Ordnance Survey
John Richardson
Jean Dalton
Rhian French

Jersey Tourism
Donna Le Marrec

Printed by TPL Printers Ltd (Worcester)
Colour origination by G&E 2000

Cover photograph © Phil Broughton   First Edition UK £9.99

Chris Juden

Contents

Introduction

If you love the open air, there are few things better for the whole family to enjoy than a day's cycling. It's easy for even the smallest legs, you can ride for as long as you want and go wherever you please.

On the other hand, there is nothing worse than finding out too late that your route is beyond your child or you are miles from the nearest toilets or shelter when nature calls or the heavens open.

So welcome to the Jordans Family Cycling Guidebook. It's everything you need for a trouble-free day out for you, your children and your bikes. Inside you will find details of more than 260 family-friendly bike trips throughout the British Isles.

The Jordans Family Cycling Guidebook focuses on the questions every sensible parent asks when planning a day out. Many of the routes are easy and traffic-free. And, because most of these are along purpose-built cycle paths, you don't need to be an ace map reader to enjoy them. They are picturesque and enjoyable too, giving you the chance to appreciate the beauty and value of nature along the way.

The book also includes details of child-friendly pubs and cafes, plus the brightest family attractions nearby, such as castles, zoos and playgrounds, for when bad weather strikes or if you want to combine riding and visiting for a full day away. Many entries also carry details of the

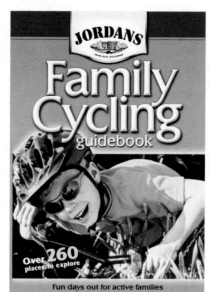

Fun days out for active families

nearest bike hire shops. So if you are not a regular cycling family or you need extra wheels for a friend, you can still enjoy a day's riding.

And just in case you really are a novice (or you need a refresher course in cycling basics) we have even included a section on bike care and cycling essentials. In fact, all YOU need to do is choose where you want to start riding. Everything else is taken care of.

About the trails in this book

Many of the trails in this guide are broad, flat and traffic-free with a relatively smooth surface of stone or gravel, suitable for all ages and for occasional and fair-weather cyclists. Typically these might be there-and-back rides on railway paths. They provide an

enjoyable day out and many novices will be very pleasantly surprised by how far they can go – easily three times the distance you might think of for a walk.

The suggested age limit for any given ride will increase with the inclusion of hills or rougher surfaces and on those rides where traffic may be encountered. Canal towpaths are given a higher suggested age limit as children will need better control of their bikes with the presence of water to one side.

The hardest trails included in this guide are those with the steepest hills and surfaces NOT made of stone and gravel, ie some of the long distance bridleways such as the South Downs Way or some of the tougher forestry rides in Wales or Scotland. These sort of trails become even more difficult to ride in the winter when the surface will become muddy. Even the flattest trail will seem difficult if you are cycling into a strong wind – so choose your days carefully!

So... if you are not sure how fit you are or how far the kids will go, start with an easy trail on fine summer days and gradually build up to tougher challenges. Never be afraid to turn around when you think the family has had enough. It is far better to have children (and novice cyclists) keen to try out another ride than to exhaust them and put them off cycling with something beyond their abilities.

How to use the book

The Jordans symbols

To help you decide whether a route is suitable for your family, each one has been given a Jordans Age Rating. For more details on matching your ride to your family's ability turn to page 20, but as a general guide the ratings work as follows:

JORDANS ALL AGES

Kids learn to cycle between four and six years old. When they start riding their own bikes, initially they will go on very short trips where the most important concern for parents is the presence of any traffic. Most routes in this category identify this and are either traffic-free or extremely quiet.

JORDANS OVER 8s

By eight years old children will be a bit stronger and a bit more experienced. Routes in this category feature gentle hills, slightly rougher surfaces and the odd road crossing or short section on quiet roads.

JORDANS OVER 12s

The remaining routes include busier roads and tough mountain bike trails as well high-distance paths.

The Ordnance Survey symbols

To help you find the routes, each entry comes with references for maps in the Ordnance Survey Landranger series. For many of the city rides it is also worth using the relevant street atlas or, better still, getting hold of a cyclists' city map. See the individual entries for details.

JORDANS FAMILY CYCLING GUIDEBOOK

Scotland

207 BORDERS FOREST TRAILS IN THE TWEED VALLEY

Why should you go?
For peace and pinewoods in the glorious Borders country, including a route which runs around the lovely River Tweed.

Where are they?
East of Peebles. Contact Peebles Tourist Information Centre (01721 720138) for details.

Where can you ride?
On one or more of the following signposted trails in the forests of Glentress, Cardrona, Elibank and Traquair.

JORDANS OVER 8s
The Anderson trail
This lies in Glentress Forest. Start at Falla Brae car park, off the A72 east of Peebles, and follow the red signs. At three miles long, the trail is suitable for fit kids.

JORDANS OVER 12s
The Highlandshiels and Wallace's Hill trails
Lying in Cardrona Forest the Highlandshiels trail is an easy five-mile route that can be picked up at Kirkburn car park, off the B7602, southeast of Peebles. Follow the red signs. The green-signposted Wallace's Hill trail is three miles longer and slightly more arduous. It's best for stronger children.

JORDANS OVER 8s
The Touring and Cheesewell trails
Find them in the Elibank and Traquair forests. The 12-mile Touring trail (yellow signs) begins at the Plora Entrance car

park, off the minor road parallel with the A72, east of Innerleithen. From the same starting point pick up the nine-mile Cheesewell trail (green signs) for stronger children.

What else can you do?
The main towns nearby are Peebles and Innerleithen. The main local places of interest are the romantic Traquair House (near Innerleithen, 01896 830323), and Melrose Abbey, a uniquely elegant 14th-century ruin off the A7 (01896 822562).

Where can you eat?
If you're looking for a family-friendly pub, the Traquair Arms at Innerleithen has a garden, children's menu and brewhouse (01896 830229).

OS *Landranger Map 73*

208 Airdrie to Bathgate rail trail

JORDANS ALL AGES

Why should you go?
For gentle pedalling along an old railway line. Good train connections allow a choice of ways to complete the trip.

Where is it?
Between Airdrie and Bathgate. Start at Craigneuk on Airdrie's eastern edge, off the A89 east of the junction with the A73. Or at Whiteside, southwest of Bathgate, off the B7002. Both Airdrie and Bathgate have stations, but they are on unconnected lines.

Where can you ride?
For 14 miles between, from the west, Airdrie, Caldercruix, Blackridge (south of Armadale) and Bathgate. A map with details of the Clyde-Forth route (NCN75) is available from Sustrans (0117 9290888).

What else can you do?
There are a number of historic sights worth visiting dotted around the route, including the Summerlee Heritage Centre (at Coatbridge), the Weavers Cottages Museum (Airdrie) and the Bennie Museum (Bathgate).

Where can you eat?
Although there's plenty of choice in the towns en route, it's wise to pack your own snacks as there are no services for the eight

miles between Caldercruix and Armadale.

OS *Landranger Map 64, 65*

209 Dalkeith and Penicuik rail trail

JORDANS ALL AGES

Why should you go?
For the enjoyment of following an easy path through wooded embankments and beside the rushing North Esk River.

Where is it?
South of Edinburgh. Start at Eskbank Post Office in Lasswade Road on the southwest edge of Dalkeith (off the A768/A6094 roundabout), or in Penicuik on

the southeast edge at the octagonal church on the junction of the A701/B6372. The nearest train station is Musselburgh (three miles north).

Where can you ride?
For eight miles, starting in the northeast, between Eskbank (on the southwest edge of Dalkeith), Bonnyrigg and Lasswade, south of Roslin and Penicuik. The NCN1 connects at Dalkeith. A cycling map of Midlothian is available from SPOKES (0131 3132114), a map with details of NCN1 can be obtained from Sustrans (0117 9290888).

What else can you do?
In Penicuik you'll find the sparkly Edinburgh Crystal Centre, offering a factory tour and a film

history (01968 675128).

Where can you eat?
Dalkeith and Penicuik offer a number of good options.

OS *Landranger Map 66*

210 Loch Katrine lakeside ride

JORDANS ALL AGES

Why should you go?
To sample a wonderful journey along the north and south banks of Loch Katrine (above).

Where is it?
In the Trossachs, north of Glasgow. Park at the Trossachs Pier car park, at the eastern end of Loch Katrine, at the end of the

A821 west of Callander and north of Aberfoyle, 30 miles north of Glasgow.

Where can you ride?
For ten miles around the loch. All but the southeastern end of the loch is open to biking and there's a pier complex at the eastern end for parking and refreshments. The ride can be extended between the southern shore and Loch Lomond on a minor road which runs past Stronachlachar (20 miles return), which is where you'll find the Inversnaid Hotel.

What else can you do?
See the SS Sir Walter Scott on the loch, stop off at the Trossachs Discovery Centre (four miles south at Aberfoyle), or visit Dunaverig Farmlife Centre, ten

170

171

The UK by region

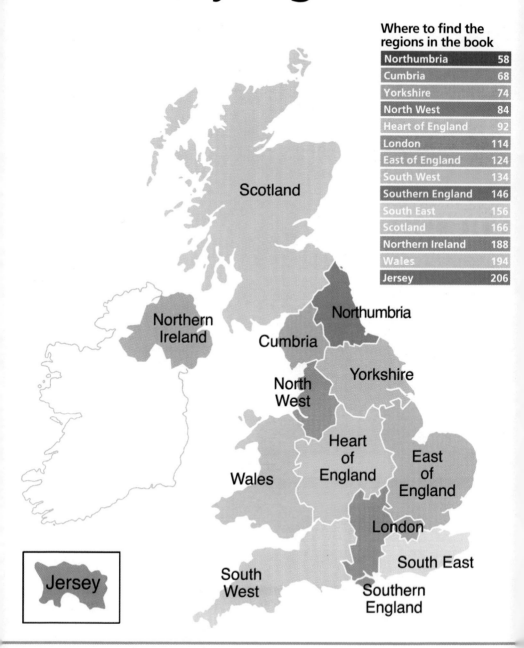

Scotland

Northern Ireland

Northumbria

Cumbria

Yorkshire

North West

Heart of England

Wales

East of England

London

South East

South West

Southern England

Jersey

A welcome from Bill Jordan

I have a confession to make. I love cycling. It's a great form of exercise and a superb way to see the best of the British countryside. So it's both a pleasure and an indulgence to introduce this book to you.

Cycling is a terrific way for families to get fit and healthy and for them to enjoy something together, but a group of mates together out for some fun exercise and a day in the country will also get a lot out of this guide.

It's not for racing cyclists, ardent club members, off-roaders or other extreme sports types. It is a genuine guidebook meant to get dog-eared and tatty from frequent use by ordinary people who like to bike.

It's based on recognised cycle paths and routes. Each of the more than 260 cycling days out is graded for suitability for children. It includes attractions along the way for adults and kids and suggests places to eat, drink and relax during and after your ride.

The maps are easy to follow and include Ordnance Survey map references for those more expert map readers amongst you. Use the Guide and before you leave home you will have a clear and informative description of the kind

of day you're going to enjoy.
If you haven't cycled for a few years, check out the 'Before you go' section on page 18. It'll make sure you're fully equipped before you make a start.

At Jordans we've always believed in the idea of wholesome, great-tasting natural food grown in a way that protects the countryside for both man and beast. That's why it seems to me there's a natural affinity for us with a healthy, outdoor leisure pursuit like cycling. And, as I confessed earlier, it's something I enjoy myself!

So choose your day out, pack your rucksacks and get pedalling.

Bill Jordan

The National Cycle Network routes open 2002

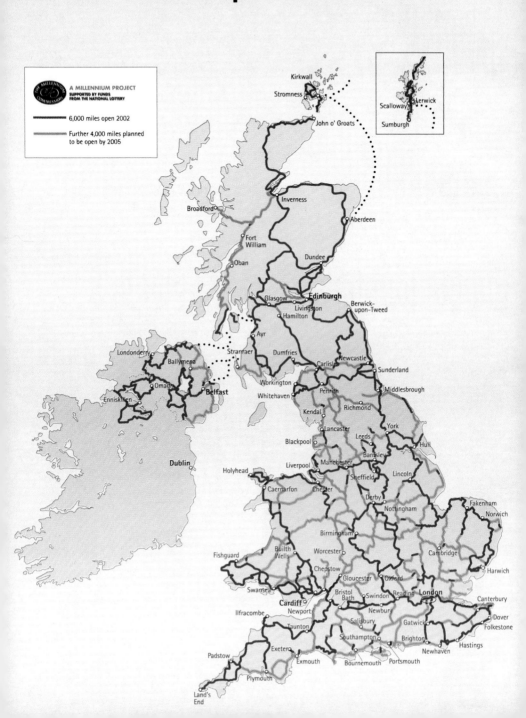

Sustrans & The National Cycle Network

There are more than 6,000 miles of safe cycling out there. What are you waiting for?

Many of the routes described in this book form part of the UK's National Cycle Network. The Network is a fantastic resource, offering over 6,000 miles of cycle routes running throughout all parts of the country. Around one-third of the Network is on traffic-free paths, such as disused railways, canal towpaths and forest trails, making it perfect for parents with young children. It's expanding all the time, too, with plans for 10,000 miles to be open by 2005.

The National Cycle Network began with the construction by engineering charity Sustrans of the Bristol-Bath Railway Path 20 years ago. Now there are traffic-free paths in every area of the country, from the Camel Trail in Cornwall to the Airdrie & Bathgate Railway Path between Glasgow and Edinburgh, and right across to the Lagan Valley Regional Park between Lisburn and Belfast.

Other parts of the network use quiet roads and traffic-calmed streets in towns and cities. These link the traffic-free sections and allow the Network to run right through urban areas and into the countryside, offering a safer and more enjoyable way to get to the shops, school or work, to visit friends or to simply get out for a ride.

All open NCN routes are numbered and signed, making them easy to follow. You may have already seen the distinctive red route number patch with a bicycle on blue road signs near you.

If you're after a little more adventure, longer sections of the network are shown on an award-winning series of route maps and make a great choice for a short break or holiday with older children. These range from the relatively easy Hull-Harwich route that travels through Lincolnshire, Norfolk and Suffolk, through the gentle hills of the Kingfisher Trail in Northern Ireland to the world-famous and challenging C2C (Sea to Sea) route through the Lake District and over the Pennines.

The National Cycle Network is co-ordinated by Sustrans, and involves hundreds of organisations, such as local authorities, businesses, landowners and environmental bodies.

As well as the National Cycle Network, Sustrans works on many other projects to encourage people to walk, cycle and use public transport more. These include creating safe routes to schools, train stations and home zones (residential areas where people have priority over cars), and developing more integrated transport systems.

■ **Visit www.nationalcyclenetwork.org.uk or call 0117 9290888 for more information about the NCN and the work of Sustrans. The website also offers free detailed on-line mapping of all the open routes that you can download, plus a wide range of maps, books and guides to buy.**

A-Z of rides

The quick-reference A-Z of rides saves you time – so you can spend longer on your bike.

Rides by age groups

Making sure you select the right route for your kids, every ride is listed by age suitability.

JORDANS
ALL AGES

Afan Argoed countryside centre **200**
Airdrie to Bathgate rail trail **170**
Alice Holt Forest **158**
Anglers Country Park & Haw Park woodland trails **78**
Ashby Woulds Moira rail trail **103**
Aviemore to Boat of Garten **186**
Ayot Greenway rail trail **132**
Bangor-Tregarth rail trail (Lôn Las Ogwen or Lôn Bach) **203**
Barmouth to Dolgellau rail trail **202**
Belhus Woods forest park trails **126**
Biddulph Valley rail trail **112**
Black Park Country Park trails **155**
Brampton Valley Way **105**
Brandon & Bishop Auckland Walk rail trail **63**
Bristol & Bath railway path **142**
Caernarfon to Bryncir rail trail (Lôn Eifion) **203**
Caernarfon to Y Felinheli rail trail (Lôn Las Menai) **203**
Callander and Brig o'Turk – via Loch Venachar **172**
Callander to Balquhidder rail trail **172**
Carsington Water reservoir circuit **107**
Castle Archdale Country Park **192**
Castle Eden Walkway rail trail **63**
Castleman rail trail **155**
Centurion Way rail trail **161**
Cheshire Lines rail trail **89**
Chippenham & Calne rail trail **145**
Churnet Valley rail trail **104**
Clumber Park **109**
Colwyn Bay to Prestatyn bike path **205**
Cowes to Newport cycleway **153**
Cudmore Grove country park tracks **126**
Dalkeith and Penicuik rail trail **170**
Deerness Valley Walk rail trail **64**
Denham Country Park trails **148**
Derby to Elvaston Castle Country Park **106**
Derby to Worthington trail **106**
Downs Link rail trail **158**
Ebury Way rail trail **120**
Edgbaston reservoir circuit **99**
Elan Valley rail trail **119**
Flitch Way rail trail **129**

Forest trails in north Scotland **181**
Forest trails in northeast Scotland **178**
Forest Way rail trail **160**
Formartine & Buchan Way rail trail **173**
Foss Island nature park trail **79**
Foyle Valley cycleway **192**
Friston Forest **163**
Glasgow to Loch Lomond **168**
Grizedale Forest trails **70**
Hadleigh Castle country park **127**
Harland Way rail trail **79**
Hatfield Forest trails **133**

Holsworthy Corkscrew **136**
Hudson Way rail trail **80**
Hull to Hornsea rail trail **82**
Hull to Patrington rail trail **81**
Ilfracombe rail trail **136**
Johnstone to Greenock rail trail **168**
Johnstone to Kilbirnie rail trail **168**
Keswick rail trail **72**
Kingswinford rail trail **97**
Lanchester Valley Walk rail trail **64**
Langdon Hills country park tracks **128**
Lisburn to Whiteabbey **190**

Tynemouth to Blyth coastal route 61
Valley Walk rail trail 129
Warrington & Altrincham towpath & rail trail 88
Weald country park 128
Weavers Way rail trail 131
West of Scotland forest trails, Highlands and Argyle & Bute 184
Whitehaven to Rowrah rail trail 73
Windsor Great Park estate roads 148
Worsbrough reservoir circuit 76
Worth Way rail trail 160
Yarmouth to Freshwater cycleway 154
York to Selby rail trail 79
York to Beningbrough cycle trail 80

JORDANS
OVER 8s

Abbeyford Woods 140
Aire & Calder Navigation 78
Alton Water circuit 129
Argyll Forest Park trails, Cowal Peninsula 187
Ashby Canal towpath 102
Ashridge Forest 150
Ashton canal 90
Auckland Way rail trail 61
Ballypatrick Forest Park circuit 190
Basingstoke Canal 152
Bedgebury Forest 165
Bewl Water 104
Birmingham & Fazeley canal 99
Birmingham Mainline Canal towpath 98
Bolam Lake Country Park circuit 60
Borders forest trails in Craik Forest 182
Borders forest trails in the Tweed Valley 170
Brechfa Forest trails 202
Bridgwater & Taunton Canal 142
Bristol-Pill riverside path 142
Cannock Chase forest trails 102
Cardinham Woods 138
Coed Y Brenin forest trails 203
Cowpen Bewley Woodland country park trail 62
Cwm Darran country park 198
Delamere Forest trails 87
Eggesford Forest 140
Epping Forest 119
Forest trails in northeast Scotland 178
Five Pits rail trail circuit 109
Forest of Dean family trail 96
Forth & Clyde Canal 176
Forth Road Bridge 176
Garwnant Forest trials 201
Gisburn Forest trails 91
Grafham Water 132
Grand Union Canal towpath 120
Grand Western Canal 141

Great Glen forest trails 177
Guisborough forest trail 83
Gwydyr Forest trails 204
Haddington to Longniddry rail trail 180
Hainault Forest country park 128
Hampstead Heath 121
Hamsterley Forest trails 64
Hyde Park and Buckingham Palace 116
Kennet & Avon Canal 143
Kielder Forest trails & trailquest 61
Langley Park Country Park 155
Leeds & Liverpool canal, Aire Valley 78
Leicester Great Central Way 104
Longdendale rail trail 113
Marriotts Way rail trail 131
Middlewood Way rail trail 90
Neath Canal towpath 200
Newport to Crosskeys canal 196
Newport to Pontypool canal towpath 196
Newry to Portadown canal towpath 192
Oakwell Hall Country Park 77
Ogmore Valley rail trail 199
Pendle towpath cycleway 91
Queen Elizabeth country park forest trails 150
Queen Elizabeth Forest Park trails 173
Rathlin Island 239
Rea Valley riverside & towpath 99
Sandwell Valley country park trail 96
Seaton Carew to Hartlepool coastal trail 62
Sherwood Pines forest trail 108
Shropshire woodland trails 81
Slough Arm of Grand Union Canal 148
Southwest forest trails of Galloway Forest Park 174
Sutton Park country park trails 102
Swansea canal towpath 201
Tame Valley rail trail 91
Tatton Park estate roads 88
Thames Towpath: Putney to Weybridge 122
The Dyke rail trail 163
The Lee Valley 118
The New Forest 154
The Nicky Line rail trail 133
The South Manchester Mersey river path 90
The Thames through Docklands 116
The Water of Leith and Union Canal path 180
Thetford Forest open tracks 130
Tyneside cycleways, north and south bank 66
Union Canal 180
Upper Derwent Valley reservoirs 112
Walsall canal towpath 98

West Walk Forest trail 153
Whitegate Way rail trail 86
Wimbledon Common 122
Worcester bike paths 96

JORDANS
OVER 12s

Aston Hill Woods trail 150
Barnes, Richmond Park & Mortlake 117
Bellever Forest 139
Blengdale forest roads 70
Borders forest trails in the Tweed Valley 170
Broughton Moor forest roads 72
Consett & Sunderland rail trail 65
Cotswold Water Park 94
Cragside country park carriage drive 60
Dalby Forest trails 82
Derwent Valley Walk rail trail 66
Ennerdale forest roads 70
Forest trails in north Scotland 181
Forest trails in northeast Scotland 178
Fulbourn Roman Road track 131
Gatehouse to Glen Trool forest route in Galloway Forest Park 182
Giant's Causeway 190
Gloucester & Sharpness canal towpath 94
Great Glen forest trails 177
Hopton mountain bike trail 100
Houghton Forest 161
Middlesbrough to Stockton (& country) 62
Miterdale forest roads 71
North Downs Way 160
Oxford Canal 151
Princetown rail trail 139
Rhondda Community Forest trail 199
Ridgeway & Icknield Way 151
Sneaton Forest trail 83
South Shields and Sunderland coastal route 67
Southwest forest trails of Galloway Forest Park 174
Suffolk Coastal road tour 130
The Isle of Dogs 117
The Quantock Hills mountain bike trails 141
The South Downs Way 162
The Speyside Way 183
The Three Forests Trail 130
The Waterlink Way 123
Waskerley Way rail trail 66
Wayfarer's Walk southerly section 152
Wayfarer's Walk westerly section 151
West of Scotland forest trails, Highlands and Argyle & Bute 184
Wey Navigation 159
Whinlatter Forest Park circuits 72

Stockfile (2)

Why should we cycle?

Despite what our instincts sometimes tell us, humans were not designed to be inactive. In other words, if you want to maintain a fit and healthy body, the basic rule is 'use it or lose it' (or in the case of excess pounds, gain it!). In fact, taking regular exercise has been scientifically proven to help cut stress and high blood pressure, reduce the risk of suffering cardiovascular disease and strokes, and make weight (or body fat) control far easier.

And you don't need to be an aspiring Olympic athlete to feel the benefits. The Health Education Authority's current minimum exercise recommendation for adults is 30 minutes of moderate exercise five times a week. A leisurely cycle fits the bill perfectly.

The body's immediate response to regular exercise includes a rise in both your heart rate and breathing rate, an increase in body temperature and increased muscular activity, as well as a heightened sense of wellbeing.

More important, however, are the longer-term changes brought about by the body adapting to repeated exercise, most notably its ability to burn off fat. For an average-weight man, an energetic mountain bike ride burns off a whopping 581 calories per hour, more than the same time spent swimming. Even less strenuous leisure cycling with the family is sufficient to burn off 413 calories per hour, which is more than an hour's golf and twice as much as the same time spent ironing. The choice is yours, but surely those creased shirts can wait a while?

What happens to my bo

When you exercise, your muscles need more oxygen in order to convert their fat and carbohydrate stores into usable energy. As you get fitter your cardiovascular system (CV) – your heart, lungs and blood – improves its ability to deliver oxygen to the working muscles. At the same time your muscles adapt and become more efficient in their use of the oxygen, which means not only do you burn off fat but your body gets tired less quickly. In essence, the more you cycle the more your body is able to keep going. Which is good news whatever you are doing. Here's what will happen throughout your body if you do cycle regularly:

• YOUR MUSCLES Your muscles become more efficient at generating energy and combating tiredness, so they can keep working for longer periods of time. This happens in a number of ways:
(1) They can tolerate greater levels of lactic acid, the substance which causes that tying up feeling in your muscles;
(2) They can store more carbohydrates (as glycogen, the muscle fuel);
(3) They increase the necessary internal substances which enables them to work harder and longer before tiring.

• YOUR BLOOD AND VEINS Exercising muscles demand more oxygen and nutrients to be delivered to them. To do this, your blood flow increases and more capillaries develop in the muscles. In addition, there's a greater opening of existing capillaries and more effective blood distribution. What's more, your resting blood pressure also decreases.

• YOUR WEIGHT To fuel your activities your body burns more calories. This results in a reduction of both your weight and the amount of actual fat in your body.

ly if I ride regularly?

• YOUR BRAIN Exercise causes the release of endorphins (natural painkillers) in the brain. This is why after exercising you feel great, almost as if you are on a high. This helps to combat the effects of stress.

• YOUR LUNGS Frequent cycling develops the body's ability to take in oxygen and then deliver it to the exercising muscles, which means you can do any strenuous work for longer periods of time.

• YOUR HEART The heart is a type of muscle, and it develops in response to exercise in a similar way to the rest of the muscles in your body. To provide for the demand for greater blood flow around the body the following happens: (1) The heart gets bigger and stronger; (2) It becomes more efficient and can pump more blood with each beat; (3) Consequently your heart-rate decreases, both while resting and exercising.

• YOUR BONES Exercise – especially when it involves impact – increases both bone and muscle density. This means there is less risk of you developing brittle bone disease.

What kind of cycling is best for fitness?

If you're serious about using cycling to get fit, think carefully about the kind of cycling you are doing. To avoid becoming incredibly bored, as well as reducing the risk of injury, you need to add variety to your routine. This is because different types of cycling have different effects. For example:

Long, slow rides are best for building your endurance or cardiovascular fitness.

Short, fast rides improve your body's ability to exercise harder for shorter periods of time. In addition, during longer outings, you'll be able to cope better with short bursts of faster riding. This is because your muscles' ability to deal with lactic acid (a by-product of hard, fast exercise) is improving. Think how your legs burn and tire if you run up stairs – that's caused by the build up of lactic acid.

Riding hard up short hills develops your leg strength and power, and also, to a lesser degree, your upper-body strength.

Riding fast downhill off-road develops your upper-body strength, coordination, balance and bike-handling skills.

Mixing hard and easy rides gives your body time to recover. That's crucial as it's during the post-exercise recovery period that your body adapts and becomes fitter.

What about kids?

Kids can benefit just as much as parents. Cycling puts less stress on growing bones and joints than most exercises, plus it helps develop motor control skills and fitness.

A perfect day out

To guarantee a perfect day out, be sure you know the distances your children can cope with and which routes best match their ability.

How to work out the distance your child can manage

It is far better to underestimate a child's strength and stamina than to overestimate it. Their energy levels can evaporate in a minute once they've reached their limits, and you can always come back another day and ride further. Children's bikes tend to be heavy and quite unwieldy – adults would probably not accept such heavy pieces of equipment. But many children will struggle on gainfully. Tap this doggedness, and nurture it.

To guarantee more time having fun together, below is a rough guide to comfortable distances for bike rides. Though distances can vary enormously depending on the surface and gradient, fitness, wind, load, type of bike and willpower, the following distances – which refer to a there-and-back journey on a flat railway path – offer a pretty useful guideline...

- CHILD IN A BIKE SEAT ON YOUR BIKE: Up to 20 miles
- CHILD ON A PEDALLING TOY: Up to 1 mile
- TRAILER: Up to 15 miles
- TAG-ALONG (THEY PEDAL HITCHED ON TO YOUR REAR): Up to 20 miles
- CHILD RIDING THEIR OWN BIKE: 3-5yrs: up to 3 miles; 5-8yrs: up to 8 miles; 8-12yrs: up to 15 miles; over 12yrs: up to 20 miles

©Sustrans

Understanding th

JORDANS ALL AGES

These routes are suitable for all ages, though when cycling with younger children (any child under eight years old), it's vital that you take several factors into consideration:

- BABIES AND TODDLERS

Lucky them, it's you who does the work. Pop your poppet in the bike seat or in a trailer, and get hauling. The extra weight restricts the distance you can ride – it's best to not go over 20 miles. Allow for their nodding off in babyseats, and expect a thump on the back as their head falls forward. Better babyseats can be set to recline.

Some people question the value of babyseats, as the child has little to do, and is exposed to the elements. In cold weather, certainly, wrap them up well.

age categories in the book

• THREE- TO FIVE-YEAR-OLDS
Start on short rides, or sections of longer rides, no more than three miles long. With all the things to see along the way, that will still take some time. Rail trails are good at this age, because they are flat and surfaced yet traffic-free and give you a travelling feel. With children on pedalling toys, however, one mile is usually as far as you should ride.

• FIVE- TO EIGHT-YEAR-OLDS
Their strength and balance is improving, and they should, after getting used to a bike in the back garden, be able to cope with rides up to eight miles long, increasing as they become stronger or just more adventurous. Always pay close attention to them near water, such as on canal towpaths.

JORDANS OVER 8s
Depending on the child, it's normally fine to tackle rides up to 15 miles long. If they are starting off cycling, go only a little way at first, try to ride most weekends, and after three months they should be able to cope with an afternoon on the bike. You may be surprised by their enthusiasm and potential – and even have trouble keeping up with them.

This is a good time to encourage girls to ride, as a fun way to keep active throughout their teens. Both girls and boys who get the bug might want to join a cycle racing club and go training – in which case they'll soon leave you behind. The Cyclists' Touring Club (0870 8730060) and the British Cycling Federation (0870 8712000) can give you contacts for your local group.

JORDANS OVER 12s
Teenagers who don't cycle much should still enjoy easy rides around five miles long. Strong teenagers, with some miles already in their legs, could tackle longer rides – as far as 20 miles in all – and maybe the rougher ten-to-15-mile forestry circuits, such as are found in the Scottish forest parks.

One of the issues for this age group is that their bikes are full size but they are not yet at full-strength. Be patient if they get gripey, and make allowances for the extra work they are having to put in. Again, encourage girls to cycle as an exciting way to get out and get fit. Exercise in teenage girls has been proven to reduce the risks of contracting osteoporosis by strengthening the bone structure.

• *Fast-growing plants can reduce a path's width by half in summer.*

• *Children will love the difference mud makes in the winter months.*

Four seasons on one trail

Let your kids experience Mother Nature's many faces.

One of the most fascinating aspects of getting to know a trail is watching the changes it undergoes with the seasons. This offers a simple and wonderful way of introducing children to the cycle of nature, as the hedgerows transform from dank and lifeless to colourful and busy – and then change back again.

If you are close to a piece of easy track, a canal or rail trail for example, which you can reach easily, try riding it with the children four times over the course of a year. The familiar A-to-B route won't change, but the atmosphere and the weather certainly will.

Winter's chill and frost-tinged twigs are replaced by spring's emerald buds and first flowers. Summer's warmth brings out the blooms and an assault by briars and insects. Come autumn's cooling temperatures, the leaves turn copper and yellow, and are dumped in piles made for speeding through, legs out wide, yelling as you go. Why, a child may wonder, must I wear gloves and a coat to cycle now, when before I was in shorts and a T-shirt?

The surface also alters drastically with the weather, often causing you to ride a different line from week to week. Children will splash through puddles and wobble through mud after wet weather. After a dry spell, likely in summer though still feasible in winter, they'll adapt to the hardness and higher speed of the track, when the puddles disappear like they never existed. Following a drought, they may taste dust kicked up by tyres, and jump as insects vroom past their ears. Nettles and brambles go mad in July with a painful effect on bare legs. They can reduce the width of a trail by half, before receding in September and October when the edges of the paths are again revealed, and you can once more choose your line.

The outdoors is like a theme park that never closes. By riding all year round, your children will be able to see, smell and feel every season, learning quickly that nature never sleeps for long.

The rules of riding

ON SHARED PATHS...
- Bear in mind that bikers yield to horses and walkers (while walkers yield to horses). Allow plenty of space to pass and be prepared to stop completely. Take extra care at junctions, bends and entrances.
- When overtaking walkers or horse riders heading in the same direction as you, call out to them or ring your bell before passing slowly. As many people are hard of hearing or visually impaired, never assume they can see or hear you. Horses may be surprised by your presence, so always check with the rider before passing.
- Use the well-worn pieces of path, and try to avoid bumping up the edges or making new tracks. This is more important on slopes, where rainwater can create a regular drainage channel out of a few tyre marks and alter the terrain.
- To avoid damaging the paths, ensure kids only ever skid on tarmac and gravelled surfaces.
- Dogs love to run alongside bikes, as they match their pace better than humans. Watch them closely, though, as they have little understanding of the line you're about to take.

ON ROADS...
- Follow the Highway Code at all times.
- As most accidents to cyclists happen at junctions, fit lights and wear conspicuous clothing and a helmet for extra safety.
- Never cycle on pavements, unless designated, and even then, use your bike bell to alert pedestrians of your presence.

IN THE COUNTRYSIDE...
- Follow the Country Code by respecting other land management activities such as farming or forestry, keeping erosion to a minimum and taking litter home.
- If cycling off-road and in remote areas, be self-sufficient by carrying food, a repair kit, map and waterproofs.
- Always cycle within your capabilities and match your speed to the surface and your skills.

How can we find the right bikes for us?

Any time spent on the wrong sized bike can be a painful experience. And never listen to anyone who says you'll eventually get used to an uncomfortable riding position. Believe us, you won't. Getting the right size frame is your first priority. Once that's right, concentrate on each of the points of contact between you and the bike, in other words, the saddle, the pedals and the handlebars.

• SADDLE HEIGHT Riding with your saddle too high or too low will cause knee pain and make you tire quickly. For both children and adults, ideally the saddle should be set so when your foot is flat on the bottom pedal, your leg is almost fully stretched. If the saddle is too low, it's like walking with your leg permanently bent. Too high and it's like walking on permanent tiptoes. Children often feel happier with a lower saddle. As soon as their confidence improves, be sure to raise it to the right height.

• ADJUSTING THE SADDLE Most people find the saddle most comfortable if it's level and central. To adjust it you will need an Allen key. To alter the angle or the height undo the bolt under the saddle until you can tilt the saddle back and forth and slide it up and down the saddle post. As a starting point, set the saddle so that the top is level and the seatpost clamps the middle of the rails.

• THE FRAME Follow this simple test. Stand aside your bike, with your feet flat on the floor. Take hold of the saddle with one hand and the middle of the bars with the other. You should be able to lift the frame 6cm before it touches your groin.

• THE SIZE If you can, find a saddle size that suits by following these guidelines. A wider saddle is better for shorter journeys and more upright positions. For a flatter riding position where your weight is supported more evenly between bars, pedal and saddle, choose a slimmer saddle – over longer journeys, a bulky saddle will chafe. There are lots of good quality women's saddles around – manufacturers have realised that women *do* ride bikes, and are a different shape!

• THE PEDALS If you are fortunate to be able to choose particular pedals and have clipless pedals, the cleats should be positioned so the centre of the pedal is fixed directly under the ball of the foot. This allows the toes to relax, while transferring power from your legs. Relaxed toes allow the blood to circulate better.

• THE BARS The handlebars can make a huge difference to your riding position. Where they sit will also affect your back. The bars need to be positioned so you can support a proportion of your weight on them without causing discomfort. If you find yourself having to stretch to reach them, they are either too far away or too low.

Do I need to adjust my child's brakes?

The brakes on many children's bikes are hard to operate with small hands. If they feature an adult hand span to the lever (many do!), they can be very difficult to reach, never mind use safely. If your child can only reach with the tips or first joints of the fingers, or struggles to pull the lever towards the handlebars, you should take the following action…

1) The bike may already be fitted with adjustable brake levers, though that's unlikely on cheaper models. If there's no screw to adjust the lever, buy an adjustable set – normally about £5 from bike shops.
2) Adjust the screw so that children can reach two joints of their fingers over the brakes while their hands still grip the handlebars normally.

3) Many children rely solely on the front brake, which is dangerous. As a test, use your third and little fingers only to pull on the back brake. If you have to use any effort, fit better brake cable, which is easier to pull.

How can we cycle with small

Even if your kids are too young to cycle, they can still go along for the ride…

Trailers

WHO ARE THEY FOR? Trailers are good for hauling children when they're still too young to ride independently or on a trailerbike. They're also ideal for taking out disabled children. The best models have a recommended weight limit of 100lbs (seven stone).

Trailers cost more than seats but are better for longer trips because the bike is more stable and the child more comfortable and less exposed. When they get bored they can play with toys or stretch out for a nap.

ARE THEY SAFE? Most trailer accidents involve tipping over on the move. It's rare, but ride carefully, remembering you're much wider at the back. You don't want to catch a trailer wheel against a rock or a kerb. Always strap your child in, and fit them with helmets.

WHICH MODEL IS BEST? Most models now hitch low down on the bike's rear triangle rather than up near the saddle, which provides extra stability. The total combined weight of trailer (20lb) and child can be quite a load, but you should trundle along quite happily. Most models fold down into their own bags very neatly.

Good makes to consider include Burley, Topeak, Winchester, BOB and S Winchester Originals, and you can expect to pay between £150 and £400.

Babyseats

WHO ARE THEY FOR? Although some parents take babies on bikes at six months or even younger, you should wait until they are a year old. By then they can take the jiggling better, and will fit properly into the straps and a helmet. Officially, babyseats take children from nine months to six years (or 22kg), but older kids tend to get too long before they get too heavy for these seats. Most models include adjustable footrests to accommodate them as they grow.

ARE THEY SAFE? One third of accidents happen when bike and baby are stopped and propped. The baby's weight is way above the bike's centre of gravity, and often right over the back wheel. One good wiggle and they're over. Take care mounting and dismounting – that's when their weight is off-centre – and always ensure they wear a helmet.

Also, try to avoid cycling while your baby rocks itself to sleep. It's not too healthy to have their heads wobbling about. If you must, ride gently, and see that they are leaning back. You can buy baby travel neck pillows – one or two models even recline slightly (including the top-of-the-range Rhode Gear, approximately £100).

children?

Trailerbikes

WHO ARE THEY FOR?

Designed for children aged four to ten (up to 85lbs) who are capable of cycling on their own, but who may slow things up or get in a pickle if they do. That gives you peace of mind and both of you a decent ride.

The child does his own pedalling on a contraption that looks like a regular bike with its front wheel missing. A bar attaches it under your saddle, but the bike has handlebars (without any steering), pedals and gears. Braking and turning are left to you, but you get a helping foot from their pedal power, which makes quite a difference.

ARE THEY SAFE? Yes, so long as you remember that you are manning a longer vehicle than usual and corner carefully, allowing more width than normal.

WHICH MODEL IS BEST?

Some models fold in half for car boots and storage, others (such as Burley's top-of-the-range models) hitch cleverly to make cornering smoother and eliminate wobbly handling. Burley's models even boast a mudguard on the main tube of the trailerbike, to keep kids clean. Other good makes include Islabike and Mongoose, and prices range from £150 to £350.

With a bit of practice all adults should be able to ride with a baby in place. The first time out, go slowly, on good dry surfaces and away from traffic. Allow plenty of time for your ride. You will find that as long as the bike is upright, you are barely aware of the extra weight or side-to-side wobble.

Do wrap up the baby thickly in cold weather. Remember, unlike you, they are completely still on the back and their legs and feet can get badly chilled.

WHICH MODEL IS BEST?

Child seat prices vary between £40 and £100, and good makes include Rhode Gear and Hamax. Think hard before choosing a seat mounted on the crossbar in front of you – some parents say it interferes with their riding. If possible, buy two mounting racks so that mum and dad can both go out with the baby and seat.

How do we choose the right boot rack?

Attach your boot rack wrongly and you'll end up with a badly scratched car – or worse still, a big fine for breaking the law whilst driving. For hassle-free racking, look out for these essential features:

- BIKE STRAPS These hold the bike onto the rack. Ideally they should be permanently fixed to the support arms so you can't lose them. They can also help keep your bikes apart, minimising damage.

- HINGES The fewer the hinges, the more rigid the rack will be once fitted. A rack with more hinges may fit more cars but that's only a concern if you plan to use it on more than one vehicle. Too many hinges can cause problems when fitting the rack to the car. Because of the vastly different boot shapes it is essential that you try before you buy.

- FITTING The rack's support arms (on which the bikes rest) should adjust so they are roughly parallel to the ground, with just a touch of upward angle. If the arms are steeply angled, the weight is taken by the bike nearest to the car, rather than the rack. Never use a rack where the support arms point downwards. When loaded, look to have at least 12 inches of space between the bike tyres and the road surface.

- RETAINING STRAPS Your rack needs six straps to anchor it firmly to the car. Any less and it will rock from side to side when the car's moving. Nearly all straps have metal hooks at the end, which should be coated in thick plastic to minimise damage to your paintwork.

The right side of the law

If any part of the bikes or rack obscures the car lights or number plate, you are breaking the law. As well as risking being stopped by the police and fined under the Road Vehicle Lighting Regulations Act (max fine £1,000) you also risk other cars running into the back of you because they can't see your brake lights. Either buy a rack which raises the bikes above your lights or fit a lighting board (£20) and a towbar (with socket, £130). High-mounted racks are more complicated to fit, however, and they also reduce fuel efficiency.

How do we choose the right helmets?

Most manufacturers have a crash-replacement warranty – if you fall off and damage your helmet they will test it and offer you a discounted replacement in return.

If you come a cropper on your bike, you need to know your helmet will protect you. It's even more important for youngsters with growing bones. The only way to be sure is to buy a quality helmet that fits perfectly. That should cost you around £30 – but you can pay more than £100 for increased strength, lightness and better ventilation. It pays to choose wisely…

What are the key features of a helmet?

• SHELL Made from shock-absorbent polystyrene with a plastic outer. The two are either fused together to make the helmet stronger and lighter – which also allows more vents to be added – or simply taped together.

• VENTS The last thing you want is a hot, sweaty head. Look for more vents, and bigger ones, to keep you cool.

• PADDING These internal strips of foam are attached by Velcro, and can be moved about for comfort.

• VISOR Keeps the rain, sunshine and flies out of your eyes. Most are 3-4cm long and removable. If it's too long, a visor can obscure your vision.

• RETENTION SYSTEM An internal head brace at the back of the helmet, attached to the polystyrene inner. Sometimes the brace can be adjusted or 'tensioned', to cradle the head more tightly.

• FASTENERS Under-the-chin fasteners lock the webbing straps that fall down in front and behind your ears. They need to be easy to adjust but secure enough to stop the helmet moving around.

How often should I replace my helmet?

Every two years. The polystyrene inner degrades in ultra-violet light, and prolonged exposure to the sun's rays will make it brittle – no good in a heavy impact. If you do bang your head in a fall, replace the helmet straight away even if it seems undamaged. When the polystyrene absorbs a blow it compresses, which will reduce its ability to absorb another heavy impact.

How do we ensure our bikes are safe?

Quick-release levers
Check these are firmly folded. They should line up with the fork blade or rear stay. Most levers have 'open' and 'closed' printed on them – make sure 'closed' is visible.

Tyres
Check tyres for bald patches and tears. Also look for shards of glass or thorns, which can work through the tyre casing. Remove before they hole the inner tube.

Spokes
Gently brush a hand over the wheels to check for broken or loose spokes. A snapped spoke will weaken a wheel, and repair is much easier if it hasn't been ridden on.

Rims
Spin the wheels to check brake blocks are not rubbing – if they are, your wheel could be buckled. Stand in front of and behind the bike to check wheels are running true.

Brakes
The front brake should lock the wheel and lift the back off the ground. Back wheel should lock and slide. Check brakes engage before lever is pulled halfway back.

How do we get the correct fit?

A well-fitting helmet will stay in place during a collision and be comfortable to wear every time you venture out. It won't give your skull maximum protection unless it sits correctly. Buy from a bike shop with experienced staff rather than a department store or supermarket. Different makes of helmet are different shapes, so try on as many as possible, following these simple tips…

1. Place the helmet on your head in a horizontal position. Before you fasten the straps, shake your head from side to side – the helmet should move with your head as it turns rather than knocking against it. If it doesn't, you'll need to try a different one.

2. Make sure the helmet is in contact with the top of your head – push down and check you can feel the pressure. You can improve the fit by trying thicker and thinner foam pads inside, but if the helmet isn't stable after those first two tests, you need to buy another.

3. Adjust the web straps so they are tight, and meet to make a Y-shape just under your ear lobes. Check they won't rub the backs of your ears. You'll be looking upwards when you ride, which loosens the straps, so make them slightly tighter than is comfortable while you are standing.

4. Push the helmet's peak upwards. If it pushes off your forehead, tighten the front straps. If you need to make these uncomfortably tight to stop the helmet pushing up, you need a different helmet. Finally, in a prone cycling position, check the back of your helmet isn't pushed up.

Brake Blocks
Check the brake blocks are not excessively or unevenly worn. Each block should be parallel to the rim and low enough to avoid rubbing against the tyre.

Chainset
Check the chain is clean and runs smoothly. Turn the pedals backwards and watch it run through the derailleur. Stiff links will cause your gears to slip under pressure.

Cables
Check all brake and gear cables for kinks in the outer casing or frays in the cable. Replace frayed cables immediately, and clean and oil rusty or dirty ones.

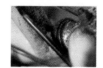

Steering
Grip front wheel with knees. Try to turn bars – they should not move independently. Check bearings by lifting wheel and turning bars – they should move smoothly.

Pedals
It's wise to regularly inspect your pedals for signs of wear and tear. Look out for any serious cracks – they can cause the pedal to break under pressure.

29

What should we wear?

You probably don't need a shiny Lycra ensemble for family cycling, but it's worth investing in some basic gear to make your time in the saddle more enjoyable.

There's nothing more miserable than getting wet on a ride, especially if it's early in the day. So choose your waterproof jacket carefully, paying close attention to the following...

• CUFFS The lightest cuff designs use Lycra or other forms of elastic to give a close fit. A press-stud or Velcro fastening will give you adjustment.

• FABRIC Super-light fabrics are now available offering excellent breathability and very high waterproofing. But you get what you pay for. Both features are equally important – especially if you sweat a lot while cycling. Check to see how noisy the fabric is too – some jackets can sound like crisp packets rustling in the wind.

• POCKETS The number and placement of pockets is down to personal preference and depends if you like to wear a rucksack or bumbag when biking. But it's good to have at least one map-sized pocket. Some jackets have a huge pocket at the back so you won't need a rucksack at all.

• LENGTH You need a jacket that's short enough to keep out of the way of the saddle, yet long enough to keep your bottom and lower back warm and dry when bent over the handlebars. That's why the back of many cycling jackets is much longer than the front.

• MAIN ZIP A full-length zip is great for ventilation control, and a lightweight one will save you valuable ounces. To prevent 'zip scratch' on the neck and chin, look for a short baffle behind the zip. Most zips are not weatherproof, so look for a storm-flap over the top to stop the wind and rain getting in.

• PACKABILITY If your jacket packs down small it will stow away easily on warm days. Some jackets come with a stuff-sack or have a pocket they can be rolled into. Some have built-in belts so you can wear the packed jacket around your waist like a bumbag.

• DRAWCORDS Hem and waist drawcords keep draughts at bay and trap warm air inside, while stopping the jacket billowing in the wind. Look for ways of tucking the cord ends away so they can't get snagged on your bike

• WEIGHT Just a couple of hundred grams can make the difference between a good sturdy jacket and a brilliant one that you'll forget you're even wearing. Expensive fabrics and simple design are the easiest ways to achieve low weight.

• HOOD If it looks like rain you might want to wear a hood over or under your helmet. It should roll into the collar or be removable – otherwise it will act like a sail in the wind. Look for a volume adjuster so you can tailor the hood's fit to your head.

• SAFETY Reflective strips on the back collar or arms are important when riding at night, especially with children.

What shoes should we wear to cycle?

• THE FIT Shoe sizes vary between manufacturers, so take your time trying on different sizes and makes. Walk them around the shop a few times before you buy. Can you feel the laces? Is the toe tough enough?

• THE GRIP Look for a sole made from durable rubber compounds to grip well on slippery terrain. If the tread pattern is too chunky, it will be heavy and awkward on the pedals; if it's shallow, it will feel better but wear more quickly. If you're likely to be walking in your shoes – perhaps pushing your bike up steep slopes! – look for an outsole with deeper cleats to bite into mud.

• THE FLEX For easy pedalling, go for a stiff sole that doesn't flex. You can test this by holding the heel of the shoe in one hand and trying to bend the toe towards the heel with the other. An ideal cycling shoe will not bend.

• SECURITY STRAP To ensure laces don't get caught in the chain, look for a Velcro strap to hold them in place. It will also provide a more secure fit.

How should we care for our jackets?

The lifetime of your jacket largely depends on its fabric and how well you look after it. Some higher priced jackets remain waterproof for at least ten years, while cheaper ones can start to leak after only two years.
• Neglecting your jacket will affect its waterproofness. Try to avoid brushing it against rocks or snagging it on branches. Hang it up to dry at room temperature to allow creases to drop out and stitching and fabric to dry.
• Some jackets can be tumble-dried – but check washing instructions first.
• If you do start feeling wet inside your jacket, it may be that it's just not breathing. Condensation forms on the inside from body sweat. The outside may also be 'wetting out' in the rain, which means water doesn't bead and roll off as it should – and breathability is drastically reduced. To avoid it, wash your jacket regularly according to the instructions.
• If your jacket still wets out, treat it with a durable water-repellency (DWR) treatment, such as Grangers Superproof or Nikwax TX10, available from good outdoors shops. If you're still not happy, return it to the shop and they'll send it back to the manufacturer for testing.

What should we pack for a picnic?

If you're planning to make a day of it, somewhere along the line you and the kids are going to have to make a pit-stop to refuel. To avoid those tired little legs running out of puff in the final stretch, carry a picnic packed full of carbohydrates, which is the fuel your muscles need when they are working hard. Although we have plenty of energy stored naturally as fat, our carbohydrate stores are relatively small. The amount of glycogen (the body's carbohydrate store) in an average man is 500g (400g in most women), which is enough for around two hours of strenuous exercise. When your store of glycogen is empty, fatigue sets in and performance suffers. Sugary snacks will provide a boost, but it will be short-lived. The secret is to eat foods packed with fast-release carbohydrate instead.

Before you go...

Eat a bowl of cereal with low-fat milk. The best cereals have carbohydrates gained from natural ingredients such as oats, barley, roasted nuts and dried fruit. And if you're tempted by a fry-up, remind yourself that cereals win hands down before a day's riding. Fry-ups give you nothing more than an extremely short-lived energy boost.

Perfect picnic food

• ISOTONIC DRINKS
These deliver glucose into your bloodstream much faster than a concentrated sugary drink. Also take at least 500ml of water and alternate between the two. And never wait until you are thirsty before you start drinking – by that point you're already dehydrated.

• BANANA
Ripe bananas may not travel as well as greener versions, but they're far easier to digest. They're also a valuable source of potassium. One medium banana provides a 35g carbohydrate boost.

• FRUIT CAKE
One thick slice provides natural sugars as well as useful minerals such as iron and calcium. Avoid icing and also marzipan; it's made from almonds and can slow digestion.

• MUFFIN
A single bran muffin (80g) provides 35g of fast-release carbohydrate and will give you a feeling of fullness without causing bloating or discomfort.

• FRESH ORANGE
One 250ml carton of fresh orange juice provides you with a useful 21g of carbohydrate. And because the sugars in the juice are in solution, they are absorbed relatively slowly which means you get a handy delayed energy boost after drinking it.

• RAISINS
Dried fruits are a concentrated source of sugars and useful minerals like potassium and iron. A single 40g pack of raisins provides 15g of carbohydrate. Other dried fruits – such as apricots – are rich in sugars, but take longer to digest.

• CEREAL BAR Cereal bars like Frusli provide 15g of carbohydrate. Avoid bars with a high fat content (more than 15g per 100g) as they will slow the absorption of carbohydrate.

• RICE PUDDING
Unlikely perhaps, but the rice and milk mix provides a fix of protein while the sugar helps to keep your brain supplied with glucose. It's a tasty final boost before you set off for home.

What about favourite snacks?
The kids may love them, but here's why you should wait until after the ride…

• SWEETS Highly processed foods like jelly beans contain carbohydrate but are also laced with a cocktail of chemicals and additives, which are far from beneficial for your body.

• ICE CREAM It's a popular mid-ride summer snack but two scoops only provide 10g of carbohydrate. The high fat content also slows down the absorption of glycogen and glucose. Fruit ice-lollies are a better choice to enjoy on a hot day.

• CHIPS A portion of chips contains a useful 49g of carbohydrate but the high fat content added from frying interferes with digestion and will result in a slow supply of glucose.

The energy-packed sandwich
Two slices of wholemeal bread with one teaspoon of honey provides 45g of carbohydrate. Use wholemeal bread rather than white (it provides more fibre and B vitamins), and avoid butter as it slows down digestion and carbohydrate absorption. As an alternative, two rice cakes sandwiching a teaspoon of jam provide 35g of carbohydrate and can be rapidly digested, making them perfect towards the end of a hard ride when you need a fast energy boost.

Why do we need fresh fruit?

If you want to make just one change to your eating habits that will positively affect your health and energy levels, eat more fresh fruit. Children especially can benefit from grazing throughout the day on apples, pears and kiwi fruit instead of swallowing sweets and guzzling cans of fizzy drinks.

WHY IS FRUIT SO BENEFICIAL?

• FRUIT CONTAINS WATER, SUGARS, VITAMINS AND MINERALS
There are three types of sugar in fruit – glucose, sucrose and fructose – all of which supply your body with energy. Fructose is absorbed much more slowly compared with the others, providing a back-up sugar supply once the others have been absorbed. However, too much fructose can cause diarrhoea, so don't eat several pieces in one go.

• MOST FRUITS ARE AROUND 90% WATER
The water helps to dilute the sugar content and, along with the fibre, helps slow down the absorption of sugars into the bloodstream. This helps to maintain a steady flow of energy into the body rather than the sudden rush of sugar you get from eating a bar of chocolate.

WHICH FRUITS ARE BEST FOR US?

• GRAPES contain a good balance of sugars and antioxidants which protect the body against the damaging effects of free radicals. The sugars are absorbed fairly rapidly so eat them as a mid-cycle snack.

• FRESH PLUMS tend to bruise easily so are not the best fruit to carry in your daypack. However, dried plums are available all year round and have a high sugar content.

• Always opt for bright orange PEACHES as they are highest in beta-carotene. This is a powerful antioxidant and helps to protect the body against harmful free radicals.

• The sugars in CITRUS FRUITS are absorbed faster than those in apples, so oranges are a useful mid-ride snack to boost your energy levels. As well as providing a good dose of vitamin C, oranges contain beta-carotene, which is essential to help maintain healthy eyes and skin.

• Choose ripe PEARS as they are easier to digest than unripe ones. When ripe, the pectin which holds the cell walls together softens, allowing the sugars to be absorbed more quickly. This makes ripe pears a useful post-ride snack to help replace carbohydrate stores.

• Weight for weight, a KIWI FRUIT contains more vitamin C than an orange and as much fibre as an apple. It also has high levels of vitamin E, which increases the body's immune response. Since strenuous exercise can depress the immune system, snack on a kiwi fruit every day when riding.

• All types of MELONS are best eaten on their own since, like grapes, they ferment rapidly in the stomach. Their high water content and dilute sugar solution make them an ideal snack for hot weather.

• The soluble fibre in APPLES slows the absorption of sugars into the bloodstream, so eat a couple an hour before you ride for a gentle energy boost. Apples also help detoxify the body

• BERRIES are a handy source of iron, calcium, potassium and magnesium. Iron is needed to manufacture haemoglobin, which transports oxygen to your muscles. Tiredness is the usual symptom if you have a low level of iron.

Why you should leave cake bars at home

If you need energy quickly, a cake bar with a high level of carbohydrate will give you a boost, but they are far from ideal. If they're not packed with masses of sugar, they are full of artificial sweeteners, additives and preservatives – none of which will help your body when out riding. Instead choose a snack bar – like a Jordans Frusli Bar, for example – made from real ingredients (like raisins, nuts and apricots) which provide energy as well as vitamins and minerals. It's an altogether more nutritious package plus a good source of carbohydrates on long cycle rides.

Which dried fruit and nuts are best?

A mix of dried fruit and nuts makes the perfect snack when out riding, and not just because they are easy to pack and won't melt in small hands. The fruit provides a mixture of the natural sugars, glucose and fructose. Glucose is absorbed quickly into the bloodstream and can provide an immediate energy boost. Fructose is absorbed more slowly and acts as a back-up-boost – handy for any unexpected hills!

The value of any mix is determined by the amount of carbohydrate it provides compared with fat. A few nuts can add some essential fats, but if more than 20% of the total calories are made up of fat then this will slow your body's absorption of the mixture. So too many nuts are a bad thing. During exercise, particularly for rides lasting longer than two hours, the priority is to top up muscle carbohydrate stores and blood glucose levels, which means even the lowest-scoring mix is better than nothing.

The truth about crisps

As great as they taste, most crisps are unhealthy on two major counts: they're often too high in both salt (as a mix of sodium and chloride) and fat to be consumed regularly.

To remain healthy, our bodies need just 1.5g of salt a day. And while a 30g bag of crisps contains a third (0.5g) of your daily ration, the fact that many natural and processed foods also contain sodium (the latter in dangerously high levels), it's all too easy to consume too much in your diet.

Because most crisps are cooked in vegetable oil, they're also high in fat. Crinkle cut crisps are the worst (more surface area = more room for fat to be absorbed), but low-fat crisps (flash-fried then blasted with hot air in an oven) remain a high-fat food, so avoid them as a daily treat. Unlike most crisps, however, Jordans Chips are made from corn, rice, wholewheat and oats and then baked – not fried. At 85% fat-free and flavoured with natural seasonings, they are clearly a healthier choice.

Know your mix...

• GOOD ON THE GO Because a mere 3% of the calories come as fat and a whopping 96% as carbohydrate, this *Pineapple and Papaya Mix* is ideal for bikers, although it does contain the preservative sulphur dioxide.

• TOO FATTY BY FAR With cashews, peanuts and almonds only 14% of the total calories come from carbohydrates and a massive 72% from fat, making *Honey-Coated Nuts* a poor choice of snack on a strenuous bike ride.

• ENERGY – BUT AT A COST If you can't carry fresh bananas on your journey, *Banana Chips* (real bananas processed to travel well) are the next best thing for a useful energy boost. Be aware, however, that the chips are sweetened and fried using coconut oil, which is highly saturated and a poor choice in health terms.

• DRIED GOODNESS Mixing dried papaya, apricots, dates, raisins and banana chips, the *Fruit Surprise* is a useful snack. The only fat comes from the fried banana chips. Omit them and you've a healthier, more beneficial mix.

- HEALTHY FAT Starring sweetened banana chips, raisins, brazil nuts, diced papaya, whole dried apricot and raw coconut chips, a *Sunset Mix* is, on the whole, a beneficial snack. Though Brazil nuts up the fat calories, they are also an excellent source of selenium, which helps boost the immune system.

- NAUGHTY BUT NICE The blend of yellow split peas, chickpeas, lentils, peanuts, cashew nuts, sultanas and chilli powder – known better as *Bombay Mix* – may be tasty, but it's too high in fat (51%) to justify its inclusion in your bag. Cyclists with breathing problems can take heart, however, as the chilli can be beneficial.

- POST-RIDE RATIONS The almonds, cashews and roasted hazelnuts in this *Super Trail Mix* provide a good dose of essential fatty acids and minerals. Alas 66% of calories in the other ingredients (sweetened banana chips, toasted coconut chips and raisins) come from fat. Save it for after a long ride.

- LOW-FAT, HIGH-CARB Because there are no nuts in this *Dried Fruit Salad Mix* of prunes, apricots, peaches, pears and apple, the fat content is low and the carbohydrate value high. It's an ideal cycle snack.

- A FATTY FEAST As 59% of the total calories in this mix of *Blanched Peanuts and Raisins* comes from fat, you would be far better off making your own mix by adding dried fruit to dilute all those nuts.

DIY MIX For the healthiest mix, combine organic, unsulphured dried fruits with walnuts and almonds – the nuts contain a good dollop of vitamin E and essential fatty acids.

Make your own cycle snacks

Why not get the kids to help make these…

Country Bran Muffins
A hearty batch ready in around 30 minutes.

What you will need
100g/4oz Jordans natural wheat bran
350g/14oz self-raising flour
2 teaspoons baking powder
2 teaspoons ground cinnamon
¼ teaspoon salt
100g/4oz raisins
2 eating apples, peeled, cored & chopped
3 medium eggs
1 teaspoon vanilla extract
100g/4oz soft brown sugar
75g/3oz butter, melted
125ml milk
45g/1½oz soft soft brown sugar (for sprinkling)

**How to make them
(for 15-18 muffins)**
1) Preheat the oven to 200°C/400°F/Gas Mark 6, or 180°C if using a fan-assisted oven. Lightly oil two 12-hole muffin tins or use paper muffin cases.
2) In a large mixing bowl, combine the Jordans bran, flour, baking powder, cinnamon and salt. Stir in the raisins and apples.
3) Whisk together the eggs, vanilla extract, soft brown sugar, melted butter and milk. Stir into the dry ingredients until just combined – but do not beat the mixture.
4) Spoon into the muffin tin or cases, sprinkling the surface of each one with soft brown sugar. Bake for 22-25 minutes or until risen and golden brown.

Flapjacks
Great for a natural energy boost and ready in half an hour.

What you will need
150g/6oz butter
200g/8oz clear honey
100g/4oz each chopped walnuts and chopped apricots
350g/12oz Jordans Oats

How to make them
1) Gently melt the butter with the honey over a low heat.
2) Stir in the chopped apricots, walnuts and the rolled oats. Mix well until the ingredients are evenly distributed.
3) Press the mixture into a greased 20cm (8in) square cake tin and bake in a preheated oven at 180°C/350°F/Gas Mark 4 for 25 minutes.
4) Leave to cool in the tin, cutting into large bars while the mixture is still warm.

Muesli Chocolate Squares
Packed with goodness – and they won't take up much space!

What you will need
400g/16oz plain chocolate
45ml/3tbsp golden syrup
25g/1oz butter/margarine
About 225g/8oz
Jordans muesli

How to make them
1) Gently melt the
syrup, butter and half
the chocolate.

2) Gradually stir in enough
muesli to make a stiff mixture.
3) Press into a greased Swiss
roll (or wide) tin.
4) Melt the remaining
chocolate into a bowl
over simmering water,
then smooth over top
of the pressed mixture.
5) Chill mixture before
cutting into squares.

Jordans Special Muesli Bread
Delicious on its own, even better spread with a little butter and honey.

What you will need
150g/6oz Jordans special
muesli
150ml/5fl oz skimmed
milk, warmed
100g/4oz wholemeal flour
1 teaspoon salt
1 tspn easy-blend
dried yeast
12g/^{1}/$_2$oz poppy
seeds (optional)
25g/1oz sultanas
280ml/9fl oz
warm water
Plus oil for greasing, milk
to glaze

How to make it
1) Mix muesli and milk
together and allow to
stand for ten minutes.
2) Sift flours and
salt into bowl, stir in yeast.
3) Make a well in the
centre, add muesli mix,
sultanas and three-
quarters of the water.

4) Mix to form a soft dough,
add more water if necessary.
5) Turn dough onto lightly-
floured work surface and
knead until smooth.
6) Place in lightly oiled bowl,
cover with cling film and
leave until doubled in size
(approx one hour).
7) Preheat oven to
200°C/400°F/Gas Mark 6
and lightly grease one

210mm x 110mm x 65mm
loaf tin or baking tray, if
making rolls.
8) Knock back dough for 2-3
minutes, place in tin or shape
into rolls. Cover with oiled
cling film; leave for 20 mins.

9) Brush top with milk,
sprinkle with poppy seeds
and/or sunflower seeds.
10) Bake for 30 minutes (20
for rolls) until bread sounds
hollow when tapped. Leave
to cool.

Staying happy in the car

Few things get a family day out off to a worse start than an uncomfortable car journey. Make sure you and the children arrive stress-free by following the simple tips below.

Travelling long distances in the car with babies, toddlers and young kids presents a number of problems, most commonly involving sickness and boredom. Take heed of Mother & Baby magazine's expert advice, however, and you are more likely to enjoy a trouble-free journey…

• BEFORE YOU GO
Because changing facilities are often few and far between, dress babies and toddlers as comfortably as possible. Loose-fitting clothes such as tracksuits, leggings and T-shirts are best.

A light, non-greasy snack one hour before you depart will help avoid travel

sleep. If you can tire your baby or toddler out during the day, they may, if you are really lucky, sleep through the entire journey.

• IN-CAR ENTERTAINMENT
Babies and toddlers will enjoy the journey more if you throw in a few nursery rhymes and sing-alongs. When your voice needs a rest, taped stories are a must. Play them on their personal stereo and you'll buy yourself a little peace and quiet.

• Games, such as 'spot the red car', help pass the time, but to avoid travel sickness, never encourage activities which involve looking down, most notably reading.

• A picture stuck to the back of your car seat or a securely attached mobile will keep your baby or toddler entertained during the journey.

• MAKING LIFE EASIER
If it's sunny, putting sunscreens on the car windows helps reduce discomfort from glare. If your toddler will wear them, sunglasses will also help.

• Stopping every hour or so allows toddlers and youngsters to stretch their legs and take a break from the car seat. Use A-roads whenever possible as the service stations on them allow regular opportunities to stop, buy refreshments and visit the toilets.

• When travelling on trains, sit near the toilet in case of an accident, and ensure youngsters have a good view out of the window to stop boredom.

■ Mother & Baby magazine has the best information on caring for your young children. It is published monthly by Emap Esprit.

sickness. Rusks and bananas are ideal, chocolate, sweets and fizzy drinks are to be avoided.

• WHEN YOU GO
If possible, begin your journey at a time when babies and toddlers would normally be sleeping. This will make it easier for them to nod off, as will packing their favourite comforter – a dummy, teddy bear or blanket.

• Night-time travelling encourages

Travel sickness

Why it happens
When conflicting messages are received by the eyes and the balance mechanisms in the inner ear, the brain becomes confused. It's because your inner ear is telling you you're moving about while your eyes are telling you differently. As a result, you experience slight nausea, dizziness or, at worst, severe vomiting. Prior to being sick, young children may go suspiciously quiet and start to look pale and clammy.

Take precautions
If your toddler is prone to travel sickness, these three simple tips will stand you in good stead…
1. Never make a fuss about the journey beforehand. This will over excite your toddler and may well make him or her feel anxious about being sick.
2. Feeding your toddler a light, non-greasy snack before you leave will help, as will packing plenty of water and diluted fruit juice for the journey.
3. Because it's better to be safe than sorry, pack a bowl and tissues.

Help is at hand
Babies and toddlers will normally feel better if they have regular stops for fresh air (if you're driving) or a drink and a nap (if you're on a train, plane or boat). But if your child does regularly become ill on journeys, your GP should be able to prescribe some pills or liquid to prevent travel sickness. If you don't like the idea of giving your child medication, however, one of the following options may help…
■ Give toddlers one tablet of the homeopathic remedy cocculus an hour before travelling. It's also worth crushing another tablet into cooled, boiled water for your child to sip throughout the journey.
■ Give Nelsons Travella tablets once an hour for two hours before setting off, and once during the journey if required.
■ Buy your child elasticated travel wrist bands which have a little stud that presses on the acupuncture point on the inside of the wrist.
■ Offer your child a drink or biscuit containing ginger if they feel queasy.

Cocculus, Travella and wristbands are available from Boots and health food stores. Always read the instructions carefully.

Where can I learn the first aid basics?

Because the odd bump or scrape is almost inevitable on a family day out, you'll need to know how to stop a drama turning into a mini-crisis…

WHAT YOU NEED TO KNOW

Everyone should know the basics of first aid. Details are given in the 'Birth to Five' book by the Health Education Authority, available free to full-time mothers. First aid books are on sale in bookshops of course, but even better is a first aid course. They are run by the British Red Cross or St John Ambulance and your local NHS Ambulance Service (details in the phone book). A step-by-step emergency leaflet – 'Save a baby's life' – is available from the Royal Life Saving Society, River House, High St, Broom, Warwickshire B50 4HN. Send a large SAE.

WHAT YOU'LL NEED TO CARRY

When cycling long distances or more than a few miles from civilisation, carry a first aid pack. The excellent Gregson Pack (available from outdoor shops) is designed for walkers and climbers, with dressings and instructions for all first aid situations packed inside a waterproof case. Even if you can't stretch to a full kit, at least carry antiseptic wipes and plasters, neither of which take up much space in your saddlebag or pocket.

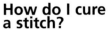

How do we guard against sunburn?

Three suggestions: protection, protection – and protection.

WHY ARE CYCLISTS AT RISK?

Because the windrush dries your skin while also making you feel the day is cooler than it really is, which means you are more likely to neglect smearing on the sunscreen.

HOW CAN YOU PROTECT YOUR CHILDREN?

Babies up to two should not be exposed to direct sunlight at all. Instead, smear their skin with a total sunblock. Toddlers and children should wear suntan lotion (factor 30) and their skin should not be exposed to the sun for more than 30 minutes, especially if they are pale after the winter or you're out riding between midday and 2pm. It's at this time that the sun is at its most intense and harmful, even though the day is not at its hottest. Also apply lip balm with sunscreen. Don't skimp on either – by the time they begin turning red, it's too late. Aftersun lotion may soothe soreness, but it won't undo the damage, so don't let your children burn in the first place.

How do I cure a stitch?

How to make that infamous sharp, stabbing pain disappear quickly.

WHAT CAUSES IT?

Some put a stitch down to being unfit or exercising too soon after eating. The most likely cause is that exercise causes repetitive bouncing of your liver and the ligaments that attach it to the diaphragm. When you breathe out, the diaphragm rises high up in the chest and the ligaments are under tension. If you land or push down heavily on your right foot, the liver bounces up and then descends rapidly. This extra tension causes the

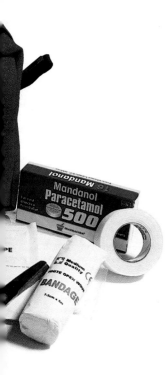

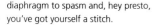

How do I treat bruises and swellings?

Follow these four simple steps and you'll be back on your bike in no time.

THE FIVE-MINUTE FIX

The key is RICE – Rest, Ice, Compression and Elevation.

• REST Keep the weight off the injury. This cuts down circulation to the area, helping reduce bruising and swelling.

• ICE This shrinks blood vessels, limiting fluid build-up. Freeze a polystyrene cup of water, then use it to massage the injured area in a rotating motion for five minutes, wetting the top of the ice to stop it sticking to the skin.

• COMPRESSION Use an elastic bandage to compress the area, it helps limit swelling and supports the injury.

• ELEVATION This reduces blood flow. Raising the injury above your heart encourages it to pump harder against gravity, helping to remove fluid from the affected area.

Can cramp be stopped?

Luckily for us all, yes it can…

WHAT DOES IT FEEL LIKE?

A sudden vicious gripping, spasm-like pain, often experienced during the night after an energetic day's exercise.

WHAT CAUSES IT?

When a muscle becomes over-tired after a period of repeated movement, instead of telling the muscle to relax, the mechanism controlling it gives up, resulting in it locking up. Other schools of thought also cite dehydration, an increase in the concentration of salts in the body, or a build-up of waste products in muscles.

HOW CAN YOU PREVENT IT?

Drink plenty of fluids if you're exercising for more than 90 minutes, and make sure you've eaten plenty of carbohydrates the night before and during the day.

WHAT'S THE BEST CURE?

Apply ice, or use your knuckles to gently massage the offending muscle in a back-and-forth motion for three or four minutes. This encourages the relax reflex to kick in. Continue exercising at a moderate pace to keep the muscle warm but not overstretched.

diaphragm to spasm and, hey presto, you've got yourself a stitch.

WHAT'S THE BEST CURE?

If necessary, stop and take deep breaths and several slow sips of water, which will help relax the abdominal area. If nobody's around, try making some loud grunting noises (yes, really), pushing your belly out as far as possible. This also helps relax the diaphragm. Doing anything to relax will help – anxiety often manifests itself in and around the tummy area.

• Right: Drinking water can help cure a stitch while also preventing the onset of cramp.

What if one of us suffers a heavy fall?

In the event of a serious accident, ask yourself…

ARE THEY UNCONSCIOUS?

If so, don't remove their helmet. If you know first aid, apply the ABC of resuscitation, if not, send for help immediately.

HAVE THEY BROKEN ANY BONES?

Don't move your child if you think their neck or spine may be injured. Unnecessary movement may cause paralysis so get expert help. Pain, swelling or a limb lying at a strange angle may indicate a broken bone. If your child can't move easily without pain, call an ambulance. If you have to move your child, be very gentle. Use both hands above and below the injury to keep it steady and well supported (using blankets and clothes if necessary). Go straight to hospital.

ARE THERE ANY CUTS OR GRAZES?

Carry antiseptic wipes and plasters with you, to clean and dress cuts and grazes. If you have none, rinse the cut with water from your water bottles, then clean and dress it carefully as soon as you arrive back at shelter. Get the child (or adult) a tetanus jab if they are not already covered.

HOW SHOULD I TREAT SHOCK IN A CHILD?

If pale, unwell or feeling faint, help your child to lie down. Keep them covered up and warm, but not too hot. If they've lost a lot of blood, keep their head down and their legs raised, to help the blood back into the head. But never do this if you suspect a head injury or a broken leg.

Protect your peepers

Sunglasses are essential to protect your eyes from the sun, flies and midges. But how can you be sure you have a reliable pair? The key is to find out how much protection they give from ultraviolet rays. The best block 100% of UV-A and UV-B light. Check they satisfy British Standard BSEN 1836 and look for the CE mark to prove they conform to European Community standards.

How do we stop insects ruining our day?

Six ways to keep pesky bugs at bay…

1) AVOID DARK CLOTHING
Contrary to popular myth, insects such as midges, horseflies and mosquitoes are more attracted to dark clothing, so in the height of summer switch to your best white cotton T-shirts.

2) TIME YOUR RIDE
Remember, midges prefer feeding during the mornings and evenings (they don't like bright sunlight) and are at their most voracious from May to August. Check your route – midges love boggy ground and sheltered, wooded areas, while mosquitoes are most prevalent around the UK coast.

3) APPLY REPELLENT REGULARLY
Most repellents contain a powerful substance called DEET. There is concern about the chemical's potential toxic effect on young children so it's best to plump for a concentration of 50% or less. Better still, spray it onto your clothes instead of your skin. Remember, the repellent will be removed by sweat or your clothes rubbing, so aim to renew the application every couple of hours for maximum effect.

4) GO EASY ON THE DEODORANT
Bees and wasps love sweet smells, so avoid wearing too much scent. And keep your sarnies wrapped up well.

5) WEAR YOUR SHADES
Racing cyclists and mountain bikers wear shades not just to look cool, but because a bug in the eye can be a bruiser – as you'll know if you've ever had one hit your forehead when travelling at top speed. Shades or goggles are less necessary for kids cycling slowly down a few miles along the towpath, but as they can easily end up with little flies under the lids or in the corner of their eyes, check if that's what's causing them to water.

6) NEVER SCRATCH A BITE
It'll only spread the irritant in the sting. Instead wash the bitten area with water (and soap, if available) and apply something soothing such as calamine lotion, a sting relief spray or aloe vera.

Take the sting out of nettles
Midsummer's main hazard is nettles overhanging the trail. True mountain bike single tracks can become completely choked during the summer, although most family trails are wide and well maintained. Even though the effect rarely lasts more than an hour, nettle stings hurt, especially if you fall off into a patch. The leaves carry tiny stinging hairs which penetrate the skin and break off, releasing an irritant liquid. Search for dock leaves, the traditional cooling remedy. Washing and dabbing with calamine lotion can also help, as can applying a homeopathic rescue remedy.

How can we stay safe in dim light?

If you're off on an evening trail ride, it's essential to take a powerful set of lights. Visibility may seem clear enough when you set out, but what if you find yourself running late or riding on the dark side of a valley?

Go for the best you can afford – a fully customisable cycle light such as the Lumicycle Ni-Met-Hy System 2000 can set you back £139.99, but it weighs just 785g and the batteries will last for up to ten hours. If you're riding on the road, a set of conventional lights will suffice, but do make sure you're carrying spare batteries for the whole family.

Don't forget to check your bikes' reflectors are clean, and wear a reflective armband to make sure you are visible in the dim evening light. Ride behind your children, and dress them in bright clothing rather than dull colours which will fade into the twilight.

What are the rules of the trail?
• Give way to horses. Greet the rider, and make sure they know you're coming by. Better still, stop completely.
• Fit a bell on your bikes, to alert walkers to your presence. Call out to let them know you are coming, slow down and allow them space to pass.

Are there special safety rules on UK towpaths?
Many of the routes in this guide follow canal towpaths. Be safe – and polite! – by following the Waterways Code:
• Give way to other people on the towpath and warn them politely of your approach.
• Access paths can be steep and slippery – join towpaths with care.
• Dismount if the towpath is busy with walkers or anglers.
• You must get off and push your cycle if the path gets very narrow, beneath low bridges, alongside locks, or close to any other hazardous areas.
• Ride at a gentle pace, in single file and do not bunch. Never race – remember that you have water on one side of you.
• If you are a young or an inexperienced cyclist, always ride with a responsible adult.
• Watch out for hidden mooring spikes or ropes across the path beside moored boats.
• Take particular care on wet or uneven surfaces and don't worsen them by skidding.
• Never cycle along the towpath in the dark. You are responsible for your own and others' safety.

What can I do to keep my children safe when cycling?

The Royal Society for the Prevention of Accidents (ROSPA) recommends that children don't ride alone on the road until they reach the age of ten. But as long as they have the balance and strength, and can control their speed and braking, they should be able to ride safely on traffic-free routes from as young as four.

• PREPARATION Follow the guide on page 28 to ensure their bike is in working order, especially the brakes and cables, and to make sure all helmets fit well. With babyseats, it's a good tip to attach a disposable cuddly toy behind the seat, facing the traffic behind you. It's a way of humanising drivers and getting them to drive considerately past you.

• ON THE ROAD Children have little sense of danger and traffic. So when you are riding with them you must be their eyes and ears. The best place to ride is outside and a little behind them.

That way you can tell them what's coming ahead and what they should do, you can let them ride ahead, round parked cars, and protect them from behind. Keep talking to them, and before you reach junctions or hazards tell them what to do.

• ON THE TRAIL The main sticky point off-road is losing control downhill, so build up slowly before you take them on sloping or rough tracks. The majority of rides in this book are flat, but some feature slopes which under-tens may need preparing for. Watch children very carefully beside canals, which can have narrow towpaths, plenty of other people around and dogs.

• GET SET 'Get Set' is the current national cycling proficiency scheme. It involves skill and safety sessions, and aims to set your child up for cycling for life in a fun way. For details of courses – which normally last for six sessions – contact your local council.

How do we read a map?

If you plan to navigate Britain using pedal power, the ability to read a map is paramount. Follow these simple tips and you'll be fine…

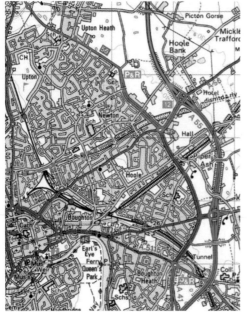

First, build confidence by using a local Landranger map…

Printed on sheets covering an area of 40km by 40km at a scale of 1:50,000, the OS Landranger map series (comprised of 204 maps) covers the length and breadth of Great Britain. To familiarise yourselves with how they work, start with an area you know well and follow these six easy steps…

• STEP ONE

Spread your OS Landranger map out on a table – it's like having a bird's eye view of the ground with the landscape laid out beneath you. Now locate your road and the approximate position of your house.

• STEP TWO

Look at the colours used to illustrate the land around your house. If you live in a built-up area this will be beige, open countryside is shown in white and woodland is shaded green and dotted with tree symbols.

• STEP THREE

Work out how high up you live. The lines you see on maps are called contours and they show how high and steep the land is. The lines are closer together on steep hills and further apart in flatter areas. An OS Landranger map shows contours every ten metres. Every 50 metres the line is in bold to help you work out the height of the land above sea level.

• STEP FOUR

Decide which direction the front of your house faces. Is it north, south, east or west? Remember that the sun is in the south at midday. Then, for practice, work out in which direction your friends live or your local shops are located.

• STEP FIVE

Identify the different types of routes you can cycle along. As well as any public road (but not motorways, of course!), cyclists are also allowed to ride on bridleways and these are shown as pink dashes. Mind how you go, though, as bridleways are usually unsurfaced and can feature such hazards as overgrown nettles during the summer. Footpaths, where you are not allowed to ride, are shown as pink dots.

• STEP SIX

Work out how far your cycle route will take you. Lay a piece of fine string or thread along your chosen route, carefully following all the twists and turns. Now hold the string or thread firmly and place it against the scale shown at the bottom of the map to work out the distance. You can get an idea of distance by using the grid squares – each square is one kilometre across.

Next, work out your own cycle route...

As well as official cycle paths, since the Countryside Act 1968 came into force, cyclists have also had the right to use bridleways in England and Wales. But always remember that pedestrians and horse riders have the right of way.

Mark the bridleways with a highlighter pen (go on, the map's a tool to help you, not an old master), then work out your circuit using lanes and other off-road routes – towpaths and former railways, for example. As a rough guide, you can work out how long your trip should take by using six miles per hour as the average speed for off-road riding.

Finally, learn to spot landmarks along the way...

Add enjoyment to your ride by using the key in the margin to find your nearest church or place of worship with a spire (or a tower); viewpoint; public telephone box; and picnic site. Plus, before you go, try the following:
• Use the map to tell the difference between embankments and cuttings on railway lines in your area.
• Identify any disused railway lines.
• Work out where disused lines once ran by following gaps through built-up areas and across fields.
• Think of a local landmark, a pylon, bridge or farm, for example, and spot it on the map.

Brush up your map-reading skills by using our online computer presentation at www.ordnancesurvey.co.uk OS maps can be ordered online at www.ordnancesurvey.co.uk/leisure, on 0845 2002712 or from all good bookshops, outdoor leisure shops and tourist information centres.

How to take a grid reference

A grid reference is a simple way of pinpointing places on a map. At the bottom of your map you'll see numbers for each square that increase from left to right. Numbers are also shown along the left-hand edge of the map which increase as you follow it up.

The numbers running across the bottom – known as 'eastings' – go along 'the corridor', those numbers running up the side – 'northings' – go up 'the stairs'. To read a grid reference you must first go along the corridor and then up the stairs. The number you use first in a grid reference appears in the bottom left-hand corner of the square you want to pinpoint.

A simple four-figure grid reference uses just the numbers of the squares. For example, '6351' is where the easting is '63' and the northing is '51'. A six-figure grid reference allows you to fine-tune the reference down to tenths of a square. So, '631 515' is where the easting is '63' plus 1/10th of a square and the northing is '51' plus 5/10ths – or half – of the square. Simple.

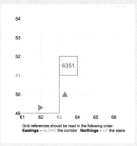

How do we ride into wind?

• DRESS THE PART Wear close-fitting clothing rather than gear that will catch the wind and drag you back. Rain jackets are often the worst culprits. Sunglasses are good protection against a drying wind and particles of dust.

• GET IN POSITION Present as small an obstacle as possible. Lower yourself down towards the handlebars; but keep your head up – you still need to look where you're going!

• USE YOUR GEARS This technique is just like riding uphill: drop down a gear

or two and maintain a good rhythm on the pedals. Cycle in too high a gear and you'll quickly wear yourself out.

• THINK AHEAD Anticipate gusts of wind by keeping an eye on the terrain. When you're close to the lee of a wall, a hedge or embankment, take a moment to ease off the pedals and preserve your energy.

• PROTECT THE KIDS Ride in front of your children, creating a slipstream so they're protected from the worst of the wind. Take turns at the front with other adults in your group.

How can I make hills seem easier?

• STAY IN THE SADDLE On a long hill, sit well back on the saddle to maximise the strong muscles in your thighs and buttocks and to give good traction to the back wheel. Sit fairly upright, holding the handlebars in a relaxed manner for easier breathing.

• SHIFT YOUR WEIGHT On steeper climbs you may need to shift some body weight forward by bending your arms and leaning closer to the handlebars. But keep your backside way back on the saddle.

• PEDAL SLOWER Select a gear that allows you to pedal at an even and comfortable rhythm that you can maintain up the hill. This will be slower than your usual pedalling rate but not so slow that you grind to a halt.

• GET IN THE SWING On steeper sections you may want to let the bike swing slightly from side to side: push down gently on the left side of the handlebars as you press down on the right pedal, and vice versa. Keep these movements small and keep your upper body relaxed.

How do I mend a puncture?

Punctures obey Sod's Law, they never seem to happen at a good time. Here's how to make the repairs as painless as possible. And relax – if you've prepared properly, it should only take five minutes.

• The trick is to carry a spare inner tube with you. It's quicker and easier to fit the spare than to patch a hole by the side of the trail. You can fix the punctured tube at your leisure when you get home. It's worth carrying a puncture kit as well though, just in case you get more than one flat.
• Ensure your pump fits the tyre valve of your bike. Your local bike shop can advise you.
• Carry the right spanner to get the wheel unbolted from the bike (unless you have

quick release levers) plus tyre levers to get the tyre off the wheel.
• Always check the inside of the tyre carefully, to remove whatever it was that caused the puncture. Also check for splits in the tyre. A split longer than 5mm will allow the tube to bulge out and burst.
• Before using tyre levers to prise off the tyre, use your thumbs to massage the bead of the tyre into the well of the rim all around the wheel. This gives the bead enough slack to slip easily over the rim.
• Put in the new tube, lever the tyre back on the rim and pump it up.
• Puncture kit glue dries up after six months once the seal's been broken, however hard you tighten the lid. It *will* need replacing.

Is there a trick to riding downhill?

• SET UP FOR THE HILL Assuming you can freewheel down the hill, flick the chain onto the big chainring to increase the tension and prevent it from bouncing off and tangling in the chainset. Next, move your pedals to a horizontal position to ensure they don't catch on the ground.

• GET IN POSITION Keep your head up at all times, looking for the best line and staying alive to any hazards. Bend your arms at the elbow and keep a firm grip on the handlebars. Now relax and let your elbows and knees act as suspension joints. The steeper the hill, the more you may need to shift your weight back to stay stable.

• CONTROL YOUR SPEED Use your body to help here. For more speed, crouch low into an aerodynamic position. To slow down, straighten your arms and sit more upright. With your weight well back you can use the front brake for most braking. If the ground is rough, use the back brake more.

How should we ride through mud?

When cycling in this country you are bound to be faced with mud and puddles sooner rather than later. Here's how to come through smiling.

GRIP FIRMLY Take a wide grasp of the handlebars – firm but not too rigid – and let the bike find its own line as much as possible. In rutted tracks, your wheels will be less likely to slip if you ride in the lower sections.

KEEP PEDALLING! This will help you to avoid getting bogged down. Choose a gear which is neither so low that you are spinning too fast to grip, nor so high that you can't pedal through more difficult sections. Ride as smoothly as possible by maintaining even pressure on both pedals.

CHECK OUT THE SURFACE Don't just blindly follow the tracks forged by previous trail users – where they are deep, there's a good chance the mud will be softer and more difficult. And beware of puddles – they can hide potholes and rocks.

KEEP STRAIGHT Don't weave all over the place. Keep changes in direction small and smooth, and keep the bike upright. Unclip one shoe from the pedals so you can easily touch a foot down and avoid a messy fall.

GET IN POSITION Keep your weight low and far back to maintain stability. Don't stand up or tilt the bike from side to side. If faced with really dire mire, pick up your bike and carry it through the worst sections. It will be quicker and less problematic than getting stuck!

AND AFTER YOUR JOURNEY... Make sure you clean your bike as soon as possible after your ride (see overleaf for how to do a thorough job). Apart from stopping it rusting and turning dirt into an abrasive paste, it'll be far easier to spot any damage inflicted during your ride.

How can we make crashing less painful?

When riding tougher trails, falls are often inevitable. Damage limitation, however, is simple…

BEFORE YOU GO
• Wear a properly-fitting helmet that won't come off in a fall. If you do hit your head, the helmet will still need replacing even if you can't see any damage.

• The padded palms of bike gloves help prevent painful gravel-rash, as do knee and elbow pads.

• Wear two layers of clothing. If you fall, the layers will slide over one another instead of causing friction burns to your skin. For that reason, a slippery polyester undervest is ideal.

FALLING SAFELY
• Try to relax as you fall. Loose muscles help the body absorb and disperse the shock of impact. When tense, the impact transfers to the point of least resistance – often causing broken bones.

• If you fly over the handlebars, tucking your arms and legs in and rolling to a halt will reduce the pain. Throwing your arms out is likely to break a bone.

• To avoid direct – and painful – impact on your head, neck and spine, try landing on a shoulder, curling your body into a ball.

• Check your body and bike for damage, but pedal off as soon as possible to prevent muscle stiffness.

What about riding round bends safely?

Whether you approach it at speed or an amble, the technique of cornering safely remains the same…

• WIDEN THE ANGLES Your approach is the key. Straighten out the curves by tackling the bend from as wide an entry point as possible. This will also give you an early view of what's coming the other way.

• SLOW DOWN Reduce speed early, before entering the corner – front brake to slow down, back brake for control. In slippery conditions brake gently (50:50) on each brake. Keep your bike fairly upright for maximum tyre traction.

• AT SPEED Older, more advanced riders taking sharp corners at speed should lean into the corner, drop their shoulders and steer with their backsides rather than with the handlebars. As you exit the corner, right your body on an even keel for traction, and accelerate away.

How do I clean my bike after

The more you ride, the more you will want to ride. But the downside of riding off-road is the time it takes to clean your bike afterwards. But your bike will be cheaper to run, last much longer, and work much better if you give it a little regular TLC. You don't need any special tools, or any previous experience, just a bit of time and a little elbow grease.

Cleaning is also useful as a regular bike check-up. It's the best time to spot worn or broken parts that would otherwise go unnoticed. Beware of using a jetwash, though. Power hoses on garage forecourts will leave your bike looking shiny, but no matter how careful you are they force water in through bearing seals, flushing grease out. This shortens the lifespan of bottom brackets, headsets and other components.

Use the routine below to transform your bike. Start with the dirtiest bits, and work up to the cleaner ones. That way you minimise the amount of recleaning you have to do.

• DRIVETRAIN Try to avoid removing the chain from the bike – it's time consuming and can weaken the link you remove. Clean it with a rag. Hold the rag around the chain and pedal backwards until the chain comes up clean, which is when you can read the writing stamped on every link. If the chain is very grubby, you will need to use a degreaser, like Finish Line Ecotech or Pedros Degreaser. For extra greasy chains, use a toothbrush.

riding through mud?

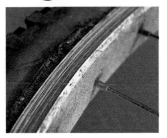

• SPROCKETS AND CHAINSET They are close to the ground, and exposed, so tend to pick up whatever is going around. If they are oily and dirty, it's worth degreasing them. Oil is sticky, and will pick up dirt as you ride along, wearing out your drivetrain. Use a little degreaser, and work it into the sprockets with a washing-up-brush. It's important to rinse everything carefully afterwards to remove all traces of degreaser. Dry the components carefully and be careful not to get degreaser into the bearings.

• LUBE THE CHAIN Drip oils allow you to direct the oil more precisely than spays, which cuts down on waste. Drip a little onto the top links of the bottom stretch of chain all the way around. Don't use excessive amounts. Leave the oil to soak in for five minutes, then carefully remove any excess with a clean rag. Don't worry about relubing other drivetrain components – they don't need any more than will be deposited by the chain into the sprockets.

• WHEELS Your brakes will work much better if your rims are clean. They pick up dirt from the ground and from the brake blocks. This stops the brake blocks from gripping the rim effectively, and can cause both the rims and the brake blocks to wear out prematurely. Green nylon washing-up pads are ideal for this job, but wire wool is too harsh. While you're in there, check for bulging rims, cracks and splits.

• BRAKES
Use a small screwdriver or knife (carefully) to pick out any shards of metal. The surface of the brake blocks can become shiny, and so not grip the rim enough. Use clean sandpaper to roughen the surface of the blocks.

• FRAME AND FORKS
The best method is to use a big bucket of warm, soapy water and a sponge. Ordinary washing-up liquid is fine, but car shampoo is much better because it contains no salt, which can corrode parts. Use the opportunity to check the frame for cracks or dents. Rinse the soapy water off with clean water.

• CABLES
Release the cables from the cable stops. Run a clean rag over the part that's normally covered by the outer casting. Relubricate with a drop of oil.

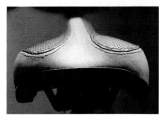

• POLISH
A wax-based polish will help to stop dirt sticking to your frame. Your saddle will benefit from a buff, too.

Chris Juden (2); Matthew Roberts

The Rides

267 paths, trails and tracks for you and your family to explore – and where to find them

Northumbria

A little cycling kingdom – that's how to describe the region between Teesside and Tyneside just 30 miles long by 20 miles wide and so richly endowed with cycle trails. On a dozen routes, where trains once blew their whistles cyclists now ring their bells. From Durham you can ride off in three directions, and from Consett in four. Long-distance trails that pass through include the Coast-to-Coast and Three Rivers, but such is the volume of short cycle hops and connections that anyone who rides all the paths in the area deserves an award.

Highlights include crossing the Millennium Bridge over the Tyne in Newcastle, seeing the Souter lighthouse near South Shields and riding the Waskerley Way up the North Pennines.

Where to cycle when you visit

FINDING YOUR WAY

OS Landranger Map maps covering these areas:
79/80/81/86/87/88/92/93

PLACES TO SEE

Arbeia Roman Fort, South Shields
Be impressed by the remains of the most excavated military supply station in the entire former Roman Empire.

Located at South Shields, the fort houses a museum of site finds including armour, coins, jewellery and weapons. Become an amateur archaeologist for the day in the museum's Time Quest. Admission to the excavations is free. Time Quest costs £1.50 for adults, 80p for children. For details call 0191 456 1369.

Cragside House
See how Tyneside industrialist Lord Armstrong lived in this beautiful building erected between 1864 and 1884 at Rothbury. The magnificent house was the first lit by electricity generated by water power. Besides the house and exquisite contents, you can explore the extensive gardens and estate most of the year round. Call 01669 620333 for further information.

Cook Museum
Films and interactive displays allow you to examine the voyages of discovery of one of history's most celebrated explorers, Captain James Cook. The award-winning museum, set in Middlesbrough's Stewart Park, lets you delve into Cook's early life and learn about the far-flung destinations he travelled to. And if all that gives you an appetite, refreshments are available in the on-site tearooms. For additional details call 01642 311211.

MAIN EVENTS

DID YOU KNOW?
The three kings of Northumbria are buried in Tynemouth Priory.

• Northumberland County Show
Based in Corbridge, this traditional show includes classes for various farm animals, showjumping and dogs. Hundreds of trade stands, arena displays, crafts and catering – a wealth of excellent family entertainment. Runs on 3rd June only.

WHAT ELSE IS ON?

• Newcastle Hoppings
Exciting 40-acre funfair (*left*) including adult and junior rides, sideshows, games of skill, fortune tellers and other attractions. (21st-30th June).

• Stockton International Riverside Festival
International artists and performers entertain in this fantastic celebration of street theatre, featuring circus acts, music, comedy, dance and carnival (26th July-4th August).

• The Sunderland International Airshow
Breathtaking displays by a varied collection of aircraft, from hi-tech military jets to vintage classics such as the legendary Spitfire. Runs on 27th and 28th July on Sunderland Promenade, Seaburn.

• Sunderland International Kite Festival
A feast of kite flying, music and street theatre from around the world, along with a huge selection of arts and crafts for sale at Washington's Northern Area Playing Fields. Takes place on 6th and 7th July.

• Wolsingham & Wear Valley Agricultural Show
Get close to prize-winning livestock, see farming displays and admire the very best in local agricultural produce at this ever-popular country fair. Great for children. Open 7th-9th September.

Northumbria Tourist Board

USEFUL ADDRESSES & NUMBERS

- **Northumbria Tourist Board** Aykley Heads, Durham DH1 5UX; tel: 0191 3753000; website: www.visitnorthumbria.com
- **Sustrans** 35 King Street, Bristol BS1 4DZ; tel: 0117 9290888; www.sustrans.org.uk
- **Northumberland National Park** Eastburn, South Park, Hexham, Northumberland NE46 1BS; tel: 01434 611521; www.nnpa.org.uk
- **Forest Enterprise** Ealsburn, Bellingham, Hexham NE48 2AJ; tel: 01434 250209 (open during Summer months only)

Northumbria

• *Kielder Forest is a wonderful wilderness destination ideal for family holidays.*

JORDANS OVER 8s

1 Cragside Country Park carriage drive

Why should you go?
Because it's a spectacular ride. Cragside estate's six-mile carriage drive leads around a rocky hillside (watch where it narrows around the outcrops), climbs to lakes and whizzes back down to the visitor centre. Cars are restricted to 15mph.

Where is it?
In Rothbury. Park at the main car park, signposted from the B6341 a mile northeast of Rothbury.

Where can you ride?
Stick to the carriage drive. Just watch for that climb and descent!

What else can you do?
If the kids have any energy left, there's an adventure playground at Cragside House plus tours of the mansion (01669 620333).

Where can you eat?
Try the restaurant at the Stable Block visitor centre.

 OS Landranger Map 81

JORDANS OVER 8s

2 Bolam Lake Country Park circuit

Why should you go?
To feel like a pioneer. Cycling is being developed in this wooded lakeside park, so expect some rough tracks unsuitable for children much under eight.

Where is it?
West of Morpeth. Park at the park on the minor road signed from Whalton on the B6524 between Morpeth and Belsay.

Where can you ride?
There's a five-mile circuit round the country park. You can pick up a leaflet at the start or write in advance to: Bolam Lake Country Park visitor centre, Belsay, Northumberland NE20 0HE (01661 881234).

What else can you do?
There are no major attractions nearby, so take your time and enjoy the surroundings.

Where can you eat?
There's a cafe at the visitor centre.

 OS Landranger Map 81

3 Kielder Forest trails & Trailquest

Why should you go?
For a huge choice of differently-graded routes in what is Britain's biggest forest park. Facilities include bike wash and hire, backpacking sites and attractions. It's like having an American wilderness holiday right here in the UK. Buy a leaflet (£2) from the Forest District Office (01434 220242).

Where is it?
Kielder Forest is a vast remote borderland area northwest of Bellingham in Northumberland. Park at Leaplish Waterside Park 12 miles northwest of Bellingham, or at Kielder Castle visitor centre seven miles on.

Where can you ride?
On your pick of routes, seven easy, five moderate, from five miles long to a 17-mile circuit of Kielder Water. There's also plenty of free trail riding plus one permanent bicycle orienteering course (covered by the leaflet detailed above). Be warned, the moderate routes are suitable for more experienced cyclists, with some climbs and descents. There are also some difficult routes and an offroad area graded 'severe' for serious mountain bikers. You can hire bikes at Leaplish Cycling Centre, Waterside Park (01434 250312), and Kielder Bikes at Kielder Castle and Hawkhope car park (01434 250392).

What else can you do?
It's more a case of what can you not do? Active families are spoiled for choice at Kielder. You can visit the Bird of Prey centre, tour the Sculpture Trail, play obstacle golf or don wetsuits for waterskiing and boating from Leaplish Waterside Park. You can even go pony trekking. When you've finished all that, calm down at the Kielder Castle exhibition at Kielder Castle visitor centre.

Where can you eat?
There's a restaurant at Leaplish Waterside Park, and a pub and cafe at the visitor centre.

 OS Landranger Maps 79, 80, 86

4 Tynemouth to Blyth coastal route

Why should you go?
To enjoy virtually car-free riding on promenades along the North Sea with en-route attractions.

Where is it?
North of Newcastle. Park at Tynemouth, Whitley Bay, Whitley Sands, Seaton Sluice or Blyth. The nearest train stations are Tynemouth, Cullercoates and Whitley Bay.

Where can you ride?
Along a seven-mile stretch of shoreline, although there are sections of roadway in the towns. The ride is part of the Coast & Castles route between Newcastle and Edinburgh, and at the Tynemouth end is connected to Tyne, Wear and Teesside's network of rail trails. Coast & Castles is part of National Cycle Route 1. Contact Sustrans for a map and more details (see p8).

What else can you do?
See the underground chambers at Tynemouth Priory & Castle (near the north pier, 0191 257 1090) or the creatures at Sea Life aquarium at Whitley Bay. The route also passes St Mary's Lighthouse to the south of Hartley (*above*).

Where can you eat?
There are cafes in Tynemouth, Whitley Bay, Whitley Sands, Seaton Sluice and Blyth.

OS Landranger Map 88

5 Auckland Way rail trail

Why should you go?
To experience some rough riding on an excellent rail trail.

Where is it?
South of Durham. Start on Princess Street in Spennymoor, turning right at the roundabout at the top of the High Street. You will find a place to park on nearby Whitworth Road.

Northumbria

Where can you ride?
The four-mile route is one of seven rail trails in Co. Durham. You can purchase a laminated route card pack for all seven by sending a £2.75 cheque, made payable to 'Durham County Council', to Environment & Technical Services Department, Durham County Council, County Hall, Durham DH1 5UQ.

What else can you do?
How about the charming 1760 deerhouse at Auckland Castle & Deer House?

Where can we eat?
For the widest choice, head for Bishop Auckland town centre.

 OS Landranger Map 93

JORDANS OVER 12s

6 Middlesbrough to Stockton (& country)

Why should you go?
For easy-going urban riding.

Where is it?
Teesside. You can park at Castle Eden Country Park visitor centre, northeast of Thorpe Thewles off the A177, or Billingham Beck Valley Country Park visitor centre. The nearest stations are Middlesbrough (a mile east of the eastern start point) and Stockton.

Where can you ride?
From Middlesbrough station the eight-mile route hugs the river as far as the tidal barrage, crosses and goes north through the Stockton suburbs. It then continues westward to the rail trail at Bishopsgarth that two miles later becomes the Castle Eden Walkway rail trail (9). You can also branch off eastward at Mount Pleasant on the segregated cycle tracks along the A19. All the trails are covered by Sustrans' 'Three Rivers Cycle Route' map. See p8 for further details.

What else can you do?
In Middlesbrough visit the museum (below), Nature's World or the Transporter Bridge. The children might enjoy the large model railway at Ormesby Hall, a Palladian mansion three miles southeast of Middlesbrough (01642 324188).

Where can you eat?
Try the visitor centres at Castle Eden Country Park or Billingham Beck Valley country park.

 OS Landranger Map 93

JORDANS OVER 8s

7 Cowpen Bewley Woodland country park trail

Why should you go?
For a taste of the 135-mile Three Rivers route between Teesside, Wearside and Tyneside (map and details from Sustrans, p8). Starting off, there's a two-mile section of the Three Rivers route through Cowpen Bewley Woodland country park. From there, follow the cycle routes on the roads through the centre of Billingham to Teesside and the Castle Eden Walkway (9).

Where is it?
The trail runs between Billingham and Hartlepool. Park in the centre of Billingham then ride one mile along the NCN14 signposted cycle route to the country park. Or park at the country park off the A1185. The nearest station is Billingham, half a mile away.

Where can you ride?
If you continue eastward on the cycle-routed roads through Hartlepool you will reach the fine traffic-free seafront cycle path between Seaton Carew and Hartlepool's historic quayside (8).

What else can you do?
Sign your offspring up for the many children's events organised by the country park. Telephone 01642 415225 for full listings.

Where can you ride?
You can get drinks at the country park centre. For a full sit-down meal head for the family-friendly Three Horseshoes pub in Cowpen Bewley village, where there's a play area and children's menu.

 OS Landranger Map 93

JORDANS OVER 8s

8 Seaton Carew to Hartlepool coastal trail

Why should you go?
For some quaint seaside cycling.

Where is it?

As you might have guessed, it runs between Seaton Carew and Hartlepool.

Where can you ride?

For a total of two miles, from the southern end at Seaton Carew seafront along Hartlepool Bay to Hartlepool quayside. Three miles further north, along Hartlepool's cycle routes, is the start of the Hart-Haswell rail trail (10), which continues virtually car-free into the heart of Sunderland.

What else can you do?

Ship ahoy! Visit Hartlepool's historic quayside and HMS Trincomalee, the oldest British warship afloat.

Where can you eat?

There are all the usual options in Seaton Carew and Hartlepool. A better option, though, is to pack a picnic and dine *al fresco* with a sea view.

 OS Landranger Map 93

9 Castle Eden Walkway rail trail

Why should you go?

Because you can cycle fully ten miles through the partly wooded Castle Eden country park.

Where is it?

Northwest of Stockton-on-Tees. Park at the visitor centre signposted off the A177 at Thorpe Thewles. Or at car parks off the A689 between Billingham and Sedgefield. There's no parking at the reservoir.

Where can you ride?

Take the trail as far as Hurworth Burn reservoir (west of the A19

east of Trimdon). Look out for the specially-built bridge across the busy A689 halfway along.

What else can you do?

Get an insight into the local landscape at the visitor centre's indoor archaeology, biology and insect displays (01740 630011).

Where can you eat?

The visitor centre serves snacks.

 OS Landranger Map 93

10 Three Rivers Route – Hartlepool to Sunderland

Why should you go?

Sustrans' wonderful Three Rivers route allows you to travel the 20 miles between Hartlepool and the centre of Sunderland almost entirely on flat, car-free tracks.

Where is it?

Between Teesside and Wearside. Park and start at Hart Station off the A1086, or pick up the route at Hesleden or Castle Eden Inn, Shotton Colliery (the old station), Haswell, South Hetton, Seaham, Ryhope, Tunstall Hills or in the Sunderland area. Part of the Three Rivers route, the ride runs on south to Middlesbrough and north to South Shields as well as to the Castle Eden Walkway (9) and Consett-Sunderland Cycleway (15).

Where can you ride?

The southern section, the lovely Hart to Haswell Walkway rail trail, is nine miles long, between north of Hartlepool and South Hetton, where the trail splits. The Sunderland route continues on a rail trail 11 miles north to

Ryhope, through the Tunstall Hills and into the heart of the pedestrianised city centre to within 100m of the station. The other branch turns northeast to Seaham on the coast, which connects back to the rail trail to Ryhope via quiet, signposted roads. For full details, the 'Three Rivers Cycle Route' map from Sustrans reveals all (see p8).

What else can you do?

Any budding mechanics in the family will love nearby Ryhope Engines Museum.

Where can you eat?

There are plenty of good pubs in the villages en route.

 OS Landranger Map 88, 93

11 Brandon & Bishop Auckland Walk rail trail

Why should you go?

For an easy pedalling rail trail.

Where is it?

South of Durham. Start on the north side of Bishop Auckland at Newton Cap viaduct car park, which lies off the A689 Crook Road, or near Durham at Broompark car park.

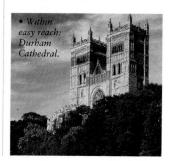
• *Within easy reach: Durham Cathedral.*

Northumbria

Where can you ride?

Alongside the Wear river. Use the laminated route cards for this and six other Co. Durham rail trails, available from Durham County Council – see Auckland Way rail trail (5) for details.

What else can you do?

You can visit Auckland Castle & Deer House or magnificent Durham cathedral.

Where can you eat?

There are cafes in Bishop Auckland and pubs in Hunwick, Willington and Brancepeth.

 OS Landranger Map 88, 92, 93

JORDANS ALL AGES

12 Deerness Valley Walk rail trail

Why should you go?

Because it's an easy rail trail, perfect for youngsters.

Where is it?

West of Durham. Start at Broompark picnic site. From the A617 take the A690 to Crook and then the first right on to the B6302 (the site is on the left). The nearest train station is Durham.

Where can you ride?

The trail criss-crosses the River Deerness for a total of eight miles. Broompark is also the start of both the Lanchester Valley Walk rail trail (14) and the Brandon & Bishop Auckland rail trail (11).

What else can you do?

There are no major attractions nearby, so take your time with the children and enjoy the ride. Durham County Council's map pack (£2.75) – see Auckland Way rail trail (5) for details – will make sure you find your way.

Where can you eat?

There's a small choice in Esh Winning and Crook (which are also the only places for toilets), otherwise it's the perfect venue for a home-made picnic.

 OS Landranger Map 88

JORDANS OVER 8s

13 Hamsterley Forest trails

Why should you go?

Because you can hire mountain bikes and explore hilly, wild Hamsterley Forest on your choice of easy, moderate or challenging signposted circuits. Hire your bikes at Hamsterley Forest Bike Hire (01388 488188). If you are a particularly adventurous family of mountain bikers you can explore the challenging bridleways that extend out beyond the forest on to the moors. Alternatively there are open forest roads which you can ride on an ordinary bike.

Where are they?

Southwest of Durham. Park at Hamsterley Forest visitor centre, one mile from Hamsterley village. There's a toll on the road from Bedburn to the visitor centre.

Where can you ride?

Select from an easy one-and-a-half mile circuit, a moderate three-mile route for children with some cycling experience and a tough three-mile route which features a good climb for experienced little cyclists. Otherwise, take out your Ordnance Survey map and roam the general forest trails and roads that wind through the trees.

What else can you do?

What more do you need? Take your time and make a day of it among the pine trees.

Where can you eat?

Either on site at the visitor centre (01388 488312) or in the beer garden at the pub there.

 OS Landranger Map 92

JORDANS ALL AGES

14 Lanchester Valley Walk rail trail

Why should you go?

Because this rural railway line conversion is suitable for all ages.

Where is it?

It runs east-west between Durham and Consett. Park at Broompark picnic site, south of Durham (from the A617 on to the A690 toward Crook, take the first right on the B6302). There is more parking at Langley Park, Lanchester and Hownsgill.

Where can you ride?

The trail runs along the River Brownley and Backgill Burn for 12 miles, from the eastern end at Broompark car park to Langley Park, Lanchester, and to the A692 south of Consett at the Hownsgill viaduct. At Broompark you can join the Deerness Valley rail trail (12) and Brandon & Bishop Auckland Walk rail trail (11). At Consett link up with the Waskerley Way rail trail (16), Derwent Valley Walk rail trail (17) and Consett & Sunderland rail trail (15). For details of how to purchase a route card see Auckland Way, above (5).

• *The spectacular Sustrans Coast to Coast route runs between the Lake District and Northumbria.*

What else can you do?

Step back in time at the Beamish Open Air Museum (0191 370 4000) with life-size Victorian reconstructions of a town, colliery village, manor and farm, railway and bank. The museum is five miles northeast of Lanchester, signposted from the A1(M) J63.

Where can you eat?

Try Lanchester or Consett.

 OS Landranger Map 88

15 Consett & Sunderland rail trail

Why should you go?

For an unforgettable combination of easy riding and the dramatic industrial sculptures and earthworks by artist Andy Goldsworthy that you pass on the way. A flagship cycle route, the Consett to Sunderland line was one of the nation's earliest railways (1834) and one of Sustrans' earliest conversions.

Where is it?

Between Co. Durham and Tyne & Wear. You can start at Hownsgill car park (off the A692 south of Consett) or at Consett or Annfield Plain, Stanley, Beamish, Chester-le-Street or James Steel Park in Washington.

Where can you ride?

This is cycling heaven. If you are feeling up to it, go the whole 22 miles from the western end at Consett all the way to Sunderland marina (where there is a link to Sunderland centre on the south side of the Wear). Otherwise, turn back at any of the other villages and towns along the way. The ride is one of two east-coast options on the long distance Coast to Coast (C2C) route to the Lake District. The other is the South Tyne cycleway (18). Consett is also the connection for three other trails: the Waskerley Way (16), Derwent Valley Walk (17) and Lanchester Valley route (14). Sustrans' excellent C2C map (p8) covers the entire route.

What else can you do?

Cycle to the Beamish Open Air Museum en route. If you have the energy, of course!

Where can you eat?

At any of the towns and villages en route, or at the cafe at the museum. There is also a cafe at Washington Arts Centre. In Sunderland's North Hylton is the

Northumbria

Shipwrights Hotel which has excellent views from the restaurant, a garden and children's menu (Ferry Boat Lane, 0191 549 5139).

 OS Landranger Map 88

JORDANS
OVER 12s

16 Waskerley Way rail trail

Why should you go?
Because you and the kids are ready to ride a rather more adventurous (and hilly) rail trail. Travelling upwards, you will need your strength and a good mountain bike. And as long as the children have good bike control, the easterly downhill after the climb is a real thrill.

Where is it?
Southwest of Consett in County Durham. Park at Hownsgill viaduct, signposted off the A692, or at Rowley station, Waskerley picnic site or Meeting Slacks.

Where can you ride?
The trail runs from Consett up into the Durham Dales to the high summit of Weatherhill over a total of ten miles. The nearest town to the hilltop finish is Stanhope down that steep descent. A laminated route card is available to make life easier. See Auckland Way (5) for details.

What else can you do?
Visit the Durham Dales Centre at Stanhope, or the animals of Cherryburn, the 19th-century farmhouse of Northumberland artist Thomas Bewick now owned by the National Trust (seven miles north of Consett near Stocksfield, 01661 843276).

Where can you eat?
There is a small choice of cafes in Consett and Stanhope, but this is a route crying out to be accompanied by a picnic.

 OS Landranger Map 87, 88 (92 for Stanhope)

JORDANS
OVER 12s

17 Derwent Valley Walk rail trail

Why should you go?
To explore the Derwent up from the heart of Tyneside through woods and old industrial sites all the way to Consett. Here the route meets three other trails, the Waskerley Way (16), the Lanchester Valley (14) and the Consett & Sunderland route (15).

Where is it?
Southwest of Newcastle-upon-Tyne (*below*). Park at Swalwell visitor centre, beside Blaydon rugby club (signposted from the A694 and B6317) or at Rowlands Gill, Pontburn Wood, Ebchester, Shotley Bridge or Lydgetts Junction. The city start is not far from the train station serving Gateshead Metro Centre.

Where can you ride?
For anything up to 11 miles (one way) from Swalwell visitor centre, passing Winlaton Mill, Rowlands Gill, Hamsterley and Ebchester before reaching Consett. For details of how to order a laminated route card pack see Auckland Way, above (5).

What else can you do?
For the body-conscious family, Newcastle's attractions include Life, which features hands-on activities and virtual reality exhibits that uncover the secret of life (Times Square, Scotswood Road, 0870 444 3364).

Where can you eat?
There are pubs at Rowlands Gill, Ebchester and Shotley Bridge, as well as a simple cafe at the campsite in Rowlands Gill.

 OS Landranger Map 88

JORDANS
OVER 8s

18 Tyneside cycleways, north and south banks

Why should you go?
To sample miles and miles of Tyneside by bike. The area is blessed with good routes either side of the river as well as fabulous town and country connections. The South Tyne cycleway runs for 14 miles, and the North Tyne cycleway is 19 miles long. A single section of the latter from Newcastle Quayside to North Shields ferry terminal is nine miles one way. Take the ferry over the river to South Shields to pick up the South Tyne cycleway and the coastal route to Sunderland.

Where are they?

On the north and south banks of the Tyne in and around Newcastle. The nearest stations are Wylam, Blaydon and Hebburn (bikes are not allowed on the Metro).

Where can you ride?

Where can't you ride? The roll-call includes Blaydon, Gateshead, Jarrow, South Shields and North Shields. The highlight is the spectacular steel-arched walking and cycling Millennium Bridge downstream of the famous Tyne Bridge, linking Newcastle Quayside and Gateshead. With dedicated cycle crossings at

Blaydon, the Tyne walking and cycling tunnels near Jarrow and the ferry between North and South Shields, any number of circular routes are possible. CycleCity's Tyneside map is available from Sustrans. Routes in and around Tyneside are covered by three Sustrans maps: 'Three Rivers Cycle Route', 'Coast & Castles Cycle Route' and 'C2C Cycle Route'. See p8 for details.

What else can you do?

At Jarrow you will find St Paul's Monastery & Bede's World, the priory home of the Venerable Bede (0191 489 2106). There are more options on the north bank: the sculpture trail on Newcastle Quayside, Wallsend shipyard cranes, Segedunum Roman Fort and the North Shields Fish Quay. At Tynemouth see the remains of the 11th-century Priory (*left*) & Castle, with its underground chambers (0191 489 2106).

Where can you eat?

No picnic? Then make for the tearoom at Souter Lighthouse.

 OS Landranger Map 88

---

19 South Shields and Sunderland coastal route

Why should you go?

Because you get to cycle down the coast past the spectacular Leas cliffs and the oldest lighthouse in the country at Souter Point.

Where is it?

Between the mouths of the Tyne and the Wear. The nearest train station is Sunderland (bikes aren't allowed on the Tyneside Metro).

Where can you ride?

For a total of nine miles, from the northern end of the route at South Shields to Marsden, Whitburn Colliery, South Bents and Sunderland. The route is connected to the South and North Tyne cycleways (18), the Consett & Sunderland trail (15) and the Coast to Coast (C2C) cycle route.

What else can you do?

Make a visit to the old 1871

Souter Lighthouse, which was the first to be powered by electric light. Or view the colourful wonders of the National Glass Centre in Sunderland.

Where can you eat?

Enjoy your own sarnies with the sea breeze blowing in your hair, or take a seat at the Souter Lighthouse tearooms.

 OS Landranger Map 88

---

20 Rising Sun Country Park rail trail

Why should you go?

So you can ride along the converted Coxlodge Waggonway to a marvellous country park created out of a former colliery.

Where is it?

North Tyneside. In the west the trail starts off the A191/A189 roundabout (South Gosforth), though there is also sufficient parking at the Rising Sun Countryside Centre.

Where can you ride?

For five miles, from the western end at South Gosforth (at the A191/A189 junction) to Little Benton Farm and the Rising Sun Country Park. Connect with the North and South Tyne cycleways (18) either side of the river.

What else can you do?

Get steamed up at Stephenson's Railway Museum nearby.

Where can you eat?

On the spot at the Rising Sun Countryside Centre. You can hire bikes there too.

 OS Landranger Map 88

Cumbria

The Lake District is England's most beautiful corner. A dramatic, colourful landscape of lakes, fells, valleys and coastlines shaped by nature and people. A unique place that has inspired poets, writers, painters and artists, and will inspire you with its peace, drama

and wide variety of landscape and activities.

Cycling is an ideal way to see Cumbria, bringing you closer to its sights, sounds and smells. With its quiet roads and friendly people, you are guaranteed a welcome wherever you ride.

Where to cycle when you visit

FINDING YOUR WAY

OS Landranger maps covering these areas:
88/89/96/90/97

Britain's national mapping agency

oS **Ordnance Survey®**
www.ordnancesurvey.gov.uk

Really get to know an area

with

Landranger®
The all purpose map

Barrow-in-Furness & South Lakeland

PLACES TO SEE

Ravenglass & Eskdale Railway
Small steam engines operate a frequent service from the Lake District coast at Ravenglass to the foot of England's highest mountains in Eskdale. An all-weather attraction, with the freedom of open spaces or the cosiness of covered carriages. You'll find a cafe and shop at both ends of the line. Cycles welcome.

The Sheep & Wool Centre, Cockermouth

The live sheep show introduces 19 breeds of sheep, Jersey cows, ducks and two breeds of working sheep dogs in an indoor auditorium. After the show meet the animals, browse the gift shop and then take a well-earned break in the cafe restaurant with home-cooked food throughout the day.

The Rum Story, Whitehaven
An excellent exhibition which

depicts the story of the UK Rum Trade, featuring a tropical rainforest, slave ship and an African village and giving you an unmissable opportunity to go on board with the Navy – all without ever leaving Whitehaven.

Muncaster Castle, Ravenglass
This historic haunted castle features the Wild Himalayan

Gardens, World Owl Centre and the Meadow Vole Maze. There's also a flying display and you can meet the birds daily, while breathtaking views of mountains and coast abound. Castle closed Saturdays. Telephone 01229 717614 or visit www.muncastercastle.co.uk

Cumbria Tourist Board

MAIN EVENTS

- **Maryport Songs of the Sea Festival**

Across the 10th and 11th August, an annual weekend of outdoor and indoor music, family fun, stalls, rides and traditional wooden fishing and sailing boats. Perfect for families.

WHAT ELSE IS ON?
- **Keswick Jazz Festival**
Though the main festival is from the 17th to 19th May, there are also five great days of jazz events at the Theatre by the Lake in the week before.
- **Holker Hall Garden Festival**
This major garden festival – the Chelsea Flower Show of the North – takes place between 31st May and 2nd June.
- **Tall Ships in Whitehaven**
Where you'll discover three tall ships to explore and numerous related events throughout the month. From 1st to 31st July.
- **Barrow Maritime Festival**
Barrow's Festival of the Sea – on 17th and 18th August – is a biennial celebration of maritime traditions.

USEFUL ADDRESSES & NUMBERS
- **Cumbria Tourist Board** Ashleigh, Holly Road, Windermere, LA23 2AQ; tel: 015394 44444; www.gocumbria.co.uk
- **Keswick Tourist Information Centre** Market Place, Keswick, CA12 5JR; tel: 017687 72645
- **Whitehaven Tourist Information Centre** Market Hall, Market Place, Whitehaven CA28 7JG; tel: 01946 852939
- **Western Lake District Tourism Partnership** www.western-lakedistrict.co.uk

69

Cumbria

21 Grizedale Forest trails

Why should you go?
Because you can choose from five signposted circuits, the easiest of which is just two miles long with one hill. Between them the circuits feature more than 80 original pieces of sculpture. You can get a free map from Forest Enterprise, Lakes Forest District, Grizedale, Hawkshead LA22 0QJ (01229 860373).

Where are they?
You will find the trails southwest of Ambleside in the southern Lakes. Head for Grizedale visitor centre, three miles from Hawkshead, and park there.

Where can you ride?
If the two-mile circuit is too easy, move up to either the two moderately difficult circuits of six and seven miles or the two demanding circuits of 10.5 miles and 14 miles. On each, older children can walk the inclines and still enjoy the rest of the ride. You can also ride freely around the bridleways and roads which cross the forest (look for the signs with grey bikes). Hire bikes from Grizedale Mountain Bikes at the visitor centre (01229 860369).

What else can you do?
If the sculptures have whetted your appetite for local culture, try the Beatrix Potter Gallery at Hawkshead (015394 36355), which features many of the author's original sketches in an unaltered building. Tourists will find plenty to do in Windermere town and Hawkshead.

Where can you eat?
There is a cafe at the visitor centre. Try also the King's Arms Hotel (garden, children's menu; 01539 436372) or the Eagle's Head pub at Satterthwaite which welcomes well-behaved children.

• *The picturesque Lake Windermere.*

 OS Landranger Map 97

22 Ennerdale forest roads

Why should you go?
To explore the forest roads of a large area of lovely Lakeland woodland.

Where are they?
East of Whitehaven in the western Lakes. Head for the car park at Bowness Knott, east off the A5086.

Where can you ride?
With an OS map work out your own routes along the forest tracks along the banks of the River Liza above Ennerdale Water, including those to Pillar and Chapel Crags. The trails of Blengdale Forest (23) lie ten miles distant. Miterdale Forest (24) is 15 miles away while Grizedale (21) is full of trails and best for facilities.

What else can you do?
With scenery like this, what more do you want? People come to this remote part of Lakeland for peace and quiet. If you are staying overnight, Ennerdale and Black Sail youth hostels lie in the valley. For anything else, head back to civilisation.

Where can you eat?
This is picnic country, so pack your own.

 OS Landranger Map 89

23 Blengdale forest roads

Why should you go?
For the smell of pine resin, the lack of cars and the freedom to navigate Blengdale's scenic forest roads yourself (the area is perfect for teaching the rudiments of map-reading).

Where are they?
Southeast of Whitehaven in the western Lakes. The roads occupy a large area of conifers beside the River Bleng east of the A595 near Seascale. Park in the village of Gosforth, off the A595. Seascale station is three miles away.

Where can you ride?
Take the OS map and work out a few routes on the slopes that run up the sides of the valley. Exhaust these and the marvellous Grizedale Forest (21) lies a little further to the south.

What else can you do?
Take a break and listen to the birdsong. There are no nearby attractions, and that's the point.

Where can you eat?
As a working forest, Blengdale has no facilities itself, so pack a picnic or head for the pub further

into the fells near Wastwater. The Screes Hotel at Nether Wasdale (01946 726262) has a garden, children's menu, real ale and accommodation. Wastwater Youth Hostel, four miles further east, offers cheap basic accommodation.

 OS Landranger Map 89

24 Miterdale forest roads

Why should you go?
To explore where you wish along the peaceful wooded forest tracks beside the River Mite.

Where is it?
Northeast of Ravenglass. Park beside the river on the minor road to Eskdale Green off the A595. The nearest train station is Drigg.

Where can you ride?
Use the OS map to work out your own routes, exploring as little or as much as you wish.

What else can you do?
Fans of Thomas the Tank Engine will love the Ravenglass & Eskdale steam railway that runs from the coast. Alternatively, show the children where the Romans once washed at Ravenglass bathhouse.

Where can you eat?
Pack your own food for the forest or head for the King George IV Inn at Eskdale Green (01946 723262). It's handily situated about half a mile from the start of the forest and has a garden, children's menu, accommodation and baby changing facilities.

 OS Landranger Map 89, 96

Tom Bailey

JORDANS FAMILY CYCLING GUIDEBOOK

Cumbria

• The beauty of Lakeland from the trail above Grasmere. Ripe for a return trip when the children are big enough.

Tom Bailey

JORDANS OVER 12s
25 Broughton Moor forest roads

Why should you go?
For the dramatic views, including glimpses of the Duddon Estuary, plus the freedom to roam the forest tracks.

Where are they?
Above Broughton in Furness, in the southwestern Lakes. Park on the road from Broughton Mills to Torver, off the A593. Foxfield station is three miles away.

Where can you ride?
Read the OS map and pick your own routes. As a rule, they get hillier towards the north.

What else can you do?
Take your time. And take in the surroundings.

Where can you eat?
You will need to take your own food and drink for a picnic lunch. For tea, head for Broughton in Furness, two miles south, and its cafes and restaurants.

 OS Landranger Map 96

JORDANS OVER 12s
26 Whinlatter Forest Park circuits

Why should you go?
To experience riding short adventurous circuits in a spectacular location. Whinlatter Forest sits dramatically atop Whinlatter Pass and is worth a visit in its own right.

Where is it?
The forest is west of Keswick in the northwestern Lakes. You can

park at the Whinlatter Forest visitor centre on the B5292. The nearest train stations are Workington and Penrith.

Where can you ride?
On two tough, hilly cycle circuits, one 1.5 miles long (orange signs) the other 2.7 miles long (purple signs), which at one point cross the high Whinlatter Pass itself. Get a leaflet from Whinlatter Forest Park (01768 778469). Easier trails in the area include the beginner's circuits in Grizedale Forest (21), Keswick rail trail (27) and Whitehaven rail trail (28).

What else can you do?
Go to the visitor centre, or escape back down to shelter in Keswick for the unique Cars of the Stars Motor Museum. You will find the youth hostel down there too.

Where can you eat?
You can get refreshments at the visitor centre, or return to Keswick and try the George Hotel, which hosts children up to 9pm with their own menu (3 St John Street, 01768 772076).

 OS Landranger Map 89

JORDANS ALL AGES
27 Keswick rail trail

Why should you go?
For easy cycling through a stretch of exceptionally beautiful countryside.

Where is it?
Between Keswick and Threlkeld in the northern Lakes. The Keswick end starts at the old station near the Leisure Pool. The nearest running railway line is at Penrith, 16 miles away.

Where can you ride?
The trail lies on the fabulous long-distance Coast to Coast route. Join at Keswick for four miles of uninterrupted cycling to Threlkeld. Hire bikes at Keswick Mountain Bikes, Southey Hill, Keswick (017687 75202).

What else can you do?
For dramatic scenery, go up Whinlatter Pass to Whinlatter Forest (26). There's also Castlerigg stone circle with its 33 monoliths, just east of Keswick.

Where can you eat?
Try the family-friendly George Hotel in Keswick (01768

772076), or the choice of cafes in Keswick. In Threlkeld the Salutation Inn has a family room, swings in the garden and a children's menu (01768 779614).

 OS Landranger Map 90

28 Whitehaven to Rowrah rail trail

Why should you go?

For easy, traffic-free cycling from the coast into the hills. Start from Rowrah and take advantage of a slight decline towards the coast. A West Cumbria Cycle Network leaflet is available by calling Sustrans Information Service on 0117 9290888.

Where is it?

Near Whitehaven in western Cumbria. There are car parks at each end in Whitehaven and Rowrah and a train station at Whitehaven.

Where can you ride?

Pick up the start of the trail in Whitehaven, signposted C2C south along Preston Street. Rowrah is nine miles away, via Whitehaven harbour, Moor Row and Cleator Moor. The trail is the start of the long-distance Coast to Coast route (see Sustrans p8), which you could return to with the kids when they're old enough.

What else can you do?

There are no major attractions nearby, so make sure you are coming for the ride.

Where can you eat?

There are pubs in Cleator Moor and Rowrah (although they are not officially family-friendly), but once you are on the trail, you will need your own food and drink.

 OS Landranger Map 88

Yorkshire

It is unfair to say cycling has returned to Yorkshire as a result of new cycle routes in the past ten years – because it never actually left. The region's beautiful uplands contrast with low-lying areas where the majority of the area's easier trails are found. Disused railway line conversions are common, as part of longer national cycle routes, and as themselves.

The eastern half of the long-distance Trans Pennine Way (TPT), created by Sustrans, arrives over the Pennines from Manchester, heads towards Barnsley and continues on to Hull. Other routes on the National Cycle Network without traffic lie further south around Sheffield.

Hull and York, both bicycle cities, feature good car-free rides in addition to road networks. And for holidays, try the North York Moors, where you can cycle in Dalby Forest one day and along the coastal rail trail between Scarborough and Whitby the next.

Where to cycle when you visit

PLACES TO SEE

Eureka! The museum for children, Halifax (07626 983191)

Everyday life is explained at this fascinating museum as your kids answer their own questions of why?, what? and how? through a series of interactive adventures. Loads of buttons to push and levers to pull mean even the little ones can have fun exploring the mechanics of household objects and the human body. For a while at least, the pressure's off the parents to provide answers!

Magna Science Adventure Centre, Rotherham (01709 720002)

Having come down off the wild and windy moors, Magna Science offers another – albeit drier and warmer – dose of the natural elements. Fire, Earth, Air and Water each have a separate area in this former steelworks that's been transformed into a celebration of science and technology. It's both hugely interactive and highly educational, and certainly the biggest and safest chemistry set available!

Cleethorpes Humber Estuary Discovery Centre (01472 323232)

Not only is there the natural beauty of this large and busy estuary to savour, but also a fantastic visitor centre that's been designed with kids very much in mind. The centre allows, even encourages, them to pretend they're an invading Viking or a lugworm crawling through a burrow, while a high-powered telescope gives great views of the busy shipping lanes. Nearby, the friendly local wildfowl will happily be fed.

www.britainonview.com

MAIN EVENTS

• Jorvik Viking Festival

York's fascinating Jorvik Centre hosts the 'Jolablot' festival each February – a Viking celebration of the coming of spring. The programme, which includes re-enactments of landmarks in Viking history, saga telling and craft demonstrations, provides excellent family entertainment. In 2002, it runs between 9th and 16th February.

WHAT ELSE IS ON?

• Sea Fever

For a taste of life on the ocean waves, head for Hull Marina between 31st August and 1st September You'll be entertained by a colourful array of shanty and sea music performers, hornpipe dancing, maritime craft demonstrations and the North Sea Classic boat.

• Arthington Show, Bramhope

This event features showjumping, classes for a variety of farm animals, dog shows and horticulture and handicraft classes. Ensuring the kids have a good time, there's also a funfair (21st July).

• World Coal Carrying Championships

West Yorkshire's world famous test of stamina and muscle grips Osset each Easter Monday. The aim is to carry a 50kg (for men) bag of coal for just under a mile. Female competitors carry a 20kg bag, and there's also a scaled-down kids class.

USEFUL ADDRESS & NUMBER

• Yorkshire Tourist Board

Tel: 01904 707961; website: www.yorkshirevisitor.com

• *Yorkshire has always been a home of cycling and now looms large on the National Cycle Network.*

Tom Bailey

Yorkshire

JORDANS ALL AGES

29 Worsbrough reservoir circuit

Why should you go?

Because it's a nice short, safe circuit around a reservoir with a working watermill and museum for visiting when you've finished.

Where is it?

South of Barnsley. Park at the car park at Worsbrough Bridge, off the M1 J36.

Where can you ride?

The circuit is a mile-and-a-half around the reservoir.

What else can you do?

Investigate the watermill. A mill has stood on this site for 900 years, and the current preserved wheel is a complex of grinding cogs and gear wheels.

Where can you eat?

If you've forgotten your picnic you can get drinks and snacks at the visitor centre (01226 774527).

 OS Landranger Map 111

JORDANS ALL AGES

30 The Burton Constable Country Park trails

Why should you go?

For the freedom of riding family-friendly tracks in the grounds of Constable Hall and around its two lakes.

Where is it?

Northeast of Hull. You get to the main car park through the campsite, signed from Sproatley on the B1238 eight miles northeast of the city.

Where can you ride?

Anywhere you like. There are short routes to suit little legs, such as the half-mile ride around the Higher Lake, as well as longer trips of up to several miles in the quiet surrounding lanes.

What else can you do?

There is a play area on the caravan site, and Constable Hall has outbuildings with a shop, cafe and exhibitions.

Where can you eat?

At the Constable Hall cafe.

 OS Landranger Map 107

31 Oakwell Hall Country Park

Why should you go?

If you live in Leeds or Bradford this is an easy day out in the local countryside. Oakwell Hall is an oasis of woodland and grassland in the middle of the Leeds-Bradford conurbation. It's perfect for cycling and there's plenty more for the children to do.

Where is it?

Northwest of Birstall, south of the M62 southwest of Leeds. There are two car parks, one at the hall and one next to the adventure playground, signposted from M62 J26, A58, A651 and A652, also from Leeds M62 J27 and A62.

Where can you ride?

For a mile-and-a-half there and back on a short linear bridleway through the park, or if you fancy a longer run, take the second bridleway that bisects the park as it runs north-south between Drighlington and Batley.

What else can you do?

Oakwell Hall is an Elizabethan mansion, with hands-on exhibits at the discovery gallery, plus holiday events, nature trails and an adventure playground.

Where can you eat?

If you run out of sandwiches there is a cafe at the visitor centre (01924 326246).

 OS Landranger Map 104

32 The Upper Don & Dove Valley rail trails

Why should you go?

For easy riding on two good grade connected rail trails on the Trans-Pennine Trail: the westerly six-mile Upper Don Trail and the easterly seven-mile Dove Valley Trail. Future developments may include riding through the currently closed Oxspring tunnel where the pair meet (currently you have to ride cross-country). As a crossroads on the National Cycle Network built by Sustrans (see p8), the area is rich in new cycle trails. You can cycle north to Leeds and south to Sheffield as well as east-west on the Trans-Pennine Trail.

Where are they?

The Upper Don Trail stretches from Dunford Bridge to southwest of Barnsley. Dunford Bridge has a family-friendly pub and parking. The nearest station that end is Penistone. The Dove Valley Trail is southwest of Barnsley. Park at Worsbrough Country Park, just off the A61, south of Barnsley. The nearest railway stations are Silkstone and Wombwell.

Where can you ride?

The Upper Don Trail is 13 miles in total from Dunford Bridge in the west; Oxspring is six miles into the trail and from there you can continue three miles southeast to Wortley station then Wharncliffe Wood and the route to Elsecar. The Dove Valley Trail runs for seven miles, from the western end at Silkstone Common through Gilroyd, Worsbrough Country Park, Aldham Junction, Wombwell and Broomhill. The Elsecar Greenway runs westward from Broomhill to Elsecar, continuing to Tankersley, becoming the Timberland Trail to Wortley where it connects with the Upper Don trail. For further details, order a Trans-Pennine Trail map from Sustrans (see p8).

What else can you do?

Visit the working Worsbrough mill (*above*) or some feathered friends at Old Moor Wetland Centre at Broomhill (01226 751593). There's the Elsecar Heritage Centre or the ambitious Earth Centre with its 26 acres of indoor and outdoor activities about sustainable living (Denaby Main, Doncaster, 01709 613933).

Where can you eat?

The Stanhope Arms at Dunford Bridge is recommended, or at

Yorkshire

Penistone there's the family-friendly Cubley Hall with a play area, restaurant and two family rooms (Mortimer Road, 01226 766086). You can also find food at the Old Moor Wetland Centre.

 OS Landranger Map 110

33 Anglers Country Park & Haw Park woodland trails

Why should you go?
Because the area offers easy pedalling for children of all ages on signposted circuits as well as open tracks.

Where are they?
At the Heronry, southeast of Wakefield. Park at Anglers Country Park visitor centre.

Where can you ride?
Choose from two signposted two-mile circuits in Anglers through grassland and young woodland, or follow any tracks in neighbouring Haw Park Woods.

What else can you do?
The visitor centre has an interactive exhibition that requires the donning of helmets. That should intrigue the kids…

Where can you eat?
The visitor centre serves refreshments.

 OS Landranger Map 111

34 Staveley to Beighton rail trail

Why should you go?
Because it's an easy rail trail

through the country park with refreshments not far away.

Where is it?
East of Sheffield. Park at Staveley (on the A619) or at Rother Valley Country Park (off the A618 southeast of Sheffield). The nearest railway station is Woodhouse Mill, two miles northeast of Beighton.

Where can you ride?
For a total of six miles, from the western end, between Staveley, Renishaw, Killamarsh, Rother Valley Country Park and Beighton. The rail trail is on the Chesterfield to Meadowhall National Cycle Network route (for details turn to p8).

What else can you do?
Besides enjoying the park, there are multiple nearby attractions. South Yorkshire Aircraft museum is close, while the remains of the dramatic 14th-century Roche Abbey lie in a landscaped park northeast of the country park (01709 812739, English Heritage).

Where can you eat?
At the country park visitor centre, also at Staveley, Renishaw and Killamarsh.

 OS Landranger Map 120

35 Aire & Calder Navigation

Why should you go?
For car-free riding along a pretty towpath, part of the impressive 18th-century canal link between the east and west coasts.

Where is it?
The trail runs out southeast from

Leeds. Park at Woodlesford railway station off the A642 southeast of the city centre. The nearest train stations are Leeds and Woodlesford.

Where can you ride?
For seven miles, from Leeds centre southeastward to Woodlesford. The kids will need good bike control.

What else can you do?
Visit Thwaites Mill Industrial museum near the halfway point, while animals await (*below*) at Home Farm, Colton, two-and-a-half miles north of Woodlesford. The Middleton steam railway runs from Belle Isle four miles south of the city centre.

Where can we eat?
Like any city centre, Leeds has all the usual eateries, but why not make this one day when you give fast food a miss?

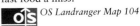 *OS Landranger Map 104*

36 Leeds & Liverpool canal, Aire Valley

Why should you go?
For a scenic journey along the

canal into Leeds from Saltaire, home of the Hockney gallery. A monumental achievement, the canal was the first waterway to cross the Pennines and connect the east and west coasts.

Where is it?
Heading west from Leeds. Park at Shipley station or Granary Wharf in Leeds. The nearest train stations are Shipley and Leeds.

Where can you ride?
For a total of 13 miles between Shipley, Horsforth, Granary Wharf and the centre of Leeds. It gets a little tricky in parts so go only if the children have good bike control.

What else can you do?
David Hockney's brightly-coloured work makes a good introduction to art for children. Find it at the 1853 Gallery on the canal at Saltaire near Shipley (01274 531163). Leeds Industrial Museum is an 1805 cotton mill with exhibits on four floors and a working spinning mill plus 1920s cinema and locomotives (Armley, 0113 263 7861).

Where can you eat?
There is a pleasant cafe at the 1853 Gallery.

 OS Landranger Map 104

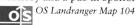

37 Harland Way rail trail

Why should you go?
Because it's a charming rail trail, with the added incentive of Spofforth Castle just a mile further on.

Where is it?
Southeast of Harrogate. Park at Wetherby old station car park, Linton Road, off the A661 northwest from town. The nearest train stations are Pannal (four miles west) and Harrogate (six miles north of Spofforth).

Where can you ride?
Along the whole trail for three miles, or four including the castle.

What else can you do?
Spofforth Castle is a manor house with an undercroft built into the rock. Otherwise, head for Mother Shipton's Cave at Knaresborough three miles north of Spofforth.

Where can you eat?
There is plenty of choice in Wetherby and a pub in Spofforth.

 OS Landranger Map 104

JORDANS ALL AGES

38 York to Selby rail trail

Why should you go?
It's one of Sustrans' earliest railway line conversions. You and the family get to cruise across a broad stretch of lowland between

the city and the town, with a signed continuation into York centre (*above*) via the racecourse and the Ouse riverside.

Where is it?
South of York. There is general parking in both York and Selby (and there's a Tesco car park at Askham Bar) and train stations at either end. To get the York City cycle map, email: walking.cycling@york.gov.uk or check details on the website: www.york.gov.uk/outabout/travelling/bike

Where can you ride?
For 15 miles, from the southern end, between the centre of Selby, Riccall, Bishopthorpe and the centre of York. The trail lies on National Cycle Route 65, going north to Middlesbrough and east to the Humber estuary and Hull.

What else can you do?
Take time to visit historic and picturesque York. Attractions include the National Railway Museum (01904 621261), York Castle Museum (01904 653611), York Minster, the largest medieval cathedral in northern Europe, and the Jorvik Viking Centre, which recreates the old Viking capital (01904 643211).

Where can you eat?
On the canalside at Selby there's the Anchor Inn with chipmunks, fish and swings (01757 270255). York's Ye Olde Starre Inn, 100m from York Minster, has an all-weather garden and kid's menu (40 Stonegate, 01904 623063).

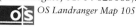 *OS Landranger Map 105*

JORDANS ALL AGES

39 Foss Island nature park trail

Why should you go?
For easy pedalling on a short

Yorkshire

green corridor on the eastern side of the city of York.

Where is it?
Start either at the old Rowntree factory or Osbaldwick.

Where can you ride?
For three miles, from the old Rowntree factory in York to Wigginton Road and on to Osbaldwick. Future plans include extensions east on a rail trail to Stamford Bridge, and possibly into York centre to link with the Millennium Bridge over the Ouse and the southerly cycle path to Knavesmire racecourse.

What else can you do?
York is full of attractions (see the York to Selby rail trail (38)). Alternatively, catch the steam train that occasionally runs from Osbaldwick to Murton.

Where can you eat?
York has a great choice of places to dine and drink. Try Ye Olde Starre Inn near York Minster (01904 623063).

 OS Landranger Map 105

 JORDANS
ALL AGES

40 York to Beningbrough cycle trail

Why should you go?
Because this lovely Ouse-side path features Sustrans' trademark open-air works of art and runs on quiet lanes to the National Trust-owned Beningbrough Hall, which is perfect for kids.

Where is it?
Heading out north of York. Use the York centre car parks, then ride to the Ouse's eastern riverbank and go northwest.

Where can you ride?
At the southern end start at Lendal Bridge in the centre of York, head northwest on the east bank of the Ouse for four miles to Skelton and, if you wish, another five miles on quiet lanes to Shipton and Beningbrough Hall.

What else can you do?
Beningbrough Hall, a Georgian mansion with a great central corridor, runs family events, has a wilderness play area, a children's guide and a cafe with a children's menu (01904 470666).

Where can you eat?
Either pick from a great choice in York or eat at that cafe at Beningbrough Hall.

 OS Landranger Map 105

JORDANS
ALL AGES

41 Market Weighton to Bubwith rail trail

Why should you go?
Because it offers gentle riding for the whole family.

Where is it?
Southeast of York. Park at Bubwith village on the A163 east of Selby. The trail starts half a mile south on the road to Breighton. The nearest train station is Wressle.

Where can you ride?
For 12 miles one way (24 miles return), on the rail trail between Bubwith at the western end, Foggathorpe and the A1079 west of Market Weighton. The Hudson Way rail trail (42) stretches east from Market Weighton.

What else can you do?
The Real Aeroplane Museum is

• In Yorkshire, riding varies from a traverse of the North York Moors to towpaths in Leeds and escapes to the North Sea.

Tom Bailey

one mile south of the start of the trail at Bubwith.

Where can you eat?
There's a small choice in villages en route, or take your own picnic.

 OS Landranger Map 106

JORDANS
ALL AGES

42 Hudson Way rail trail

Why should you go?
Because it offers cruising along the southern edge of the Yorkshire Wolds on an easy old railway line.

Where is it?
Between Market Weighton and

Beverley, northwest of Hull. Park at Market Weighton at the old station, north of Station Road off St Helen's Square behind the church. At Beverley, park off the bypass north of town. Beverley is the nearest station.

Where can you ride?

For 11 miles, between Market Weighton in the west and Beverley. Another rail trail runs westward from Market Weighton to Bubwith (41).

What else can you do?

Skidby windmill lies four miles south of Beverley on the A164, or head for the centre of Hull eight miles south for the Fish Heritage Trail plus the Hands-On, Streetlife and Maritime museums.

Where can you eat?

Beverley has a good family pub, the White Horse Inn, where children are welcome away from the bar; it has a garden too (22 Hengate, 01482 861973).

 OS Landranger Map 106, 107

JORDANS
ALL AGES

43 Hull to Patrington rail trail

Why should you go?

To make an easy-going escape from the city to the North Sea.

Where is it?

East of the city. Start in Hull at Southcoates Lane, also Hedon and Patrington.

Where can you ride?

The full trail runs for 13 miles.

What else can you do?

Hull offers a Fish Heritage Trail, Hands-On museum, Streetlife museum and Maritime museum, also the Spurn Lightship in Humber dock marina.

Where can you eat?

In Hull there is a good family-friendly venue along the Beverley Road, the St Johns Hotel. It has music, family rooms and a garden and is situated about a mile north of the centre (10 Queens Road, 01482 343669).

 OS Landranger Map 107

Yorkshire

44 Hull to Hornsea rail trail

Why should you go?
Completing the ride from the centre of Hull to the seaside town of Hornsea makes a good afternoon run for older, more advanced children, while younger ones can do shorter sections.

Where is it?
The trail begins in the northeast of the city. Find the start at Dansom Lane off Holderness Road east of the city centre, west of the junction of Holderness Road and Mount Pleasant.

Where can you ride?
For a total of 13 miles, between the centre of Hull, heading east to New Ellerby and Hornsea.

What else can you do?
Once you get there, enjoy the pleasures of seaside Hornsea.

Where can you eat?
You will find all that you need in Hull and Hornsea if you haven't packed your own.

 OS Landranger Map 107

45 Dalby Forest trails

Why should you go?
To experience wild pinescapes on the North York Moors on family trails suitable for older, more advanced children.

Where are they?
Northeast of Pickering on the North York Moors. The entrance to the forest lies off the minor road one mile north out of Thornton le Dale (on the A170 two miles east of Pickering). Note, there is an entrance fee. Park at Dalby Forest visitor centre at Low Dalby two miles along the forest drive. The trails are signposted off the forest drive. The nearest station is Malton, seven miles south.

Where can you ride?
On two trails: a six-mile beginner/family green trail on grass tracks and forest roads on the high plateau; and an eight-mile blue route on forest roads and grass tracks, which is steep in places. Two other tougher routes are designed for 'head down' riders and can give the children something to aspire to in the future. There is a trail map available at the visitor centre (01751 460295).

What else can you do?

There are play areas dotted around the forest at Snerdale and Adderstone Field. Or climb aboard the North Yorkshire Moors steam railway (*above*) which runs right across the high moorland plateau north-south from Pickering to Grosmont. Try also Pickering Castle which offers a free activity sheet for the kids (01751 474989).

Where can you eat?
At the visitor centre at Low Dalby (weekends only in winter).

 OS Landranger Map 94, 101

46 Scarborough to Whitby rail trail

Why should you go?
Because you get to see at first hand the cherished North Yorkshire coastline, passing the Ravenscar Cliffs and Robin Hood's Bay. There are plenty of pickup points if you are riding with little children, but note there is a taxing 130m slope from Whitby to above Robin Hood's Bay, and gradually up from Scarborough to Ravenscar.

Where is it?
On the coast beside the North York Moors. Park at Safeways in Scarborough. Pick up at Scalby, Cloughton, Ravenscar and Robin Hood's Bay. The nearest stations are Scarborough and Whitby.

Where can you ride?
For 18 miles, between Manor Road in Scarborough in the south, Scalby, Cloughton, Ravenscar, Robin Hood's Bay, High Hawsker and Whitby south side (near Larpool Hall). Get a route leaflet (30p) from Scarborough DC, TIC Unit 3, Pavilion House, Valley Bridge Road, Scarborough North Yorkshire YO11 1UZ (01723 373333) and hire bikes from Trailways Cycle Hire, the Old Railway Station, Hawsker (01947 820207).

What else can you do?
Scarborough's wealth of

attractions includes the beach, Sea Life Centre, Watersplash World (*below*) and Kinderland. Also worth a trip are the giant shaggy steeds at Shire Horse Farm at Staintondale six miles north of Scarborough.

Where can you eat?
Child-friendly places include, on the north side of Scarborough, the Scalby Mills Old Hotel which has great views, a children's room and open-air drinking. At Cloughton get tea at Cober Hill. At Ravenscar you will find the Foxcliffe tearooms and Raven Hall which serves teas and has a bar. At Robin Hood's Bay is the Dolphin Hotel. At High Hawsker is the Woodlands tearoom.

 OS Landranger Map 94

JORDANS
OVER 12s

47
Sneaton forest trail

Why should you go?
To give older children a taste of a long cross-moorland trail.
Where is it?
South of Whitby, North York Moors. The trail runs north-south from Sneaton Forest to the Dalby circular trails (45). Park at Falling Foss car park (on the B1416 five miles south of Whitby) or at Dalby Forest visitor centre. The nearest train station is Malton, which is six miles south of Thornton le Dale.
Where can we ride?
If the children are fit enough, take on the full 18-mile stone-based signposted trail through the forest (there are some steep slopes and you should arrange to be picked up at the far end). A family on the north side of the moors at Sneaton may extract a couple of miles of there-and-back fun from the trail, and also see Falling Foss waterfall. A cycling pack (£2.50) is available from Forest Enterprise, North York Moors District, Outgang Road, Pickering YO18 7EL (01751 472771).
What else can you do?
Apart from the waterfall, there are play areas in Dalby Forest.
Where can you eat?
The Wilson Arms is a family-

friendly pub in Sneaton serving good food with a garden (01947 602552). Walk from there along the Monks Path into Whitby

(*below left*) for a choice of eateries. You can also get refreshments at the Dalby Forest visitor centre.

 OS Landranger Map 94, 101

JORDANS
OVER 8s

48 Guisborough forest trail

Why should you go?
To cruise a combined rail trail and forest track on the northern slope of Guisborough Moor. The rail trail is easy and good for little ones. Adding the forest circuit extends and toughens the route somewhat for older children.
Where is it?
South of Middlesbrough on the edge of the North York Moors. Park at Pinchinthorpe car park, south of the A173/A171 junction, west of Guisborough. The nearest station is at Nunthorpe, three miles west.
Where can you ride?
For three miles (six miles return) along the well-surfaced rail trail. Or for five miles along the connected steeper, rougher forest circuit, which requires a sturdy bike and pedalling.
What else can you do?
Visit old Tocketts Watermill which lies two miles northeast along the A173 Saltburn road. Saltburn by the Sea boasts a Smugglers Heritage Centre full of tales of dirty dealing that should thrill little children.
Where can you eat?
If you haven't packed a picnic, try Guisborough.

 OS Landranger Map 93

North West

The new Trans Pennine Trail gets special mention in this chapter. Built by Sustrans, it runs from coast to coast on a series of old railways, parkland trails and canals, using as little roadway as possible. Quite an achievement considering the trail runs right past Liverpool and Manchester, over the Pennines to Sheffield, York and Hull. Parts of the TPT are broken down into separate trails, such as the Cheshire Lines path, the Sankey Valley path and the Warrington-to-Altrincham route.

Plenty of other gentle rural rides exist. Cheshire does well, and Lancaster features the Lune River cycle path from old Glasson docks to the big bend at Crook o'Lune.

Where to cycle when you visit

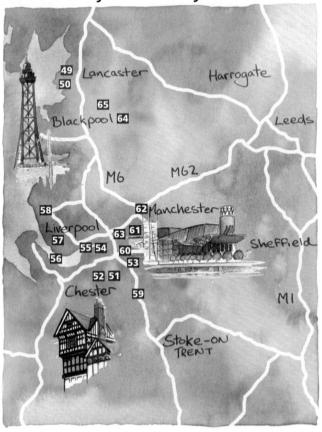

FINDING YOUR WAY

OS Landranger maps covering these areas:
96/97/103/108/109/110/117/118/119/190

Britain's national mapping agency

Ordnance Survey®
www.ordnancesurvey.gov.uk

Really get to know an area with **Landranger**
The all purpose map

PLACES TO SEE

National Football Museum, Preston (01772 908442)
Celebrate the history of our national game and bewilder the kids with ye olde fashioned football kit. Let them try their hand at being a *Match of the Day* pundit, then they can have their table footy skills analysed on video. There's almost as much to do as see, and of course, you can refuel in the museum's cafe.

Gulliver's World, Warrington (01925 444888)
It's a theme park aimed exclusively at kids, with lots of great rides for toddlers as well. There's so much to fire their imagination; from pirate ships and spooky castles, to rides on giant ladybirds and the Mad Hatter's Tea Party. Given the amount of entertainment on offer, it's best visited after a morning ride.

Planet Aquarium, Ellesmere Port (0151 3578800)
Sharks are always popular with kids, and this place boasts the largest collection of sand tiger sharks in Europe. Also, by taking one of the longest underwater walkways in the world, you can travel from a Scottish Glen, down the Amazon and across Lake Malawi to the sparkling depths of the Caribbean. There are also loads of interaction opportunities for the kids.

Greenacres Farm Park, Deeside (01244 531147)
All the usual farm park animals and attractions are on offer here, including tractor rides around the farm's 80 acres. To add a little exotic spice there are ostriches, wallabies, llamas, polecats and chipmunks, while clowns and puppets put on magic and comedy shows to give the kids a chuckle.

MAIN EVENTS

• Martell Grand National, Aintree
One of the highlights of the sporting calendar, the Grand National is a thrilling day out for horse lovers. The meeting runs for three days, culminating in the big race on Saturday afternoon (4th-6th April).

WHAT ELSE IS ON?
• Spirit Of Friendship Festival, Manchester
Run to coincide with the Commonwealth Games, and to tie in with the Queen's Golden Jubilee, the Spirit of Friendship Festival aims to combine sport, arts, culture and education to create an "unforgettable celebration of the Commonwealth" (11th March and 10th August).
• Cheshire County Show
Includes dog display teams, showjumping, handicrafts and a cheese show. Something, as they say, for everyone (18th-19th June).
• Aquafest
Onboard a variety of vessels floating down the city's waterways throughout July and August, Aquafest aims to entertain visitors to Manchester with a wide and diverse range of music.
• World Worm Charming Championships
Join hundreds of other baffled spectators for this unique annual event and watch as worms are charmed from the soil using every trick known to man (22nd February).

USEFUL ADDRESS & NUMBERS
• Northwest Tourist Board
Tel: 01942 821222; website: www.visitnorthwest.com

North West

49 Morecambe-Lancaster rail trail

Why should you go?
For gentle family riding either to or from the seaside. You could ride one way by bike and come back by train.

Where is it?
The Lancashire coast. The trail branches off the Lune rail trail (50) over the new Millennium Bridge in central Lancaster and on to the delights of Morecambe four miles away.

Where can you ride?
In Lancaster, start by riding across the Millennium Bridge over the River Lune in the city centre and bear left on to the rail trail. In Morecambe you can park at Morrisons store, or free on the promenade if you are lucky. The trail starts near Morrisons round the corner from the promenade. The trail also connects with the Lune cycleway. Hire bikes from Duke of Lancaster cycle hire (01524 849484).

What else can you do?
In Morecambe try the Megazone indoor laser adventure and Superbowl. For little children

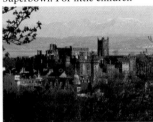

there's the Happy Mount Park at the east end of the promenade with a paddling pool, roundabouts, swing boats and

little trains. In Lancaster (*below left*) the Maritime Museum on the quayside has interactive displays on four levels that tell the story of Lancaster as a port through the ages (01524 64637).

Where can you eat?
There is a good choice at both ends, but if you get peckish halfway along you will need your own snacks.

 OS Landranger Map 96, 97

50 Lune rail trail: Glasson Dock to Bull Beck

Why should you go?
To experience gentle family cycling along an atmospheric stretch of old riverside railway.

Where is it?
On the Lancashire coast. Park at Glasson Dock, in Lancaster or at the Crook o'Lune picnic site (signed from the A683). Lancaster has a train station.

Where can you ride?
The trail stretches for five miles from the historic Glasson Docks at the mouth of the Lune estuary, through the centre of Lancaster via the quayside, as far as the Crook o'Lune near Caton, where the Lune carves a turning path through rocky cliffs (as depicted in the famous painting by Turner). In Lancaster, you can branch off to Morecambe along the rail trail (49). For full route details send for a leaflet from Lancaster City Council (01524 582902). Bike hire is available at Duke of Lancaster cycle hire (01524 849484).

What else can you do?
Why not give the little ones a fright at Lancaster Castle's court and prison? It's where Lancashire witches were once tried and condemned to death (01524 64998). Otherwise, there's the Lancaster Maritime Museum (01524 64637).

Where can you eat?
Take tea in Glasson, dine in Lancaster or try the pub in Caton beyond the Crook.

 OS Landranger Map 103

51 Whitegate Way rail trail

Why should you go?
For the perfect rural ride. Cycling as it used to be. The Whitegate Way trail boasts lovely views as it gently drops eastwards through the Cheshire countryside on an old salt-carrying railway line.

Where is it?
East of Chester (*below*). The best place to park is halfway along at

the old Whitegate Station (signed from the A54). There is also parking in Winsford at Bradford Road. The nearest train stations are Cuddington (two miles) and Winsford (one-and-a-half miles).

Where can you ride?

Start at Whitegate station and you can explore the trail in both directions and have a picnic on your return. The route in full is six miles between Cuddington (Oakmere Hall on the A556, four miles west of Northwich) to the minor New Road between Winsford and Whitegate. The Weaver Wanderer is a local road-based family cycle route that uses part of the Whitegate Way and quiet country lanes on an 11-mile circuit. Route leaflets are available from: Rural & Recreation HQ, Room 291, County Hall, Chester CH1 1SS (01244 602833).

What else can you do?

The children might enjoy Joe Crows play barn at Blakemere Craft Centre on Chester Road, Sandiway, south of Cuddington (01606 883261). And nearby is the spectacular Anderton Boat Lift, one mile north of Northwich. Children also get their own activity sheet at Beeston Castle, a huge 13th-century castle on a craggy outcrop ten miles southwest of Winsford (01829 260464). Otherwise the children will be thrilled by all the hi-tech interaction on offer at the Jodrell Bank Science Centre, home of the Lovell radio telescope (01477 571339). The centre lies 12 miles east of Winsford.

Where can you eat?

In Winsford High Street just south of the eastern end of the route you will find the family-friendly Golden Lion pub, which

• *The Crook o'Lune is the perfect spot for a family picnic at the end of the Glasson Dock to Bull Beck stretch of the Lune rail trail.*

has a bouncy castle at weekends and a children's menu (01606 592750). There is a limited choice of eateries in Whitegate.

 OS Landranger Map 117, 118

JORDANS OVER 8s

52 Delamere Forest trails

Why should you go?

To ride in some pretty woodland on two all-weather signposted forest trails which won't make you sweat too much. In part at least, the shorter route is suitable for little children.

Where is it?

East of Chester. Park at Linmere visitor centre near Delamere train station or at Hatchmere a mile further north on the B5152.

Where can you ride?

On two trails totalling 11 miles, the four-mile easy circuit (following blue signs) and the seven-mile circuit (white signs) for children over ten. The Delamere Forest Guide Map is available from Forest Enterprise, Linmere visitor centre, Delamere CW8 2JD (01606 882167). The Whitegate Way rail trail (51) lies four miles east.

What else can you do?

The visitor centre hosts lots of children's events, including birthday parties, Easter Bunny hunts and play schemes.

Where can you eat?

At the Abbey Arms pub, which has a garden and children's menu,

North West

south of the forest on the A556.

 OS Landranger Map 117

JORDANS OVER 8s

53 Tatton Park estate roads

Why should you go?
Because you get the run of eight miles of estate road in a grand 1000-acre deer park.

Where is it?
Southwest of Manchester. Tatton Park lies between Altrincham and Knutsford east of the A556 (signposted from the M56 J7/8 and M6 J19). The nearest train station is Knutsford.

Where can you ride?
All over the estate roads used by slow-moving traffic. Get a map of the park from Estate Operations Manager, Tatton Park, Knutsford, WA16 6QN.

What else can you do?
Take a tour of Tatton Park stately home and gardens (01625 534400). The kids will absolutely love its working farm and adventure playground.

Where can you eat?
There is food available in the estate's stableyard near the house.

 OS Landranger Map 118, 190

JORDANS ALL AGES

54 Warrington & Altrincham towpath & rail trail

Why should you go?
For easy navigation and car-free pedalling, although you'll need good bike control.

Where is it?
Between Warrington and Altrincham. Pick up the Manchester Ship canal at London Road, Stockton Heath on the south side of Warrington (A49 north from the M56 J10) or at Heatley, northeast of Lymm on the A6144 (east of the M6 J21). Park at the eastern end where Black Moss Road meets Seamons Road, west of Broadheath. The nearest train stations are Warrington and Altrincham.

Where can you ride?
For a total of seven miles along a section of the Manchester Ship Canal and then a rail trail. From the west, start at Latchford Lock on the Manchester Ship Canal (southeast of Warrington) through Lymm and Heatley to the minor road one mile northeast of Dunham Town/west of Broadheath. The route continues westward (to Sankey Valley Park) and eastward (to Sale Water Park) along the 205-mile Trans-Pennine Trail. Get a leaflet on the Trans-Pennine Trail from The Trans-Pennine Trail Officer, c/o Planning, Barnsley MBC, Kendray Street, Barnsley S70 2TN (01226 772574).

What else can you do?
Visit Dunham Massey House which has wonderful restored Edwardian interiors, a garden and park trails. There's a quiz for the children too (01619 411025). For more games and a zoo, head for Walton Hall & Gardens, three miles south of Warrington at Higher Walton (01925 601617).

Where can you eat?
Two family-friendly real ale pubs lie close to the eastern end of the route. At Little Bollington, one mile southeast of Heatley, is the Swan With Two Necks which has a garden, children's menu and good food (0161 928 2914). The cosy Axe & Cleaver is at Dunham Massey village and has a garden and children's menu (0161 928 3391).

 OS Landranger Map 109

JORDANS ALL AGES

55 Sankey Valley Park & St Helens canal towpath

Why should you go?
For gentle riding for the whole family. The towpath is a short traffic-free section of the long-distance Trans-Pennine Trail, although you will need good bike control for some sections.

Where is it?
Between Widnes and Warrington, east of Liverpool. Start at Sankey Valley Park (near Bewsey Old Hall). There is a big car park at the Catalyst Museum in Widnes. The nearest train stations are Widnes and Warrington.

Where can you ride?
For seven miles, from the west, from the Catalyst Museum on Spike Island, Widnes to Sankey Bridge in Sankey Valley Park (on the west side of Warrington). Details of the Trans-Pennine Trail are available from the Trans-Pennine Trail Officer, (see 54).

What else can you do?
Children will get scientific fun at the Catalyst Museum at the west end, which has a great view from the external glass lift (Mersey Road, 0151 420 1121).

Where can you eat?

Either at the Bewsey Farm Inn near Bewsey Old Hall at the eastern end, or the Ferry Tavern at Fiddlers Ferry. There is also a good little coffee shop at the Catalyst Museum.

 OS Landranger Map 108

56 Liverpool & Wallasey Promenades

Why should you go?

For an easy yet spectacular afternoon's pedal along both sides of the Mersey waterfront.

Where is it?

On the Mersey and the seafront between Liverpool and Wallasey. Start at Pleasure Island, Albert Dock, Pier Head. The nearest train stations are James St, St Michaels, Cressington and New Brighton.

Where can you ride?

For a total of nine miles. The Liverpool route is five miles long, from the south, from Otterspool Promenade to Dingle, Albert Dock and the Pier Head ferry terminal. Take the ferry for the Birkenhead route which is four miles long from the southern end to New Brighton on the sea. There is a cycle route road link through Liverpool from Otterspool Promenade via Sefton Park to the Liverpool Loop Line rail trail (57) which connects north with the Cheshire Lines rail trail (58) and south with the Sankey Valley Park & St Helens canal towpath (55) – all part of the long-distance Trans-Pennine

Trail. The general Liverpool city cycling map can be bought at the Liverpool Cycle Centre at 9 Berry Street (0151 708 8819).

What else can you do?

Try the Liverpool Loop Line (57), or go see the historic ships and tramways in Birkenhead.

Where can you eat?

There are cafes and bars all along the route if you haven't brought your own lunch.

 *OS Landranger Map 108*

57 Liverpool Loop Line rail trail

Why should you go?

Because you get to ride through town for ten miles on a predominantly traffic-free route.

Where is it?

Between Halewood and Aintree. Start at Halewood Country Park (southwest of the M62 J6), or at the Walton Loop Line nature park (near the A580 four miles west of the M57 J4) or on the A59 at Aintree. The train stations are Halewood, Broad Green, Walton and Rice Lane.

Where can you ride?

For ten miles, from Halewood in the south through Knotty Ash and Walton to Aintree. The trail is part of the 205-mile Trans-Pennine Trail. You can get details from the Trans-Pennine Trail Officer (see 54 for details). The general Liverpool city cycling map is available from the Liverpool Cycle Centre, 9 Berry Street (0151 7088819).

What else can you do?

Liverpool has numerous

attractions including the Mersey ferry and riverfront with the nearby restored Albert Dock which houses the Tate Gallery (0151 702 7400) and the Beatles Story exhibition (*below*).

Where can you eat?

Stock up at Halewood Country Park visitor centre before you go.

 OS Landranger Map l08

58 Cheshire Lines rail trail

Why should you go?

To cruise on a rural former railway line through pleasant open areas from the outskirts of Liverpool to the sand dunes and amusements of the seaside town of Southport.

Where is it?

North of Liverpool. At Maghull (off the A59 north of the M57 J7), the trail starts on a sharp right bend on the minor road between the A5147 and B5195. At the Southport end, start at Marine Drive, near the Shoal of Fish sculpture and the Traumatiser ride. The nearest stations are Maghull, Ainsdale and Southport. Details of the Trans-Pennine Trail are available, see 54 above for details.

North West

Where can you ride?
For 13 miles, from the southern Maghull end via Ainsdale to Southport, the terminus of the Trans-Pennine Trail. From the southern end, the Trans-Pennine Trail continues along the Liverpool Loop Line (57) towards Halewood Country Park.

What else can you do?
Chill out in Southport, a seaside resort with a beach, rides, children's boating, a zoo and an annual flower show.

Where can you eat?
You are spoilt for choice in seaside Southport.

 OS Landranger Map 119

59 Middlewood Way rail trail

Why should you go?
To enjoy an easy and popular old railway line near the course of the Macclesfield canal along the western edge of Lyme Park.

Where is it?
East Cheshire. At Marple, follow the sign off the A626 Stockport-Glossop road opposite the post office into Railway Road. The sign for the trail is in the far left-hand corner of car park. Higher Poynton has car parks at Jackson's Brickworks and Nelson Pit. There are more at Poynton Coppice and Higher Poynton (east of Poynton and the A523) and in Bollington, in Adlington Road car park by the viaduct. In Macclesfield park at the railway station. The nearest train stations are Marple, Marple Rose Hill, Middlewood and Macclesfield.

Where can you ride?
For as fas as ten miles from Marple in the north (the southeastern outskirts of Manchester) to Higher Poynton, Bollington and Macclesfield. You can get the trail leaflet from Macclesfield Borough Council Leisure Services Department (01625 504504) and hire bikes at the Lyme View Cafe (en route close to Adlington).

What else can you do?
Follow the children's guide and quiz at Lyme Park, the great Italianate palace and medieval deer park. The entrance is just off the A6 near Disley (01663 762023)

Where can you eat?
There is a cafe at Higher Poynton, and the family-friendly Miners Arms (01625 872731) one-and-a-half miles north of Bollington at Adlington near the canal.

 OS Landranger Map 118

60 The South Manchester Mersey river path

Why should you go?
To give the kids a genuine countryside hit along a green/blue urban corridor.

Where is it?
Suburban south Manchester. Park at East Didsbury church (off A5145 west of A34, north of M63 J10). The nearest stations are Sale and East Didsbury.

Where can you ride?
For ten miles, from Sale Water Park in the west, through Chorlton Water Park, West Didsbury, the Mersey riverbank and East Didsbury. A Manchester city cycling map is available from CycleCity Guides, Wallbridge Mill, The Retreat, Frome, BA11 5JU (01373 453533).

What else can you do?
You are sure to find something in the free brochure of family activities organised by Arts About Manchester (0161 953 4238).

Where can we eat?
Sale Water Park visitor centre has a family-friendly cafe.

 OS Landranger Map 109

61 Ashton canal

Why should you go?
For the joys of travelling through the city along the old waterway. Children, however, need decent bike control to negotiate sections of the narrow towpath.

Where is it?
Between Ashton-under-Lyme and Manchester. Start in Manchester at Ducie Street Basin, and in Ashton at Portland Basin.

Where can you ride?
It's a seven-mile stretch all the way to Ashton-under-Lyme.

What else can you do?
The impressive Lowry gallery is one-and-a-half miles west of the

city centre at Salford Quays
(0161 876 2000).

Where can you eat?
The Station pub in Ashton has a
conservatory and a garden
(Warrington St, 0161 330 6776).

 OS Landranger Map 109

JORDANS
OVER 8s

62 Tame Valley rail trail

Why should you go?
For great riding… not forgetting
all those family-friendly pubs
en route.
Where is it?
East of Manchester. Park in
Ashton at Portland Basin, or
the canalside Tesco (Stalybridge),
also at Brownhill visitor centre,
Roaches Lock pub car park
or the Royal George lay-by
at Greenfields.
Where can we ride?
For ten miles between Portland
Basin in the southwest at Ashton-
under-Lyme, through Stalybridge,
Mossley, Roaches, Greenfield,
Brownhill visitor centre at
Uppermill and Diggle.
What else can you do?
The Portland Basin Industrial
Heritage Museum is good for
kids and the Saddleworth
Museum (Uppermill) has
a whole host of children's
holiday activities.

Where can you eat?
There's The Station pub in
Ashton, also the Royal George
Hotel (Greenfield), Woodend
Tavern (Manchester Rd, Mossley)
and Roaches Lock pub.

 OS Landranger Map 109, 110

JORDANS
ALL AGES

63 Salford Looplines rail trail

Why should you go?
Because it offers easy riding for
even the smallest children.
Where is it?
West of Manchester. Start at
Monton Green (east of M63 J1),
Walkden (west of M62 J14) or
Little Hulton (southeast of M61
J4). Park in Monton Green at
Duke's Drive Park off Parrin Lane
west of the junction with Monton
Green. The station is Walkden.
Where can you ride?
It's five miles one way.
What else can you do?
It's worth heading for the new
Lowry gallery, Salford Quays
(0161 876 2000).
Where can you eat?
Try in Monton Green and
Worsley Basin.

 OS Landranger Map 109

JORDANS
OVER 8s

64 Pendle towpath cycleway

Why should you go?
For classic towpath riding along
the Leeds & Liverpool canal.
Where is it?
Between Colne and Brierfield,

Lancashire. Park at Greenfield
Road, Colne, follow the road
over the junction with Whitewalls
Drive to Barrowford Locks, go
left onto the towpath. Stations
are Colne, Nelson and Brierfield.
Where can you ride?
It's five miles. Colne has quiet
roads, and the children will need
some bike control for the towpath.
What else can you do?
Try the British In India Museum,
the Pendle Heritage Centre in
Colne or the restored Elizabethan
Gawthorpe Hall and tea room at
Padiham (01282 771004).
Where can you eat?
The family-friendly Hare &
Hounds has a children's menu
(two miles northeast of Colne at
Black Lane Ends, 01282 863070).

 OS Landranger Map 103

JORDANS
OVER 8s

65 Gisburn Forest trails

Why should you go?
For great views and the fresh
scent of pine in your nostrils.
Where is it?
North of Clitheroe. Start at
Cocklet Hill, on the minor road
that crosses the B6478 four miles
northeast of Slaidburn.
Where can you ride?
On three signposted forest trails.
What else can you do?
Of general interest is Salley Abbey
at Sawley three miles northeast of
Clitheroe off the A59.
Where can you eat?
Pack a picnic. There are no
facilities in this remote landscape.

 OS Landranger Map 103

Heart of England

Great industrial centres and swathes of countryside are split down the middle by the Pennine hills in central England. Good weekend destinations include the excellent rail trails of the Peak District and there are forest rides in Cannock Chase and

Sherwood Pines. Hereford and the Marches boast dedicated MTB trails for some serious legwork, while the residents of Birmingham and the Black Country are blessed with miles of car-free riding on canals, rail trails and parkland which can be easily navigated.

Where to cycle when you visit

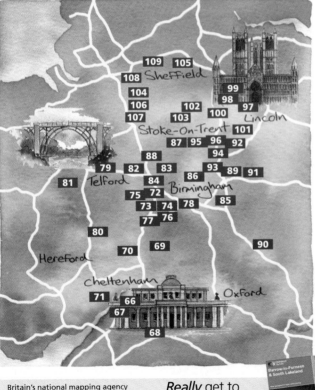

FINDING YOUR WAY

OS Landranger maps covering these areas:
110//118/119/120/126/127/128/129 /137/139/140/150/151/152/162/163/199

PLACES TO SEE

The National Heritage Corridor, Derbyshire (01332 255802)
The Derwent Valley is a World Heritage site and recognised as the birthplace of the Industrial Revolution. Belpher North Mill is one of the world's most important industrial buildings and a central feature of the Derwent Valley Mills World Heritage Site.

The Workhouse, Southwell (01909 486411)
This 1824 workhouse is the best preserved in England and records the history of the site and the people who worked there. Visitors can experience, just for a short time at least, what life was like for 19th-century paupers.

Thinktank and IMAX Theatre at Millennium Point, Birmingham (0121 643 2514)
Where ten themed galleries on four floors bring science and history to life in a variety of new and innovative ways. The Power Up section has a working display of the steam engines that made the Midlands one of the most productive manufacturing areas in the world. Entertaining and informative in equal measure.

Iron Bridge Museum, Shropshire (01952 432166)
Nine exceptional, award-winning museums are spread along the beautiful valley beside the River Severn – still spanned by the world's first iron bridge. Costumed craftsmen work iron, fashion china and glass, and bring alive the people who once lived and worked here.

MAIN EVENTS

www.britainonview.com

• Gold Leaf Competition, Forest of Dean
To celebrate the Queen's Golden Jubilee the Forest of Dean has organised this special competition. A mobile of copper leaves will be hidden in the forest and whoever finds it will win a unique, handmade real gold leaf. The competition runs from this March until 31st October 2002.

WHAT ELSE IS ON?
• British motorcycle grand prix, Donington Park, Leicestershire
The British leg of the World Championship. Riders on awesome 200mph bikes battle to take the chequered flag (14th July).
• Coventry Jazz Festival
The Coventry Jazz Festival is now in its fourth year and uses a range of different venues in the city centre. Past festival stars have included Courtney Pine, McCoy Tyner, Georgie Fame and Jimmy Smith (21-26th August).
• Ludlow Marches Food & Drink Festival, Shropshire
Britain's foremost food and drink festival includes demonstrations by celebrity chefs, the butchers' Sausage Trail, local food and drink displays and stalls selling excellent food (7th-9th September).
• Westonbirt Festival of Gardens, Nr Tetbury, Gloucestershire
This new three-month, design-led event featuring more than 20 unique gardens runs from June until the middle of September.

USEFUL ADDRESSES & NUMBERS
• **Heart of England Tourist Board** Tel: 01905 763450; website: www.visitheartofengland.com
• **Derbyshire Tourist Information** Tel: 01332 255802
• **Leicestershire Tourist Information** Tel: 0116 2998888
• **Shropshire Tourist Information** Tel: 01743 281200
• **Birmingham Tourist Information** Tel: 0121 6432514

Heart of England

66 Gloucester & Sharpness canal towpath

Why should you go?
For easy riding along a historic waterway. The canal keeps the barges running in and out of Gloucester when the tide on the Severn is low.

Where is it?
Gloucestershire. For the most convenient parking, try either Frampton on Severn on the B4071 west of Stroud or central Gloucester. The nearest stations are Gloucester, Cam and Dursley.

Where can you ride?
You can follow the towpath for a total of 15 miles one way. At the southwestern end start at Sharpness Docks and ride to Purton, Frampton on Severn, Quedgeley and on to Hempsted Bridge on the southwest edge of Gloucester. Beware though, some sections are a bit bumpy.

What else can you do?
See flamingos and other colourful birds at the Slimbridge Wildfowl & Wetlands Centre. There's also Ratty's Tunnel and a number of hands-on displays at the visitor centre (01453 890333). Or, several times a year, you can combine your ride with a sighting of the Severn Bore, one of the highest tidal bores in the world. Gloucester Tourist Information centre (01452 421188) provides details of dates and times of the tidal wave and the best viewing points.

Where can you eat?
If you head into Slimbridge you'll find a good child-friendly pub – Tudor Arms – which has a family room, toys and a children's menu.

 OS Landranger Map 162

---

67 Stroud rail trail

Why should you go?
To explore an old valley line with no risk of getting lost!

Where is it?
South of Gloucester. At the southerly end, park near the Railway Hotel/Egypt Mill in Nailsworth (near the clock tower). Park at the far end of the car park. The nearest stations are Stonehouse and Stroud.

Where can you ride?
The six-mile rail trail starts in the north from Stroud and runs via Dudbridge to Nailsworth.

What else can you do?
Admire the birds at Slimbridge.

Where can you eat?
Just a short distance from Nailsworth, the Old Lodge Inn at Minchinhampton, has a fine garden, skittle alley and children's menu (01453 832047); otherwise head for Stroud.

OS Landranger Map 162

---

68 Cotswold Water Park

Why should you go?
For a cracking countryside break. You're in the south Cotswolds near the source of the Thames, where old gravel pits have been turned into a park with trails, lakes and holiday facilities.

Where is it?
South of Cirencester in Gloucestershire. Park at Keynes country park or at the car park on the B4696 south of South Cerney, four miles south of Cirencester, then follow the signs for the bridlepath circuit. The nearest train station is Kemble.

Where can you ride?
Older children who can manage nine miles can tackle a flat circuit around the lakes on quiet lanes and a rail trail. From the west the route runs from Keynes Country Park via Hailstone Hill and South Cerney to the car park on the B4696. The leaflet, Cycle Routes in the Cotswold Water Park, details two routes (one is on roads) and is available by sending an SAE to Rangers Office, Keynes Country Park, Shorncote, Glos GL7 6DF. You can hire bikes from Cerney Cycle Hire, Cotswold Hoburne Holiday Centre, Broadway Lane, South Cerney, Glos (01285 860216) and Go By Cycle, Keynes Country Park, Shorncote, Glos GL7 4DE (07907 419208).

What else can you do?
Steam along to the Swindon & Cricklade railway, or the nostalgic Great Western Railway Museum in Swindon. Wannabe gladiators may like to tread the earth-covered mound that was once a Roman amphitheatre at Cirencester.

Where can you eat?
Head for the Eliot Arms Hotel one mile south of Cirencester, signposted off the A419 at Clarks Hay, where you will find a riverside inn and garden with

• *For English country cycling at its very best, few regions match the beauty of The Cotwolds.*

skittles and assistance with nappy changing, as well as a children's menu (01285 860215).

 OS Landranger Map 163

69 Stratford Greenway rail trail

Why should you go?
Because it offers a lovely, easy rail trail trip for all ages.

Where is it?
Southwest of Stratford-upon-Avon. The route starts in the centre of town, half a mile west from the Avon. Your nearest train station is Stratford-upon-Avon.

Where can you ride?
From the northeast, from Stratford to Long Marston (five miles one way, ten miles return). Look out for the fine bridge over the Avon along the way.

What else can you do?
The area has plenty of child-friendly diversions. Come face to face with giant horses at the Shirehorse Centre (two miles south of Stratford) or go gooey at the Teddy Bear Museum with its rarities and celebs at 19 Greenhill St, Stratford (01789 293160). Big, beautiful butterflies and insects cohabit at the Butterfly Farm in Swans Nest Lane, Stratford (01789 299288). The Tudor mansion connected with Elizabeth I and Shakespeare, at Charlecote Park, five miles east of Stratford, has a nice children's play area and cafe (01789 470277).

Where can you eat?
You are spoilt for choice in tourist-friendly Stratford.

 OS Landranger Map 151

95

Heart of England

70 Worcester bike paths

Why should you go?
Because the wide choice of paths means you can tailor your day perfectly. You can cycle along the River Severn, around the racecourse and off to the Worcester & Birmingham Canal.

Where is it?
The starting point is in the centre of Worcester, half a mile west from the Avon. Park at the long stay car park. From the city centre follow signs for the A44 Leominster over the Severn Bridge to the west bank, take the next left and the car park is next to the petrol station. The nearest train station is Worcester.

Where can you ride?
Path 1 is north from the bridge around the racecourse. Cross the road at the lights to the north side of the bridge (west bank), follow the river, cross on the pedestrian bridge (east bank) and away you go around the racecourse.
For **path 2** follow the river south (down the west bank) for a mile.
For **path 3**, the link to the Worcester & Birmingham Canal at Diglis basin, cross the bridge towards the city centre (east bank). Walking along the pavement, go right on the riverside path and continue to the Diglis basin. Cross the lock and turn left on to the Worcester & Birmingham Canal towpath.

What else can you do?
Worcester played a major role during the Civil War when Cromwell fought the Royalists

led by Charles I. The Commandery in the city centre was the Royalist HQ and today displays handsome exhibits (01905 361821). Worcester Cathedral contains the tombs of King John and Prince Arthur.

Where can you eat?
Head for the perfect family-friendly canalside pub, The Anchor Inn, south of the cathedral on Diglis Road near Diglis basin. It has a garden, children's menu and real ale (01905 351094).

 OS Landranger Map 150

71 Forest of Dean family trail

Why should you go?
To ride through the heart of the wild and wonderful Forest of Dean on a track specifically designed with children in mind.

Where is it?
The highlands of Gloucestershire on the Welsh border. Head into the heart of the forest for the Pedalabikeaway cycle centre and hire shop at Cannop (01594 860065), east of Coleford, one mile north of the B4234/B4226 crossroads. The nearest station is Lydney seven miles to the south.

Where can you ride?
On a 12-mile-long signposted family cycle circuit that starts and finishes at Pedalabikeaway. There's a leaflet on the cycle route available from Forest Enterprise, Bank House, Bank St, Coleford, Glos GL16 8BA (01594 833057).

What else can you do?
Visit the dramatic beauty spot of

Symonds Yat, where the River Wye forms a great curving gorge on the northwest edge of the forest. Or for a hearty dose of themed entertainment try Fairytale Land & the Splendour of the Orient park near Whitchurch on the A40 on the north side of the forest. Train buffs young and old will enjoy the Great Western Railway Museum at Coleford, and wannabe miners can explore passageways and caverns at Clearwell Caves & Ancient Iron Mines, south of Coleford (01594 832535).

Where can you eat?
Either at Pedalabikeaway, which is the hub of cycling here, or try the Speech House Hotel nearby.

 OS Landranger Map 162

72 Sandwell Valley country park trail

Why should you go?
Because you get a choice of differently-graded trails in a great green space plus a Victorian farm and tea room too!

Where is it?
West Bromwich, West Midlands. Park on the eastern side of Sandwell Valley at Swan Pool car park off Forge Lane, south off the A4041 Newton Road. On the western side, park at Sandwell Park Farm car park off Salter's Lane, West Bromwich.

Where can you ride?
For all ages, there's a two-mile A-to-B section through the park. The Sandwell Valley trail itself has two loops. Stronger children can ride the four-mile Hill House

• To find out how to make hills seem easier turn to p52.

73 Kingswinford rail trail

Why should you go?
For tranquility, a good surface, no hills and absolutely no cars.

Where is it?
Southwest of Wolverhampton. At Wombourne turn off at the A449/A463 roundabout signposted for the trail. Follow signs for Trysull on to Billy Buns Lane. Just before a railway bridge there's a right turn onto the track.

Where can you ride?
The trail from the south starts at Pensnett and runs for ten miles via Himley to Wombourne, Castlecroft, Tettenhall and Aldersley Stadium.

What else can you do?
Visit Dudley Zoo & Castle, or inspire childhood interest in history at Boscobel House & Royal Oak (01902 850244), the hunting lodge where Charles II hid from Cromwell's troops. It's on the minor road from the A41 to the A5, eight miles northwest of Wolverhampton, M54 J3.

Where can you eat?
Cake or beer, you choose. There's a good tea shop at Wombourne Station, and in Wombourne the Round Oak pub on the canal has garden toys (01902 892083). On the Dudley Canal at the southern end of the Netherton tunnel (walk through only) is the fascinating Little Dry Dock pub with a galleon and tiling interior, as well as a garden and children's meals (01384 235369).

 OS Landranger Map 139

Farm loop, and children over 12 with mountain bikes can have a go at the Jubilee Wood loop, a mile-and-a-half circuit graded difficult. The track is shared with horses. There's a leaflet available from The Visitor Centre, Salters Lane, West Bromwich, West Midlands B71 4BG (0121 553 2147).

What else can you do?
Lovers of wildlife will be in heaven. You can either visit the animals at the authentic Victorian farm at Sandwell Park Farm or head for Dudley Zoo, which is just seven miles away. If you have little children, there are play areas at both Dartmouth Park and Forge Mill Farm.

Where can you eat?
Both the visitor centres at Sandwell Park Farm and Forge Mill Farm have cafes, and there's also a family-friendly pub northwest of the park, The Manor House, complete with knights in armour (Hall Green Road, Stone Cross, 0121 588 2035). Churchfield Tavern is a family-friendly pub with climbing frames. It's south of the park (18 Little Lane, Sandwell, 0121 5885468).

 OS Landranger Map 139

Heart of England

74-78 BIRMINGHAM & BLACK COUNTRY CANALS

Chris Juden

Birmingham New Street, Tipton and Wolverhampton.

Where can you ride?
Start at Gas Street Basin, point your bikes northwards and you're off towards Smethwick and through Tipton, Coseley and on to Wolverhampton.

What else can you do?
No trip to the Black Country is complete without a visit to Dudley Zoo & Castle. It's just southeast of Tipton.

Where can you eat?
Make a bee-line for the curious Manor House pub at West Bromwich, which features knights in armour and a garden. It's north off-route near Smethwick (0121 588 2035).

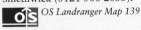 *OS Landranger Map 139*

Famed for having a greater waterway network than Venice, Birmingham's canals are coming back to life. An estimated 150 miles of towpath through Wolverhampton, Walsall, Dudley, Sandwell and Birmingham are currently rideable, although parts are rough and mucky in places. The grand plan is to restore all towpaths to a good standard. With a map of the network you can weave your own routes around the canals, using roads to create circuits and links.

Only children with good bike control should tackle towpaths. The paths are often narrow. And you will need a permit, available with an information pack from the canal network office at British Waterways, Birmingham & Black Country Canals, Bayleys Lane, Tipton, West Midlands, DY4 0PX (0121 506 1300). You will need to dismount at two busy central spots, Brindley Basin and Farmers Bridge (for the sake of the people and slopes), as well as at flights of locks.

Finding your way: There is a superb map of the Birmingham canal network (with roads) for £4.75 from GeoProjects, 9 Southern Court, South Street, Reading RG1 4QS (0118 939 3567). Also useful is the Birmingham cycling map from CycleCity Guides, Wallbridge Mill, The Retreat, Frome BA11 5JU (01373 453533), or from Sustrans, PO Box 21, Bristol BS99 2HA (0117 929 088).

JORDANS
OVER 8s

74 Birmingham Mainline Canal towpath

Why should you go?
For the joys of riding beautifully-

restored, easy towpaths. The kids will love the adventure.

Where is it?
The path runs for fully 14 miles between the fashionable Gas Street Basin in the heart of Birmingham city and Broad Street Basin in Wolverhampton. The nearest train stations are

JORDANS
OVER 8s

75 Walsall Canal towpath

Why should you go?
Simply to be able to explore miles of the region's traffic-free waterway network.

Where is it?
This seven-mile towpath stretches north-south between the Mainline Canal just south of West Bromwich as far as Walsall and the Wyrley & Essington canal. Stations are Sandwell & Dudley, Dudley Port and Walsall.

Where can we ride?
From the south, pick up the towpath at Pudding Green Junction where the Walsall Canal meets the Mainline Canal south of West Bromwich, and continue

to Ocker Hill. Go west of Wednesbury to Darlaston, Walsall and Birchills Junction, where the Walsall Canal meets the Wyrley & Essington Canal.

What else can you do?
What more do you want? The day is all about the waterway.

Where can you eat?
There are no particular venues, so carry snacks and stock up on arrival at town centres.

 OS Landranger Map 139

76 Rea Valley riverside & towpath

Why should you go?
For gentle riding along a green corridor of parkland, riverside and towpath.

Where is it?
The route runs eight miles south from central Birmingham. In the north, park at the Midlands Art Centre, Cannon Hill Park. The nearest train stations are at King's Norton and Northfield not far from the route.

Where can you ride?
The route spins out via Stirchley to the Birmingham & Worcester canal towpath, King's Norton and Northfield.

What else can you do?
View the exhibitions and play area at the busy and interesting Midlands Arts Centre.

Where can you eat?
The Midland Arts Centre is the star with its child-proof cafe.

 OS Landranger Map 139

77 Edgbaston reservoir circuit

Why should you go?
For a short and easy-to-navigate ride around water, with a traffic-free connection to the Birmingham Mainline Canal.

Where is it?
Central west Birmingham. The reservoir lies southeast of Summerfield Park (the cycle path continues south to Harborne) and you reach it from there by hopping across a couple of roads. Approach via Reservoir Road off Monument Road one mile west of Five Ways, where the nearest railway station is.

Where can you ride?
Ride the Edgbaston reservoir circuit, and, if you feel like it, the neighbouring parkland cycle path through Summerfield Park to Harborne. You can hire bikes at Bearwood Cycles (428 Bearwood Road, Bearwood, 0121 429 2199), Harborne Cycle Surgery (60 Wood Lane, 0121 428 5040) or Major Nicholls Cycles (48 Durban Road, Smethwick, 0121 558 2044).

What else can you do?
There are no other attractions in the area, so why not jump back on and try to beat your time on a second turn?

Where can you eat?
Take some snacks with you because there's no venue within striking distance.

 OS Landranger Map 139

78 Birmingham & Fazeley canal

Why should you go?
It's great cycling for the whole family. Older children might manage the full return trip, younger ones may enjoy a one-way ride, and adults will be spurred on by the existence of a good pub halfway through.

Where is it?
Southeast of Birmingham in the countryside. Pick up the canal anywhere along its length, and park in the surrounding roads. The nearest train stations are Water Orton (at the southwestern end) and Tamworth (northeastern).

Where can you ride?
Start at Minworth at the Caters Bridge, at the junction of the A38/A4097 southeast of Sutton Coldfield and cycle to Fazeley Junction, south of Tamworth at the northeastern end.

What else can you do?
For more natural wonders, visit the 200 species of animals at Twycross Zoo, 12 miles north east of Tamworth, on the A444 Burton-Nuneaton road, M42 J11 (01827 880250).

Where can you eat?
There's nowhere better than the family-friendly, real ale-serving Dog & Doublet, which has a garden and children's menu. It's one-and-a-half miles northwest of Marston.

 OS Landranger Map 139

Heart of England

JORDANS
ALL AGES

79 Silkin Way ex-canal trail

Why should you go?
For two hits in one. The easy-to-ride Silkin Way is a rail trail that also follows the course of an old canal between Telford and the birthplace of the industrial revolution, Ironbridge, on the River Severn (*above*).

Where is it?
Telford, Shropshire. The trail starts at Coalport, at the China Museum on the minor road beside the river parallel with the A442, south of the M54 J4. Or you can park in Telford town centre, and start from there. The nearest train stations are Telford and Wellington.

Where can you ride?
From the southern startpoint at Coalport, the full trail is 14 miles long. A good day trip is riding from Telford station to Ironbridge for lunch and the sights. There and back is about ten miles.

What else can you do?
Question: why is Ironbridge a World Heritage Site? Because it's as beautiful as it is historic. It's the home of the ironworks that created the first iron wheels, rails and steam locomotive as well as the elegant 1779 bridge that

spans the Severn gorge in the middle of town. Nine museum sites make up the Ironbridge Gorge Industrial Museum, for which a single ticket is available from the tourist centre. Booklets are also available from Leisure Services, Telford & Wrekin Council, PO Box 211, Darby House, Telford TF3 4LA (01962 202745). Elsewhere Telford Wonderland, featuring a giant playground, lies southeast of Telford centre, and there's a children's activity sheet for Wroxeter Roman City, the impressive remains of the fourth-largest Roman settlement in the country. It's five miles east of Shrewsbury (01743 761330). Steam train buffs will love the picturesque route of the Severn Valley steam railway from Kidderminster to Bewdley to Bridgnorth (01299 403816).

Where can you eat?
Ironbridge, which lies on the tourist trail, is full of family-friendly cafes and restaurants.

 OS Landranger Map 127

JORDANS
OVER 12s

80 Hopton mountain bike trail

Why should you go?
To give your older children a genuine taste of hardy mountain biking in the Shropshire hills.

Where is it?
West of Ludlow. Head for Hopton Castle. From Ludlow take the A4113, then the B4385 and the minor road north and west to the car park in Hopton. The nearest station is Ludlow.

Where can you ride?
You have the freedom to roam anywhere on a signposted network through hilly pine forests. The routes leaflet is essential reading and available from Forest Enterprise, Marches Forest District, Whitcliffe, Ludlow, Shropshire SY8 2HD (01889 586593).

What else can you do?
Stokesay Castle near Craven Arms is the best preserved 13th-century fortified manor house in England (01588 672544). Or give the children a dose of country life at the Acton Scott Working Farm ten miles away, just south of Church Stretton. Meanwhile wannabe knights will enjoy Ludlow Castle (01584 873355).

Where can you eat?
There's a good inn six miles northwest at Clun, The White Horse, where children are welcome if eating, also in the games room and the garden (The Square, 01588 640305). Ludlow and Church Stretton have plenty of cafes, too.

 OS Landranger Map 137

JORDANS
OVER 8s

81 Shropshire woodland trails

Why should you go?
Because the choice of four different forest trails here means there's a ride to suit any child.

Where is it?
Southwest of Shrewsbury, Shropshire. For Bury Ditches take the B4385 southeast to Brockton. After two miles go right on the

minor road to Brockton and continue to the car park. For Eastridge Woods use Poles Coppice car park: from Minsterley (ten miles southwest of Shrewsbury) take the minor road eastward towards Habberley. The car park is on the left halfway up the hill. The nearest train stations are Church Stretton and Craven Arms.

Where can you ride?

Bury Ditches has a single three-and-a-half mile circuit graded moderate (for teens). Eastridge Wood has three trails. The first is an easy four-miler for stronger under-tens and teens (marked with brown signs); the second is a seven-mile beast for teens (pink signs); and the third, graded hard, is three miles but for dedicated bikers only (grey signs). A helpful leaflet entitled Countryside & Woodland Cycle Trails is available from Shropshire Books, Column House, 7 London Road, Shrewsbury SY2 6NW (01743 255043).

What else can you do?

Welshpool is 16 miles to the west and is home to Welshpool Llanfair light railway, Powysland Museum and Powis Castle.

Where can you eat?

If you're at Eastridge Woods try the Horseshoe Inn at Ratlinghope (it's near Bridges) where children are welcome in the lounge and garden (01588 650260). Near Bury Ditches there's the Three Tuns & Brewery at Bishop's Castle, which has ancient buildings and welcomes children but not in the public bar (Salop Street, 01588 638797).

OS *Landranger Map 126, 137*

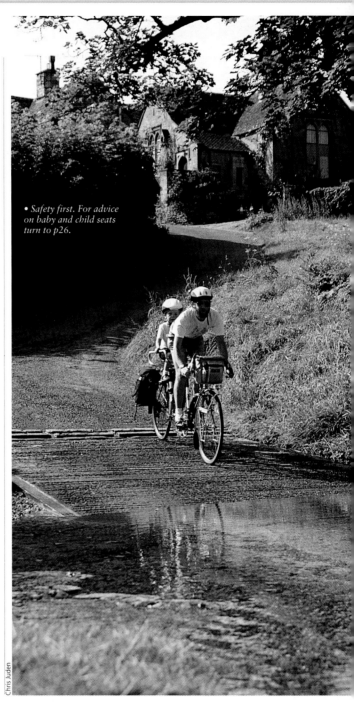

• Safety first. For advice on baby and child seats turn to p26.

Chris Juden

Heart of England

JORDANS
ALL AGES

82 Stafford-Newport Greenway rail trail

Why should you go?
Because it's easy riding with no cars and lots of nature. It's also short enough for older kids to complete in both directions.

Where is it?
From Stafford take the A518 to Telford. At the new housing estate at Castlefields turn off, follow Martin Drive from the first roundabout and go straight ahead at the second roundabout on a narrow lane (signposted 'No Through Road'); the car park is on the left. On the bikes, turn left out of the car park along the lane. The trail is on the right at the end of the row of factories.

Where can you ride?
From the eastern Stafford end, it's three miles to Derrington.

What else can you do?
The kids will find plenty to do at the magnificent Shugborough Estate & House at Milford: animals, a games gallery, a playground and a large puppet collection (01889 881388).

Where can you eat?
you've a choice in central Stafford and at Shugborough.

 OS Landranger Map 127

JORDANS
OVER 8s

83 Cannock Chase forest trails

Why should you go?
To find rides to suit all ages. The wonderfully wild open spaces of Cannock Chase form one of the largest country parks in Britain.

Where is it?
North of Birmingham. Cannock Chase visitor centre lies three miles north of Cannock, off the A460 Rugeley road. The nearest train station is Rugeley.

Where can you ride?
Younger children with some pedalling behind them might finish the four-and-a-half-mile long Pepperslade route, while older children with some stamina might enjoy the full nine-mile Sherbrook Valley route. The difficult, four-mile Lady Hill route with steep climbs is for enthusiasts only. There's a leaflet available from the visitor centre (01543 871773) or the County Countryside Officer, Shire Hall, Market Street, Stafford ST16 2LQ (01785 277264).

What else can you do?
The Shugborough Estate & House is nearby. Its playground and games gallery are perfect for burning off any energy the kids have left (01889 881388).

Where can you eat?
At the visitor centre, or at a fine family-friendly pub at Gentleshaw called the Old Windmill (around four miles southeast from the visitor centre, Windmill Lane, 01543 682468). If you fancy a canalside drink, try the Moat House pub at Acton Trussell (eight miles northwest of the visitor centre). It's a 14th-century listed building at the south end of the village with a garden and children's menu (01785 712217).

 OS Landranger Map 127, 128

JORDANS
OVER 8s

84 Sutton Park country park trails

Why should you go?
For the chance to explore the tracks and bridleways of a big moorland park. Sutton Park is an oasis of calm slap-bang in the middle of a built-up area.

Where is it?
North of Birmingham. Park at the Sutton Park visitor centre, off the A5127 west of Sutton Coldfield.

Where can you ride?
All over. Simply make up your own routes using a map of the trails and the signboards en route. Just be aware that some tracks get rough after rain and the park slopes in most places. For a useful route leaflet, contact the visitor centre at Sutton Park, Sutton Coldfield, West Midlands B74 2YT (0121 355 6370).

What else can you do?
Teach the kids Roman bathing habits, at Wall Roman Site. It's on the old Roman Watling Street, now the A5, nine miles north of Sutton Park.

Where can you eat?
On site, at the visitor centre cafe.

 OS Landranger Map 139

JORDANS
OVER 8s

85 Ashby Canal towpath

Why should you go?
Because it's almost impossible to get lost on this countrified towpath – plus you get to choose how far to go.

Chris Juden

• *For tips on planning the perfect day for you and your children turn to p20.*

Where is it?
North of Coventry. Pick up the route anywhere as it runs through rural countryside, parallel with the A447 Hinckley-Coalville road. The nearest train stations are Nuneaton and Hinckley.

Where can you ride?
From the southern end, southeast of Nuneaton on the B4114, the towpath runs 20 miles to Hinckley, Stoke Golding, Congerstone and Snarestone.

What else can you do?
Visit Twycross Zoo (four miles west at Twycross, on the A444 Burton-Nuneaton road, M42 J11, 01827 880250) or take a ride on the Battlefield Line steam railway. The Snibston Discovery Park in Coalville is amazing – a children-friendly science park created from disused mineworkings.

Where can you eat?
There are pubs in the villages along the route.

 OS Landranger Map 128, 140

JORDAN'S ALL AGES

86 Ashby Woulds Moira rail trail

Why should you go?
For the chance to stretch those little legs on a flat three-miler. The rail commemorates the Moira blast furnace, one of the best preserved from the Napoleonic period.

Where is it?
West of Ashby-de-la-Zouch. Park at the Moira Furnace car park, off the B5003 six miles southeast of Burton-on-Trent.

Where can you ride?
From the northwestern end at Moira, simply head off towards Donisthorpe and Measham (there's a short stretch of lanes at Donisthorpe).

What else can you do?
The stately Calke Abbey is a

Heart of England

wonderful illustration of an English country house in decline. Preserved as it was in the 19th-century, the house has a spectacular natural history collection and interiors. The entrance is at Ticknall five miles north of Ashby (01332 863822). Otherwise head for Snibston Discovery Centre in Coalville, a science park created from old mineworkings.

Where can you eat?
In Smisby two miles north of Ashby is the Mother Hubbard pub, where there's a garden with toys and a children's menu (01530 413604).

 OS Landranger Map 128

Trent, head along the rail trail to Alton Towers and Denstone.

What else can you do?
Make a weekend of it, by visiting Alton Towers theme park (*above*) just north of Alton. Or catch a scenic five-mile ride on the Foxfield steam railway, six miles west of Oakamoor (01782 396210). Animals await at Blackbrook Zoo Park, a moorland attraction with children's pets, a farm and under-fives indoor jungle playroom. It's at Winkhill six miles southeast of Leek (01538 308293).

Where can you eat?
Try the pubs in Denstone and Oakamoor, otherwise take snacks or a picnic along with you.

 OS Landranger Map 119, 128

---

87 Churnet Valley rail trail

Why should you go?
Because it's the natural alternative to the stomach-churning rides down the road at Alton Towers.

Where is it?
West of Ashbourne in the Peak District. In Oakamoor, the car park is off the B5417 west of the river bridge by the Cricketers Arms. On the bikes, ride past a second pub, The Admiral Jervis, to the end of the second car park and turn left for the trail. In Denstone use the village hall car park on the B5032. Ride the bikes from the car park past the petrol station and left before the phone box to the trail. The nearest train station is Uttoxeter.

Where can you ride?
From the northwest, the Oakamoor end east of Stoke-on-

---

88 The Manifold Trail rail trail

Why should you go?
For rail trail riding at its most spectacular. This ex-railway line runs through a dramatic fissure in the rock formed by the River

Manifold. There are cafes at half and full distance and bike hire nearby. With the Tissington and the High Peak trails (103), it forms a trio of superb Peak District car-free rides.

Where is it?
In the south Peak District. At the southern end, park at Waterhouses nine miles northwest of Ashbourne off the A523 Ashbourne-Leek road. The car park is near Ye Olde Crown Hotel. At the northern end, at Hulme End 12 miles southwest of Bakewell, turn off the B5054 west of the Manifold Valley pub. The nearest train station is Uttoxeter, ten miles south. There are two places to hire bikes at Waterhouses: Peak National Park cycle hire (01538 308609) and Brown End Farm cycle hire (01538 308313).

Where can you ride?
For eight miles from Waterhouses via Wettonmill to Hulme End.

What else can you do?
Go to Blackbrook Zoo Park. For details see 'Churnet Valley rail trail' (87).

Where can you eat?
There's a good pub in Waterhouses and a perfect family-friendly cafe on the trail near the southern end. You'll also reach a cafe/pub at Wettonmill and a pub in Hulme End.

 OS Landranger Map 119

---

89 Leicester Great Central Way

Why should you go?
For a great mix of riding. Enjoy

the river corridor through the heart of Leicester on rail trail, towpath and riverside. The ten-mile route suits all children (the only limit is their endurance) plus it's great for quick trips in the fresh air in and out of town.

Where is it?
Through the heart of Leicester.

Where can you ride?
From the north, start at Watermead country park (Birstall) and head south through Abbey Park, down Great Central Way, along the Grand Union Canal to Crow Mill car park/Blaby on the southern edge of Leicester. One central starting place is St Margaret's Pasture car park near the sports centre off St Margaret's Way near Abbey Park. To ride north, go round one-and-a-half sides of the sports ground, then right over the concrete river bridge and right again along Riverside Way. To ride south, return to the main road and go left down the steps to the towpath. A very useful map, produced by CycleCity, is available from Wallbridge Mill, The Retreat, Frome BA11 5JU (01373 453533).

What else can you do?
Hitch a ride on the Great Central steam railway, Britain's only mainline steam railway, between Birstall and Loughborough (01509 230726) or visit the new National Space Centre, complete with real-life lunar rocket, north up the river from Abbey Park.

Where can you eat?
Try the child-proof Gazebo cafe in Abbey Grounds. There are also pubs at Birstall and Blaby.

 OS Landranger Map 140

JORDAN'S ALL AGES

90 Brampton Valley Way

Why should you go?
For easy, peaceful riding through fine countryside. Older children can try making the full 14-mile distance – and back if they're particularly adventurous.

Where is it?
Between Northampton and Market Harborough. The start at Market Harborough is at The Bell Inn (on the left coming out of town on the A508). The trail lies behind the pub. To start from Northampton follow the A5199 for four miles. Once you are in the country, go first right into Brampton Lane and immediately right again into the car park.

Where can you ride?
Follow the old railway line, from the north at Market Harborough via Great Oxendon, Brixworth and Chapel Brampton to the A5199 north of Northampton. You will need lights on your bikes to see your way through the two tunnels en route.

What else can you do?
Fans of Thomas the Tank Engine will like the locomotives and

rolling stock at Chapel Brampton to the south. Fans of Princess Diana can visit Althorp, her family estate and final resting place, where there is a commemorative exhibition. It's on the A528 Northampton-Rugby road (01604 770107).

Where can you eat?
No contest! Head for The Bulls Head at Clipston (near Great Oxendon) two miles west of the route towards the northern end, for real ale, skittles, a garden and children's menu (Harborough Road, 01858 525268).

 OS Landranger Map 141, 152

JORDAN'S ALL AGES

91 Rutland Water reservoir circuit

Why should you go?
A honeypot for family cyclists, the 17-mile Rutland Water reservoir circuit is easy to ride, has great views, lots of facilities and, if you're feeling particularly energetic, the chance to pursue any number of watersports.

Where is it?
East of Leicester, between Oakham and Stamford. There are pay & display car parks at Normanton, Barnsdale, Whitwell and Empingham. The nearest station is Oakham, one-and-a-half miles away.

Where can you ride?
Find your way to the water's edge, and go clockwise or anti-clockwise, passing through Egleton (near Oakham), Manton, Edith Weston, Whitwell and Upper Hambleton. There are bike hire shops at Whitwell (01780

Heart of England

460705) and Normanton (01780 720888), both of which sell maps of the cycle routes.

What else can you do?
Around Rutland Water (*above*) you will find plenty of diversions en route: watersports, fishing, play areas, the Butterfly & Aquatic centre, a nature reserve, a climbing centre (with tuition) and boat trips between Whitwell and the Normanton Church Museum (details from the Tourist Centre at Empingham, 01572 653026). Train buffs will love Rutland Railway Museum four miles northeast of Oakham, near Cottesmore.

Where can you eat?
Check out the waterside cafe near Normanton. There are also cafes in Oakham and pubs at Edith Weston, Empingham, Whitwell, Hambleton and Manton.

 OS Landranger Map 141

JORDANS
ALL AGES

92
Nutbrook rail trail

Why should you go?
For peace and quiet for you and gentle pedalling for the kids.

Where is it?
Southwest of Nottingham. At

Long Eaton, the trail starts at Midland Street (near the A6005/B6540 southwest of Nottingham) with parking near the council offices. At Kirk Hallam, start on the A6096 south of Ilkeston. Long Eaton is the nearest train station.

Where can you ride?
From the south, from Long Eaton past Sandiacre to Kirk Hallam. There's a useful leaflet available from Erewash Borough Council (0115 9072244).

What else can you do?
If it rains, head for the Donington Grand Prix collection (Donington Park west of Castle Donington, two miles from the M1 J23a/24, 01332 811027).

Where can you eat?
At Sandiacre is the canalside pub, The Plough, where children are welcome in the lounge. There's also skittles and garden toys (Town Street, 0115 949 9190).

 OS Landranger Map 129

JORDANS
ALL AGES

93 Derby to Worthington trail

Why should you go?
Because you're unlikely to get too breathless on this flat route along rail trail, riverpath and canal.

Where is it?
It's a north-south rail trail and canal towpath that totals 24 miles return. From central Derby the route follows the River Derwent then turns south along a former canal to Melbourne, and continues another four miles along a rail trail to Worthington. Start in Derby by the Council

House. The car park is on the A6 two miles southeast of the centre at the Alvaston recreation ground. Derby is your nearest station.

Where can you ride?
From the northern end at Derby city centre the route runs through Crewton, Allenton, Chellaston, Swarkestone and King's Newton to Worthington. Note that the three-quarters of a mile stretch of road from Swarkestone to Weston-on-Trent gets busy. For more details, order the 'Derby Cycling Map' from Derby CC Planning Department, Roman House, Friar Gate, Derby DE1 1XB (01332 255021).

What else can you do?
Car-mad kids will love the Donington Grand Prix collection (Donington Park west of Castle Donington, two miles from the M1 J23a/24, 01332 811027). Calke Abbey is a preserved 19th-century country house with a spectacular natural history collection and interiors. The entrance is at Ticknall five miles north of Ashby (01332 863822).

Where can you eat?
You will find indoor and outdoor play areas at Swarkestone on the A514 at The Crewe & Harpur pub, plus a children's menu (01332 700641).

 OS Landranger Map 128

JORDANS
ALL AGES

94 Derby to Elvaston Castle Country Park

Why should you go?
For the pleasure of riding an easy green route between the country

and the city centre. There's no traffic either.

Where is it?
The trail runs from Derby city centre east along the river Derwent and into Elvaston Castle Country Park, where there is another rideable circuit. If you are driving it is better to start at Elvaston Castle, off the B5010 which runs between the A6 and A6005. The start in Derby city centre is at the council offices on the south side of the bridge over the River Derwent.

Where can you ride?
It's a four-and-a-half mile trip via the Bass recreation ground. For more details, order the 'Derby Cycling Map' from Derby CC Planning Department, Roman House, Friar Gate, Derby DE1 1XB (01332 255021).

What else can you do?
Visit Elvaston Castle & Museum, or Shardlow canal village two miles away.

Where can you eat?
There's a cafe at Elvaston Castle, and a family-friendly pub on the canal at Shardlow village, two miles east of the park. The Malt Shovel was built in 1779 and has a garden, children's menu and real ale (01332 799763).

 OS Landranger Map 128, 129

JORDAN'S
ALL AGES

95 Carsington Water reservoir circuit

Why should you go?
For the challenge of completing an eight-mile circuit of the reservoir, or in the case of little

ones, going as far as they can manage.

Where is it?
Northeast of Ashbourne in the Peak District. Park at the visitor centre (turn off the B5035 Wirksworth-Ashbourne road at the Knockerdown pub).

Where can you ride?
In either direction round the reservoir from the visitor centre.

What else can you do?
There are watersports on the lake and attractions nearby. Try prospecting for gems and fossils at the National Stone Centre at Middleton Top Engine House (northwest of Wirksworth) or feel the fear on the white-knuckle rides at Gullivers Kingdom theme park (01629 580540). For more gentle thrills try a cable car ride at the Heights Of Abraham country park or catch an old-fashioned ride at the National Tramway Museum (01773 852565).

Where can you eat?
At the visitor centre.

 OS Landranger Map 199

JORDAN'S
ALL AGES

96 Shipley Country Park trails

Why should you go?
Because you can pick your own routes, over any distance, around the estate's roads, lakeside and woodland tracks.

Where is it?
West of Nottingham. Park at the information centre at the entrance to the park, one mile south of Heanor (off the A6007 west of the M1 J26). Heanor is the nearest train station.

Where can you ride?
Wherever you like using the map from the information centre. You can hire bikes there too (01773 719961 for prices).

What else can you do?
Nottingham city centre attractions include the Tales of Robin Hood and the Galleries of Justice, or head six miles north towards Ripley for a ride on the Midland steam railway.

Where can you eat?
If you haven't brought your own picnic head for the cafe at the information centre.

 OS Landranger Map 129

JORDAN'S
ALL AGES

97 Southwell rail trail

Why should you go?
Because it makes perfect riding for even the smallest legs. It's a disused railway line in the Nottinghamshire countryside near Sherwood Forest which can easily be divided into shorter, more manageable sections for younger children.

Where is it?
East of Mansfield. It starts at Bilsthorpe at a roundabout in the southeast corner of town. The other end is at Southwell, in the northeast corner of town on the minor road to Hockerton (off the A612). Fiskerton, three miles southeast of Southwell, is the nearest train station.

Where can you ride?
From Bilsthorpe at the western end, the trail runs for eight miles to Farnsfield and Southwell, west of Newark.

Heart of England

What else can you do?

Admire thousands of animals at the White Post Modern Farm centre, including llamas and reptiles. You'll find it at Farnsfield (01623 882977).

Where can you eat?

If you head for Upton, two miles east of Southwell, you'll reach The Cross Keys pub, where families are welcome in an area away from the bar. The pub holds regular beer festivals, has a small garden and boasts a good children's menu.

 OS Landranger Map 120

JORDANS OVER 8s

98 Sherwood Pines forest trail

Why should you go?

Because it's an easy-to-follow family trail. It's also the perfect route for indulging those Robin Hood fantasies.

Where is it?

The car park is off the B6030, five miles northeast of Mansfield.

Where can you ride?

Follow the six-mile-long signposted forest circuit. Just note that some tracks are unsurfaced and sloping. There's a useful leaflet available at the visitor centre and bike hire at Sherwood Pines Cycles (01623 822855).

Chris Juden

What else can you do?

Talk to the animals at either Sherwood Forest Farm Park (off the B6035 Market Worksop road north of the forest) or the intriguing White Post Modern Farm Centre (see Southwell trail).

Where can you eat?

Your best bet is to either pack a picnic or head for the Sherwood Pines visitor centre.

 OS Landranger Map 120

JORDANS
ALL AGES

99 Clumber Park

Why should you go?

For great cycling choice. You can choose between exploring the forest, or tackling either the easy or the more challenging signposted cycle routes.

Where is it?

Southeast of Worksop. Clumber Park has several entrances. From the north off the A57, from the west off the B6034 and from the east off the A614. The main car park is near the chapel, restaurant and shops, and the nearest station is Worksop (three miles west).

Where can you ride?

Families with younger children can zip off round the five-mile lake circuit, while big, fit kids could tackle the full 13-mile circuit. For everyone, there's a wonderful choice of surfaced tracks and estate roads throughout Clumber Park. Simply follow the map leaflet from the visitor centre (01909 474468). You can hire bikes at Duke's Garage (01909 476592).

What else can you do?

Clumber Park is full of features; the Great Lake, a Gothic chapel, Hardwick village and, for any green-fingered family members, a famous walled kitchen garden with the longest greenhouses in the National Trust's possession (estate office, 01909 476592). Otherwise, visit the animals at the White Post Modern Farm Centre. Or visit the Discovery Centre at Bolsover Castle, a 400-year-old house built with romance and chivalry in mind, where children

also have an activity sheet to guide and entertain them. It's ten miles southwest off the A632 Bolsover road (01246 822844).

Where can you eat?

No sandwiches? Then head for the visitor centre.

 OS Landranger Map 120

JORDANS
OVER 8s

100 Five Pits rail trail circuit

Why should you go?

Because you get to ride a pleasant and slightly hilly six-mile trail that loops back on itself, plus a seven-mile loop to make 13 miles if you're up to it. Grit your teeth and think of the family-friendly pub nearby at Doe Lea.

Where is it?

Southeast of Chesterfield. Park at the Birkin Lane car park on the little road between Temple Normanton and Grassmoor. The nearest train stations are Alfreton (three miles south of Tibshelf) and Chesterfield (three miles northwest of Grassmoor).

Where can you ride?

From the north, the circuit runs through Grassmoor, Holmewood, Tibshelf Ponds, Highfields (crossing the A6175) and back to Grassmoor. There are two steep climbs, one near the start, the other near Tibshelf.

What else can you do?

See the fabulous interiors and grounds of Hardwick Hall, built by the redoubtable Bess of Hardwick, one of the Elizabethan Age's most powerful and wealthy women. It's at Doe Lea (01246 850430). Bolsover Castle is also

Heart of England

nearby and has plenty to keep the kids amused. See Clumber Park (99) for details.

Where can you eat?

Just two miles away, is the family-friendly Hardwick Inn, which offers family rooms, a garden and games (next to Hardwick Hall, off the M1 J29, 01246 850245).

 OS Landranger Map 120

JORDANS ALL AGES

101 Pleasley rail trails

Why should you go?

It's an ingenious, and safe, five-mile circuit made up from three rail trails. The good news is there's no way you can lose the children, and nearby Elizabethan Hardwick Hall provides cultural entertainment for the afternoon.

Where is it?

Northwest of Mansfield. Start at Pleasley in Pit Lane just off the A617 roundabout (take the exit for Pleasley and then the first right). Or in Skegby use the Teversal Trail car park on Buttery Lane, off the B6014. The nearest train stations are Mansfield and Mansfield Woodhouse.

Where can you ride?

The five-mile circuit starts at Pleasley, goes to Skegby and Teversal and back to Pleasley.

What else can you do?

For details see the 'Five Pits' rail trail (100).

Where can you eat?

Stop off at the Hardwick Inn (it's right next to Hardwick Hall, 01246 850245).

 OS Landranger Map 120

JORDANS ALL AGES

102 Monsal Trail

Why should you go?

Perfect for little ones, this four-mile section of rail trail heads out from the comforts of Bakewell across the high country.

Where is it?

Bakewell in the Peak District. Start at Bakewell station or at Monsal Head and head back one-and-a-half miles by road to Little Longstone to the rail trail.

Where can you ride?

Once you reach Monsal Head you can, if you wish, continue on the road from there for one-and-a-half miles to one of Britain's

great beauty spots, the viaduct at Monsal Dale. There's a useful leaflet available from the Information Group, Peak National Park Office, Aldern House, Baslow Road, Bakewell DE4 1AE (01629 816200).

What else can you do?

Why not take the children to see the underground splendours of Poole's Cavern at Buxton? One of the great attractions in nearby Matlock is the Heights of Abraham cable car ride.

Where can you eat?

Tarts proliferate in Bakewell, of course. If you have less of a sweet tooth, there are pubs in Great Longstone and Little Longstone.

 OS Landranger Map 119

JORDANS ALL AGES

103 The High Peak & Tissington Trails

Why should you go?

To explore the heart of the Peak District under your own steam on a pair of classic rail trails. Great views too. The two trails, which join at Parsley Hay, can be broken down into sections for little ones to ride in short bursts, or you can let older ones off the leash to explore the routes in their entirety. Start at Parsley Hay on the top and enjoy an easy, scenic ride back down either trail. Of the two, the Tissington Trail gradient is gentler.

Where are they?

The Peak District. The nearest train stations are Matlock, Buxton and Uttoxeter. For car parking, see below.

Where can you ride?

The High Peak trail is 17.5 miles long. At the lower southeastern end, start at High Peak Junction (near Cromford, south of Matlock) and ride via Black Rocks, Middleton Top, Minninglow, Friden and Parsley Hay (where it meets the Tissington Trail) to Hurdlow. The flattest section is the 12 miles between Middleton Top and Parsley Hay. There is a stiff 800ft climb with steep sections from near Matlock to Middleton Top.

• *A full load. To find out exactly what to take on your ride see p32 onwards.*

If you are not riding the full length, there is parking at Parsley Hay, Friden, Minninglow, Middleton Top (at the visitor centre) and Black Rocks.
The Tissington Trail is 13 miles long. The lower southerly end starts at Ashbourne (Mapleton Lane) and spins through Thorpe, Tissington, Alsop and Hartington before finishing at Parsley Hay. There is a steady 700ft height gain over the trail's distance. Find car parks at Parsley Hay, Hartington, Alsop, Tissington and Thorpe. For a leaflet write to: Information Group, Peak National Park Office, Aldern

House, Baslow Road, Bakewell DE4 1AE (01629 816200). Bike hire: Parsley Hay (01298 84493), Middleton Top (01629 823204) and Ashbourne (01335 343156).

What else can you do?

Engineering enthusiasts might like a look at Middleton Top Engine House and the restored beam winding engine that used to haul trucks up the Middleton Incline (01629 823204). For attractions in Matlock and Wirksworth see Carsington Water (95).

Where can you eat?

At the visitor centres at Parsley Hay, Middleton Top and Hartington, also at Black Rocks

and High Peak Junction. There are pubs at Hurdlow, just off route in Middleton, at Thorpe and Biggin and teas at Bassett Wood Farm at Tissington.

oS *OS Landranger Map 119*

JORDAN'S ALL AGES

104 Rudyard Lake rail trail

Why should you go?

For cruising along an easy linear rail trail beside a reservoir. The return trip is nine miles long and should suit older children.

Heart of England

Where is it?

Northwest of Leek, Staffs, below the western edge of the Peaks. At the northern end, park at the Knot Inn at Rushton Spencer, off the A523, eight miles south of Macclesfield. In the middle of the route, turn off the A523 two miles northwest of Leek on to the B5331 (signposted 'Rudyard Lake') and turn left after the railway bridge. From Leek, turn off the A523 Macclesfield road opposite Supersports Manufacturing beside the Dyers Arms. The lane becomes track, and you join the trail at the bridge. The nearest train station is Congleton.

Where can you ride?

From the northwest at Rushton Spencer (off the A523 south of Macclesfield) head to the east side of Rudyard Lake and on to Leek.

What else can you do?

Steam buffs should head for Cheddleton railway centre off the A520, three miles from Leek.

Where can you eat?

There's a general pub at Rushton Spencer and a choice in Leek.

 OS Landranger Map 118

---

105 Upper Derwent Valley reservoirs

Why should you go?

For easy riding in a dramatic Peak District setting.

Where is it?

Between Manchester and Sheffield. The best parking is at the Fairholmes visitor centre. Turn off the A57 Sheffield-Glossop road on the west side of the viaduct over Ladybower reservoir, and drive for two-and-a-half miles to the centre. The nearest train station is Hope, south of Ladybower reservoir.

Where can you ride?

Choose from three circuits around the Ladybower, Derwent and Howden reservoirs. You will be cycling anywhere between five miles (Ladybower) and 16 miles (all three).

What else can you do?

In this remote highland area, beautiful Edale is the next valley south (eight miles by road) and the Hope Valley the next after that. There you will find the Blue John and Speedwell show caverns and Winnats Pass, which leads to the foot of Mam Tor, 'the shivering mountain'

Where can you eat?

If you haven't packed your own, head for the visitor centre.

 OS Landranger Map 110

---

106 Biddulph Valley rail trail

Why should you go?

For easy pedalling on a high old railway line that passes beneath a great viaduct near Congleton.

Where is it?

Congleton in Cheshire. From Congleton, drive half a mile east on the A54 Buxton road. The trail is to the right of the Brunswick Wharf depot, opposite Brook Street garage. Driving from Biddulph, on the south side of town, turn right from the A527 at the lights for Mow Cop. The trail starts after 200m at the railway bridge. The nearest train station is Congleton.

Where can you ride?

It's five miles between Congleton and Biddulph.

What else can you do?

If you are after a heritage fix, visit Britain's finest half-timbered manor house, Little Moreton Hall, four miles from Congleton along the A34 (01260 272018).

Where can you eat?

The family-friendly Egerton Arms pub at Astbury has a tower and battlements, garden play centre and children's menu. It's two miles west of Congleton on the A34 (01260 273946).

 OS Landranger Map 118

---

107 Salt Way rail trail

Why should you go?

Perfect for smaller children, Salt Way rail trail is a short and pleasant stretch of old railway line in wooded countryside.

Where is it?

Northwest of Stoke in Cheshire. For the northwest end, turn right off the A533 two-and-a-half miles south of Sandbach, continue under the motorway and take the first right into the car park. The nearest train station is Alsager.

Where can you ride?

Follow the trail for two-and-a-half miles from the northwest at Hassall Green to Alsager, northwest of Stoke.

What else can you do?

Go to Little Moreton Hall (see the Biddulph Valley rail trail above) or visit Stapeley Water Gardens, which features a huge glasshouse with birds, animals, fish and reptiles. It's one mile southeast of Nantwich on the A51 (01270 523868).

Where can you eat?
There's a lockside cafe in Hassall Green, or try the Wilbraham Arms pub 200m along the B5078 towards Alsager at the southeastern end of the ride.

 OS Landranger Map 118

---

108 Sett Valley rail trail

Why should you go?
For pleasant, easy riding for all ages. You ride along a short branch of the old Manchester-Hayfield line (closed as late as 1970), which lies below the western edge of the Peak District. Make the time, in New Mills, to walk the spectacular 150-metre elevated steel Millennium Walkway through Torrs Gorge above the River Goyt. A path leads to it from the Heritage Centre (also worth a visit).

Where is it?
Hayfield, Derbyshire, southeast of Manchester. In Hayfield, park at Sett Valley visitor centre off the A6015 (New Mills road), or at New Mills, which has several car parks. Pick up the trail at the Heritage Centre. The nearest stations are New Mills Central and New Mills Newtown.

Where can you ride?
From the eastern end in Hayfield for three miles to New Mills. You can hire bikes from the Hayfield

visitor centre (01663 746222). For full details on the area send for a leaflet from Hayfield Information Centre, Hayfield, Derbyshire (01663 746222) or New Mills Heritage Centre, Rock Mill Lane, New Mills, Derbyshire SK22 3BN (01663 746904).

What else can you do?
As well as crossing over the New Mills Millennium Walkway, children can crawl through a mineshaft with sound effects at the New Mills Heritage Centre (01663 746904). At the end of the trail, dismount for the dramatic Riverside Park and Torrs waterfalls (there are steps) or go round on the road.

Where can you eat?
At the Hayfield visitor centre or the New Mills Heritage Centre. There's a reasonable choice in New Mills, too.

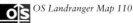 *OS Landranger Map 110*

---

109 Longdendale rail trail

Why should you go?
For easy riding in a spectacular setting in Longdendale, an important Pennine pass. For seven miles, the old Woodhead line trail runs beside a chain of five reservoirs, which provide a quarter of Manchester's water. Strong children (and parents) could aim to reach the family-friendly pub over the moorland at Dunford Bridge.

Where is it?
It crosses the Pennines, east of Manchester. In the west there is a dedicated car park in Hadfield

(it's near the railway bridge). Halfway along is parking at the Torside Information Centre on the B6105. At the eastern end, there is parking near the Woodhead tunnels entrance at Audernshaw Clough on the A628, and at Winscar reservoir near Dunford Bridge. The nearest station is Hadfield.

Where can you ride?
At the western, civilised end, start at Hadfield station and follow the rail trail past the reservoirs for several miles to the Woodhead tunnels/Salters Brook on the A628. The tunnels were a wonder of the railway age, but are now closed and carry only pylons. The ride tracks the tunnels, using a high moorland road, for two miles over Windle Edge, then drops to Dunford Bridge, which is the start of the Upper Don rail trail (32). With younger children, a good place to start is the Torside visitor centre about halfway along, where you can go east, perhaps as far as the entrance of the tunnels and back, or west. A leaflet on the route is available from the Trans-Pennine Trail Office (01226 772574).

What else can you do?
This is prime cycling country, make the most of it – and pray it stays dry!

Where can you eat?
Either at the start in Hadfield, at Torside visitor centre halfway along, or at the eastern end at Dunford Bridge, where you will find the family-friendly Stanhope Arms, with a family room, garden, play area and children's menu (01226 763104).

 OS Landranger Map 110

London

Good cycling in London is far easier to find than most people think. In almost every part of the city green patches and corridors form a parallel world to the busy streets and the countryside slides into the urban area unnoticed.

On the roads follow blue signposts for the London Cycle Network, which provides quieter routes around traffic blackspots. While the Thames Cycle Path along the river both east and west makes a picturesque escape route to the West Country and Kent.

Where to cycle when you visit

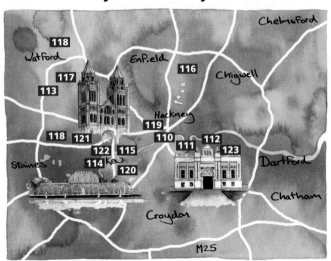

FINDING YOUR WAY

OS Landranger maps covering these areas:
152/165/166/167/176/177

CYCLE MAPS AND BOOKS FOR LONDON

• The definitive street map showing all cycle routes and bike shops is published by the London Cycling Campaign (020 79287220), in Central, North and Northwest editions.
• The London Cycle Network Map shows the entire official network, free from the London Cycle Network Project Team (0208 5475907).
• Two books of weekend cycle rides based on the city's riversides, canals and commons are *The London Cycle Guide* (published by Haynes) and *Cycling Without Traffic – London* (Dial House).
• Covering the picturesque Thames in West London is *Cycling The Thames*, published by the Thames Landscape Strategy (020 89400654), a pack of ten routes with rides 5-12 miles long between Weybridge and Hammersmith.
• Maps with full details of the National Cycle Routes 1 and 4 are published by Sustrans (0117 9290888).

BIKES ON TRAINS IN LONDON

You can take bikes free on the London Underground on the District, Hammersmith and City, Circle and Metropolitan lines outside rush hours (7.30am-9.30am and 4pm-7pm). On London's other underground lines you can only take bikes where the line runs above ground. Bikes are not allowed anywhere along the Victoria or Jubilee lines or the Docklands Light Railway. For an overground line that is geared for cyclists, look up the Gospel Oak-Barking line through north and east London, which is known locally as the Rolling Cycleway. Ramps, cycle parking and space on trains encourage cyclists to use the service, which has connections with many other lines.

www.britainonview.com

PLACES TO SEE

London Zoo (020 77223333)
Open since 1847, London Zoo currently, and quite rightly, ranks as one of the finest zoos in the world. It's home to some 650 animal species, many of which are threatened in their natural habitat, and focuses strongly on conservation. Catering for kids of all ages, it's certainly worth an afternoon visit.

London Aquarium (020 79678000)
For a glimpse of what goes on beneath the surface of the world's oceans, London Aquarium is essential. The depths of the Atlantic and Pacific oceans can be explored, along with coral reefs, swamps, rainforests and, closer to home, British rock pools. Educating and entertaining in equal measures.

MAIN EVENTS

• The Lord Mayor's Show
A fun day for all the family follows the Lord Mayor's procession – this year's is the 675th – as it winds through almost 800 years of London's history, taking in everything from the Black Death to the Blitz as it goes. The fireworks finale bring a spectacularly fitting end to a memorable day (9th November).

WHAT ELSE IS ON?
• National Street Arts Festival
Now into its tenth year, the touring National Street Arts Festival takes its mix of music, comedy, theatre and circus onto the streets of London, entertaining all ages at a variety of locations throughout the Capital during the month of May.

• The Queen's Jubilee
As part of the Golden Jubilee celebrations which will run throughout the UK this year, visitors to London can enjoy the Royal Guided Tour, seeing aircraft and artefacts used by members of the Royal Family and indulging in a royal cream tea in the process. From 1st to 4th June.

CONTACT
• London Tourist Board
Tel: 0207 9322000; website: www.londontouristboard.com

London

110 Hyde Park and Buckingham Palace

Why should you go?
Because it's sightseeing the healthy way. Plus all the fun of the Serpentine in Hyde Park. Give the children a romp in the Princess Diana Memorial playground or make a day of it by combining your ride with a visit to the Natural History Museum.

Where is it?
In central London. Enter Hyde Park by any gate in the eastern section. You can park your car underground at Marble Arch.

Where can you ride?
For two-and-a-half miles on a paved path around the Serpentine lake in Hyde Park, with a half-mile spur alongside Green Park to Buckingham Palace (*above right*). Follow the London Cycle Network (LCN) signs for two miles to the Thames at Chelsea and you can pick up the Thames Cycle Path (**122**). To hire bikes head for Bikepark Chelsea, 63 New Kings Road, SW6 (020 7565 0777).

What else can you do?
You are truly spoiled for choice. Head for the Princess Diana Memorial playground (Broad Walk), see the Changing of the Guard at Buckingham Palace (daily May-August 11.30am) or visit the State Rooms (open August-September). A mile south of the park are the Natural History Museum and the Science Museum (down Exhibition Road), or visit the changing art shows at the Serpentine Gallery. The State Rooms at Kensington Palace are also open to the public.

Where can you eat?
At the Serpentine cafeteria on the south side, and at kiosks and restaurants around the lake. Nearby hostelries that admit babies and children are Le Metro, a bar/brasserie (28 Basil Street, via Albert Gate) and the Wilton Arms (71 Kinnerton Street, via Albert Gate). The Mitre pub (24 Craven Terrace) has a no-smoking family room while The Ranoush Juice Bar (43 Edgware Road) serves delicious fruit juices and pastries.

 OS Landranger Map 176

111 The Thames through Docklands

Why should you go?
Because it's the most dramatic way to see the east of the city and the old docks. You can pick out a section of backroads and pathways or travel the whole way from Tower Bridge via Rotherhithe and Greenwich to the Thames Barrier. Children can pat the animals at Surrey Docks farm, scamper around the Cutty Sark and gape at what's left of the Millennium Dome.

Where is it?
East London. Pick up the signs near the river. Parking is on-street only, and limited, so travel by train to London Bridge, Greenwich and Charlton.

Where can you ride?
For anything up to nine miles (there are LCN and NCN signs to follow but carry your A-Z for backup). Start from the city end at Tower Bridge and you will pass Rotherhithe (two miles), Surrey Docks (three miles), Greenwich (five miles), the Dome (seven miles) until you eventually reach the Thames Barrier (nine miles). On Your Bike (52 Tooley Street, half a mile west of Tower Bridge, 020 7378 6669) has 15 bikes per day for hire (summertime only).

What else can you do?
Cross the high walkways on the Tower Bridge tour, or savour the tranquility of the ecological park at Rotherhithe, where in-filled docks form a haven-like nature reserve. Surrey Docks city farm (020 7231 1010) is full of animals in an unlikely site. The glorious Cutty Sark, the original clipper ship complete with figureheads, awaits at Greenwich, as does the Old Observatory with its unbeatable views. Learn about the powerful Thames Barrier at the barrier visitor centre at the eastern end of the route.

Where can you eat?
At a dozen places en route. The Angel pub (one mile east of

Tower Bridge, 101 Bermondsey Wall East) admits children and babies to the eating area, and The Blacksmith's Arms (three miles, 257 Rotherhithe Street) has a family room. You can get snacks at Surrey Docks farm, while at Greenwich the Gipsy Moth pub (four miles, 60 Greenwich Church Street) has a riverside terrace and offers colouring books and nappy changing facilities. The famous riverfront Trafalgar Tavern at Greenwich (five miles) has a children's menu. And at the end of the route, there is a cafe and picnic area at the Thames Barrier visitor centre.

 OS Landranger Map 177

112 The Isle of Dogs

Why should you go?
Because it's the perfect way to see London's spectacular peninsula of docks and skyscrapers. For the children it's a day of contrasts: show them the highest office buildings in Europe and then the llamas at Mudchute Farm. Greenwich, with its cafes and sights, lies over the river via the foot tunnel. The route does involve two miles of main road without cycle signposting.

Where is it?
East London. Start in the south at the Greenwich foot tunnel (there's a lift, no cycling in the tunnel). In the north it's via Limehouse (NCN1, for details turn to p8) and from the east you start on cycle paths across the Lower Lea Crossing. There's car parking at

the ASDA supermarket in East Ferry Road. The best tube stations are Greenwich and Bromley-by-Bow on the District Line (a mile to the north). You can't take bikes on the Docklands Light Railway or Jubilee Line.

Where can you ride?
Using an A-Z and following the cycle signs, ride for four miles from Westferry Circus to the Greenwich foot tunnel. Take Saunders Ness Road east from the tunnel for half a mile, turn left into Seyssel Street and right into Manchester Road/Preston Road. After two miles, at the roundabout turn left and go straight through the Canary Wharf buildings.

What else can you do?
There are those llamas at Mudchute Farm. Alternatively, cross to Greenwich for all that it has to offer including the Cutty Sark (see The Thames through Docklands, (111).

Where can you eat?
The choice is vast. Canary Wharf has a Café Rouge on the waterfront, which is open weekdays and Saturday lunchtimes, and an All Bar One (next to the Jubilee Line station) which is open all weekend, although children can only sit outside. Get cheap and cheerful eats at the ASDA supermarket cafe (East Ferry Road) and the family cafe at Mudchute Farm. The Ferry House pub (26 Ferry Street, near the foot tunnel) admits children for lunches in a separate room. For food in Greenwich see The Thames through Docklands above.

 OS Landranger Map 177

113 Barnes, Richmond Park and Mortlake

Why should you go?
To combine cycling with a visit to the Wetland Centre. The nature reserve lies right on this circuit of backroads and tracks that run through Barnes, Richmond Park and beside the Thames.

Where is it?
West London. Start at Hammersmith Bridge on the south side. On the north side there's car parking underground on Hammersmith Broadway (half a mile away), also in Richmond Park at Roehampton Gate and East Sheen Gate. Send for a map of Richmond Park from Royal Parks, Richmond Park, Surrey TW10 5HS (020 8948 3209). The best train stations are Mortlake, Barnes, Barnes Bridge and Hammersmith. For bikes, The Original Bicycle Hire Company in Richmond Park (0800 0138000) charges £4.50 per hour, £8 half day, £12 all day.

Where can you ride?
There are two options. If you choose the longer eight-mile route, start from the south side of Hammersmith Bridge and cycle southeast on the river towpath towards Putney. Turn inland towards Barnes at Queen Elizabeth Walk (this is where you will find the Wetland Centre). Follow the National Cycle Network signs through Barnes to Richmond Park. In Richmond Park continue to the crossroads, turn right and exit at East Sheen Gate. Follow the road and signs

London

for a mile-and-a-half to reach the river again at Mortlake. Go right then cycle with care along the towpath; it is narrow in places and gets covered by high tides. Continue for two miles to Hammersmith Bridge.

The shorter four-mile route through Barnes cuts back to the river in half the distance. Follow the directions from Hammersmith Bridge to the Wetland Centre. At the road junction beyond that, go straight ahead along Church Road/Barnes High Street for half a mile to rejoin the river. Turn right on the towpath for a long mile to Hammersmith Bridge.

What else can you do?
The Wetland Centre (Queen Elizabeth Walk, Barnes) is a converted reservoir now home to butterflies, amphibians and wild birds. Play in the Pondzone, pet the ducks in the farmyard, see traditional craftmaking and go spotting at the 'bird airport'. There is also a children's shop and cafe. Entrance is £6.50 for adults, £4 for children; a family ticket is £17.

Where can you eat?
There are outdoor tables at two good riverside pubs – The Rutland Arms and The Blue Anchor – on the north side of Hammersmith Bridge. The Coach and Horses (27 Barnes High Street) has a courtyard and climbing frame that will appeal to your children. There is a cafe at the Wetland Centre, and cafes inside Richmond Park at the Roehampton Gate and – with a lovely view – on the far western side at Pembroke Lodge.

 OS Landranger Map 176

JORDANS ALL AGES

114 Tamsin Trail, Richmond Park

Why should you go?
For the best family cycling in London. The eight-mile circuit was built courtesy of an anonymous benefactor and named after his daughter. Surfaced and traffic-free, a full circuit is an enjoyable ride for young teens.

Where is it?
West London. You can find ample car parking (clockwise from the northeast) at Roehampton Gate, Robin Hood Gate, Kingston Gate and Pembroke Lodge. Your stations are Kingston, Richmond and Mortlake.

Where can you ride?
You can start absolutely anywhere on the circuit. It's eight miles all the way round with a short cut through the centre. Hire bikes from the Original Bicycle Hire Company which is in the park near Roehampton Gate. For a map of the park write to: Royal Parks, Richmond Park, Surrey TW10 5HS (020 8948 3209).

What else can you do?
Relax in the park or seek out the red & roe deer herds (rutting in autumn, fawns in spring) and the flocks of green parakeets gone feral. Otherwise visit stately 18th-century Ham House (a mile west on the Thames) and the world-renowned Kew Gardens is two miles to the west.

Where can you eat?
The park was made for picnicking but if you haven't pre-packed or you need a cuppa,

the finest cafe seats are outside at Pembroke Lodge (west side), with more at Roehampton Gate (northeastern edge). The White Cross pub (Water Lane, Richmond) is a mile from Richmond Gate down Richmond Hill. It has a family room upstairs with a balcony.

 OS Landranger Map 176

JORDANS OVER 8s

115 The Lee Valley

Why should you go?
For a glorious ride along a green corridor used by migrating birds and weekend people alike. There are narrowboats and watering holes along the way. The kids will need good bike control.

Where is it?
In East London. Lee Valley Country Park at Waltham Abbey is at the northern end. Your stations are, from the south, Stratford, Hackney Wick, Clapton, Tottenham Hale, Northumberland Park, Ponders End, Brimsdown, Enfield Lock, Waltham Cross, Cheshunt and, finally, Broxbourne.

Where can you ride?
For up to 20 miles. Start at the southern end, from the Hertford Union Canal on the southeastern side of Victoria Park in Hackney, and you can ride to Walthamstow Marshes, Tottenham, Edmonton, Enfield and Waltham Abbey and on to the northernmost point at Broxbourne, Hertfordshire. If you need to hire bikes head for Lee Valley Cycle Hire at Broxbourne Meadows, Mill Lane (01992 630127), which is open between

• Tower Bridge marks the start of a great ride along the river through Docklands to Greenwich and back.

March and October. It's a £20 deposit and £1.20 per hour.

What else can you do?
The Museum of Childhood in Bethnal Green is worth visiting for its display of old toys, model trains, theatres and the royal dollhouses (Cambridge Heath Road E2, 020 8983 5200). House Mill near the Bow flyover is the oldest and largest tidal mill in the land and also the location of the Big Brother house. It's at Three Mill Lane E3, behind Tesco, one mile southeast of Victoria Park by road. Guided tours take place Sundays 2-4pm between mid-May and the end of October. Admission: adults £2, children £1. At Waltham Abbey, the 14th-century abbey church has a chequerboard front, original walls, a gatehouse and bridge.

Where can you eat?
There are plenty of atmospheric pubs nearby that admit children. In London, the Dove Freehouse (24 Broadway Market) has a separate family area. You will find it half a mile west of the western end of Victoria Park. The Royal Inn On The Park (111 Lauriston Road E9) admits children and babies to the restaurant. The Falcon & Firkin (north side of Victoria Park) has chess and Jenga and outside tables. There is also a cafe at the corner of Springfield Park, Stamford Hill, near the footbridge and Springfield Marina. In the country, there is The Riverside Cafe on the towpath at Haselmere Marina near the M25, plus a wealth of eateries in Waltham Abbey centre

(leave the towpath within sight of the abbey church along Station Road). The Red Cow (Windmill Lane, Cheshunt) is a real ale pub with a children's area in the lounge and gardens.

 OS Landranger Map 166, 177

JORDANS
OVER 8s

116 Epping Forest

Why should you go?
To set your city-dwelling family free on the plains, woods and pebbled tracks of Epping Forest. They will never finish exploring the depths or tire of the seasonal colours in one of England's few remaining ancient woodlands. Keep your sense of direction and watch for horses!

London

Where is it?
On the London-Essex border. One place to start is High Beech (a mile west of the A104 Chingford-Epping road) where there is parking and a pub. There is also parking off the A1069 from Chingford, and at Hill Wood and the Epping town end. The nearest train stations are Chingford and Highams Park, plus on the Underground, Epping, Loughton (Central Line, no bikes into the centre after Leyton).

Where can you ride?
Anywhere you like in the forest, on the grasslands or horse tracks. Things get busy at weekends though, and it's wise to give way to horses and pedestrians. You can do a lengthwise circuit on surfaced, marked tracks. A map of Epping Forest is available from the Conservation Centre (020 8508 0028) and you can hire bikes from Top Banana at the southern end of the forest (7b Johnston Road off the A11 High Road, Woodford Green, 020 8559 0170). Mountain bike hire is £15 per day.

What else can you do?
Go to Epping Forest Information & Field Centre (at High Beech) for forest displays, leaflets and events (020 8508 0028). Queen Elizabeth's Hunting Lodge is on the A1069 outside Chingford (open afternoons Wed-Sun). Or view the unlikely cricket pitch on top of the motorway at the Epping end.

Where can you eat?
The King's Oak pub at High Beech has a big garden and is popular with families. There's a tea hut at Hill Wood, a cafe at Butler's Retreat adjoining Queen Elizabeth's Hunting Lodge on the southerly edge, and some eateries in Epping town to the north.

 OS Landranger Map 167, 177

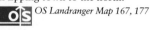
JORDANS ALL AGES

117 Ebury Way rail trail

Why should you go?
Because there's lots for children to do at Batchworth canal centre and at Cassiobury Park at either end of this short and easy rail trail. The route crosses the Colne, Chess and Gade rivers as well as the Grand Union Canal.

Where is it?
Between Rickmansworth and West Watford, northwest of London. The start at the Rickmansworth end is at Church Street. At the Watford end head for Watford Football Club at Vicarage Road. There are car parks at Rickmansworth and Rickmansworth Aquadrome, but none near West Watford. Your BR stations are Rickmansworth, Watford Junction, while on the Metropolitan Line it's Rickmansworth and Watford.

Where can you ride?
Along a three-mile stretch between Rickmansworth, Croxley Green and West Watford. The Grand Union Canal is also rideable in both directions (Cassiobury Park is three miles from Batchworth). There is a useful leaflet available from Three Rivers DC (01923 776611).

What else can you do?
Sunday is children's day at Batchworth Lock canal centre at Rickmansworth, so there's plenty to keep the little ones entertained. Or head for the playground, sailing and canoeing at Rickmansworth Aquadrome (Easter to October); it's further west on the canal. Cassiobury Park in Watford has an adventure playground, paddling pools and children's railway. It's one mile from the Watford end or three miles along the Grand Union Canal from Batchworth.

Where can you eat?
There's a simple cafe at Rickmansworth Aquadrome, while the Batchworth Brasserie is a family-friendly narrowboat restaurant at Batchworth Lock. If you are feeling particularly hungry, order the Full Monty meal at the Scotsbridge Mill Beefeater (half a mile from the Rickmansworth end).

 OS Landranger Map 166, 176

JORDANS OVER 8s

118 Grand Union Canal towpath

Why should you go?
It's 110 miles of family cycling heaven, where you can ride for an hour or for three days. You can't get lost and the canalside pubs are a delight. The kids just need good bike control for safety.

Where is it?
The towpath runs on and on between London and Northamptonshire. Nearby stations along the route are (from the London end) Uxbridge, Denham, Watford Junction, Hemel Hempstead, Berkhamsted, Leighton Buzzard, Milton Keynes and Northampton.

Where can you ride?

Of course we don't expect you to ride it all in one go. Pick your own section. From the London end, the path starts at Ladbroke Grove and passes Uxbridge, Rickmansworth, Watford, Hemel Hempstead, Tring, Leighton Buzzard, Milton Keynes and southwest Northampton until it reaches Norton Junction (three miles northeast of Daventry). Just keep a close eye on the children near the water's edge.

What else can you do?

At Stoke Bruerne canal village there are double locks and the Waterways Museum, also boat trips to Blisworth Tunnel. Children can follow the study trail around Woburn Abbey stately home, which also boasts grounds open to the public and a cafe; it sits five miles east of the canal. You will need your car for driving through the wild animal enclosures at Woburn Safari Park, which also features fabulous adventure playgrounds (01525 290407) – perfect for the kids.

Where can you eat?

There are plenty of pubs en route catering for children. On the southern section, on the canalside at Hunton Bridge, the Kings Head has exciting play equipment and a family room; at Bulbourne The Grand Junction Arms has an adventure playground; at Wilstone The Half Moon offers a climbing frame and swings; at Linslade The Hunt Hotel has a garden; at Leighton Buzzard The Claypipe has swings and a Wendy house; The Barge at Little Woolstone welcomes children away from the bars and log fires; at Great Linford, next to the

canal, The Black Horse inflates a bouncy castle in the summertime and stokes fires in winter; at Deanshanger, three miles west of the canal, The Fox & Hounds has a garden and patio, while The Boat Inn on the canalside at Stoke Bruerne canal village is particularly good; at Gayton the Queen Victoria Inn has a restaurant, and at Weedon the best choice is the Globe Hotel while it's said the Heart of England Hotel is haunted by a noisy child! It puts on Punch and Judy shows too.

 OS Landranger Map 152, 165, 166, 176

JORDANS OVER 8s

119
Hampstead Heath

Why should you go?

Because if you live in London it's a great opportunity for the kids to experience off-road cycling on beautiful heathland. Cycling on Hampstead Heath is permitted on a total of just three miles of heath, on four marked tracks surrounded by open space for play and picnics. The tracks are not surfaced, and there is an upward slope to the north.

Where is it?

North London. There are seven start points (at Spaniards Road, East Heath Road, Millfield Lane, Highgate Road, Nassington Road, West Heath Road and North End Way). You will find car parks at East Heath Road, Jack Straws Castle pub (at the top of Hampstead) and near Gospel Oak station. The nearest train

stations are Hampstead Heath and Gospel Oak.

Where can you ride?

It's difficult to make up a circuit because cycling on the heath is limited (strictly) to the following four linear routes: 1) a long mile south-to-west on the upper side, from the top of Hampstead at Spaniards Road to the bottom of East Heath Road; 2) a short mile west-to-east through the middle of the heath from near Hampstead Ponds (via Highgate Ponds) to Millfield Lane; 3) for half a mile along the southern lower side, from Highgate Road to Nassington Road; 4) for half a mile between Golders Hill Park and West Heath on Sandy Road.

What else can you do?

In summer, you can go swimming in Hampstead mixed pond or Highgate men's or women's ponds. Fly a kite and enjoy the views from Parliament Hill (no cycling), or see a decent collection of animals at the children's zoo at Golders Hill Park (you can cycle there on Sandy Lane). Kenwood House on Hampstead Lane is a beautiful neo-classical house and art gallery featuring works by Rembrandt and Turner.

Where can you eat?

There are three pubs to suit families. The Freemasons Arms (opposite the car park on East Heath Road) has a beer garden and separate area for kids, plus nappy changing. The fine Spaniards Inn (Spaniards Road, half a mile by road from the top track) was Dick Turpin's pub, and has a separate children's area, garden and aviary. Jack Straws Castle (on North End Way on the west side of the heath) welcomes

London

children and has highchairs. Alternatively, eat cake in the elegant surroundings of the old coachhouse, now the Brew House cafe, at Kenwood House (on Hampstead Lane on the north side of the heath. No cycling from the heath, go by road). There is also a cafe on the southern side of the heath below Parliament Hill, and public toilets on Millfield Lane (east side).

 OS Landranger Map 176

JORDANS OVER 8s

120 Wimbledon Common

Why should you go?
For exploring fine heathland on broad sandy tracks.

Where is it?
Southwest London. You can start at a dozen points around the common. There is parking at the Telegraph pub near Tibbett's Corner (at the north end on Putney Heath), at the windmill car park (off Parkside on the east side) or the Richardson Evans Memorial Playing Fields (off the A3 at the Robin Hood roundabout). Best stations are Wimbledon BR and Underground and Putney Bridge (District Line).

Where can you ride?
On five miles of open tracks shared with horses, also on signposted routes. Get a free cycle map at the signboards and at the Rangers Office at the windmill. Be sure to give way to walkers.

What else can you do?
Visit the windmill and museum. There's also a playground in Wimbledon park a mile eastward.

Where can you eat?
The Windmill cafe in the middle of the common also houses a little museum. There is a tea stand on Putney Heath (at the northern corner of Tibbett's Ride and Putney Heath Road opposite the Green Man) and pubs at Wimbledon village. Two pubs en route to the south are the Crooked Billet and the Hand in Hand, which have grassy areas for outdoor drinking.

 OS Landranger Map 176

JORDANS ALL AGES

121 Osterley Park

Why should you go?
For the chance to ride and play in the grounds of the wonderful 18th-century Osterley Park, a National Trust property.

Where is it?
West London. Cycle in from the north from Osterley Lane or from the south from Jersey Road. There is a car park near the house, via the main Jersey Road entrance. The nearest stations are BR Southall and Syon Lane. On the Underground use Osterley (Piccadilly Line, bikes permitted only between Hounslow West and Hammersmith).

Where can you ride?
Anywhere in the park grounds.

What else can you do?
The kids might enjoy the children's quiz at the house (famous for its beautiful Robert Adam interiors) built in the 18th century. There's a farm shop too.

Where can you eat?
There is a rather special cafe, with bicycle hitching posts, in the

converted Tudor stables, and a walled tea garden at the house (open main periods only, baby changing in the toilets).

 OS Landranger Map 176

JORDANS OVER 8s

122 The Thames Towpath: Putney to Weybridge

Why should you go?
Because this lovely riverside path continues unbroken for fully 24 miles, passing many sights on the way. You can ride a section there and back or arrange for someone to meet you at the end. The path is part of NCN4, the Thames Valley Cycle Route, which continues to Reading and Oxford. The path also connects via the Wey Navigation to the Basingstoke Canal for a 50-mile route from Putney Bridge to Basingstoke. At the eastern end you can link up with Richmond Park's eight-mile family circuit (**114**). There are plenty of places to hire bikes too. Richmond Cycles has branches at King Street, Hammersmith (020 741 0115) and Richmond Road (020 8892 4372). Moore Bros has two branches, at Isleworth (020 8560 7131) and Twickenham (0208 744 0175). Try also Walton Cycles (01932 221424).

Where is it?
Between west London and the country. Pick your starting point, but note there is limited street parking along the way (these are busy town centres). It is better to take the train. Choose from the following BR stations: Kew

Bridge, Brentford, Chiswick, Barnes Bridge, Mortlake, Richmond, Twickenham, Teddington, Kingston, Surbiton, Thames Ditton, Hampton Court, Walton-on-Thames and Weybridge. At the London end, there's the Underground too: Putney Bridge, Kew Gardens and Richmond (on the District Line).

Where can you ride?
For up to 24 miles from Putney Bridge, past Kew, Richmond, Kingston, Hampton Court and Walton-on-Thames to Weybridge. The A-Z covers the eastern two-thirds of the ride. Contact Sustrans for details of the Thames Valley Cycle Route (details p8).

What else can you do?
See monster steam pumps in action at the weekends at Kew Bridge Steam Museum, while Kew Gardens glasshouses are always a hit. Syon Park House is a stately home with lots for children to do, including an indoor adventure playground and reptile and butterfly houses. Entrance is free to the grounds of Hampton Court palace, and charged to the maze and the magnificent house.

Where can you eat?
There are pubs at Kew Bridge and in Richmond, with more family-friendly hostelries including the Castle Inn at Old Isleworth which has a conservatory, garden and children's menu. The White Swan on Twickenham riverside has a garden and children's menu. The Anglers Hotel, which lies on the riverside at Teddington Lock, has rides and climbing frames, plus nappy changing and a children's menu. There is a cafe inside Hampton Court palace grounds

• The sights and sounds of the West End lie half a mile north of the spectacular Thamesside cycle route.

(entrance to the grounds is free).

OS *OS Landranger Map 176*

JORDANS
OVER 12s

123
The Waterlink Way

Why should you go?
For peaceful cycling along a sliver of greenery through London's eastern suburbs.

Where is it?
Southeast London, between the Cutty Sark at Greenwich and South Norwood country park, which is the best place to park. Stations include BR Greenwich (bikes aren't allowed on the Docklands Railway) and Elmers End.

Where can you ride?
For a total of ten miles north-south along the Ravensbourne and Pool rivers. Ride the length or a small section. The northern end starts at Greenwich and heads south via Lewisham through Catford, Sydenham and New Beckenham to Elmers End. The Waterlink Way is soon to become NCN21, continuing via Hailsham and East Grinstead to the south coast at Eastbourne.

What else can you do?
At the northern end, board the Cutty Sark to see the sailors' quarters and figureheads. Further south, three miles east of the route, see the restored Eltham Palace & Grounds (020 8294 2548), the opulent 1930s home of the Courtaulds spliced to an important medieval royal palace.

Where can you eat?
At Greenwich the Gipsy Moth pub has a riverside terrace and nappy changing (Greenwich Church Street). The famous riverfront Trafalgar Tavern, 100m from the Cutty Sark, has a children's menu, while at Catford the Black Horse & Harrow has a separate area and garden (Rushey Green, half a mile east of the route at Catford Bridge).

OS *OS Landranger Map 177*

East of England

For family cycling the landscape of eastern England is ideal. Hills can be counted on the fingers of one hand and the views are often exceptionally pretty. The best holiday destination is arguably Suffolk, for its pretty lanes and fascinating coastline, while there are long car-free rides on the rail trails near Norwich, and Thetford Forest is one of the largest offroading areas in the country. Essex benefits from small picturesque country parks in locations as varied as the Thames Estuary and the London borders.

Where to cycle when you visit

FINDING YOUR WAY

OS Landranger maps covering these areas:
133/134/142/144/153/154/155/166/167/168/169/177/178

www.britainonview.com

PLACES TO SEE

Dinosaur Adventure Park, Lenwade (01603 870245)
Follow the dinosaur trail and encounter the T-Rex as he rears up from the undergrowth, then sneak quietly past the angry Stegosaurus and hope he doesn't spot you. The dinosaurs come to life in this fantastic fantasy world (well, almost!), where all ages can climb, run and play to their heart's content. And after that, you can refuel at Dippy's Diner!

Norfolk Shire Horse Centre, Cromer (01263 837339)
A fascinating insight into life before tractors, with a good collection of European breeds and a number of native ponies, while demonstrations show the kids how hard farm life used to be.

MAIN EVENTS

• Duxford 2002 Air Show
This annual aviation extravaganza this year celebrates the 60th anniversary of the US 8th Air Force's arrival in the UK with the 'We'll Meet Again' display. Free for kids to enter, the show will see fighters and bombers, transport aircraft and modern combat planes take to the skies. From 7th to 8th August.

WHAT ELSE IS ON?
• The East Of England Show
Mixing agricultural displays with country crafts, flower shows and entertainments, this ever-popular event is perfect for the family. Held at the East of England Showground, Peterborough, 14th-16th June.

• The English Civil War
Travel back to the English Civil War at this annual two-day event in Waltham Abbey's Royal Gunpowder Mills. The event recreates the environments and battles of the time through lectures and demonstrations. And to keep youngsters entertained, there's a host of kids' activities on offer. From 6th to 7th April.

CONTACT
• East of England Tourist Board
Tel: 01473 822922; website: www.eastofenglandtouristboard.com

East of England

124 Peterborough Green Wheel

Why should you go?
For easy riding through pretty parkland, plus the opportunity to cycle along the River Nene in both directions or tour the city on traffic-calmed roads.

Where is it?
The city of Peterborough in Cambridgeshire. The Green Wheel runs through Ferry Meadows country park and the visitor centre is signposted off the A605 Oundle Road three miles west of the city centre. The country park forms the core of Nene Park which runs either side of the river for six miles out from the centre. Peterborough is the nearest train station.

Where can you ride?
Start off at Ferry Meadows (hire your bike here too, at Lakeside Leisure, 01733 234418). Ten miles of cycle paths connect with another 30 miles of paths westward along the Nene to the A1 and eastward through the city to Flag Fen prehistoric site. The Green Wheel as a whole is a network of signposted bridleways and lanes that link the city centre via 'spokes' to a circular rim around the city. A map is available from Peterborough Environment City Trust, High Street, Fletton, Peterborough, PE2 8DT (01733 760883).

What else can you do?
Drop the bikes at the children's play area and water sports centre at Ferry Meadows, or take a seven-mile ride with Thomas the Tank Engine on the Nene Valley steam railway from Wansford station next to the A1 (01780 784444). Whether or not you are interested in the ancients, the Flag Fen prehistoric fenland centre is an interesting trip when the weather is good. The museum houses the oldest wheel in England, and there are rare breeds to admire, plus a visitor centre with refreshments.

Where can you eat?
There are cafes at the Ferry Meadows visitor centre, the water sports centre and at Flag Fen.

 OS Landranger Map 142

125 Belhus Woods forest park trails

Why should you go?
To enjoy a dose of easy country riding close to London and the M25 – on a track with no mud!

Where is it?
On the London/Essex border. Find the entrance to the park on Romford Road, two miles from junction 30 of the M25, north through Aveley. The nearest stations are Purfleet (three miles) and South Ockendon (two miles).

Where can you ride?
Either ramble by bike over flat open land in the park, or on the one-and-a-half mile-long stone-based track, ideal for youngsters.

What else can you do?
The visitor centre runs Family Mayhem fun days in June, as well as guided nature walks. Otherwise, explore the long ramparts of Tilbury Fort, a great 17th-century riverside fortification, the last built to defend the Thames and London; it's ten miles to the southeast.

Where can you eat?
You can stock up on drinks at the visitor centre, but for food it's best to pack a picnic.

 OS Landranger Map 177

• Make the most of the pretty River Nene on good paths through Ferry Meadows Country Park.

126 Cudmore Grove country park

Why should you go?
For a scenic ride plus picnicking on the beach.

Where is it?
On the seaward side of Mersey Island in Essex's Blackwater Estuary. The entrance to Cudmore Grove country park is

at Bromans Lane at East Mersey, ten miles south of Colchester.

Where can you ride?
Anywhere on the 35-acre grassy, mostly flat land that adjoins the seawall. Cyclists have also been known to ride around the sea wall itself, which is shared with pedestrians.

What else can you do?
Grab a basket and harvest your

own supper at the Pick Your Own fruit, vegetables and flowers site

at East Mersey. In the summer the Mersey Museum features local artefacts. Nearby Colchester Zoo (*below left*) and the children's creative play and family days at the Minories Art Gallery (74 High Street, 01206 577067, open Mon-Sat) are worth a visit.

Where can you eat?
At Cudmore on summer Sundays you can get drinks at the information room, or there is the nearby Dog & Pheasant Inn, which has a garden with toys, and Hasten's Halt tea room (both at East Mersey). For a special treat, go to the Company Shed cafe at the harbour in West Mersey for fresh fish off the boats.

 OS Landranger Map 168

127 Hadleigh Castle country park

Why should you go?
Because it's easy riding for little legs. The paths are on surfaced horse tracks above and along the Thames Estuary.

Where is it?
West of Southend, with free parking at the stations of Benfleet (to the west of the park) and Leigh (to the east).

Where can you ride?
You have a choice of tracks in the park plus the Thames sea wall, making six miles total. For little ones, try the one-mile horse track on Two Tree Island in the estuary near Leigh station. Or there is a

East of England

two-mile (four-mile return) surfaced path from close to St Mary's Road near Benfleet station. Meanwhile the sea wall runs through flat marshland for three miles between Benfleet and Leigh Station.

What else can you do?
The 13th-century towers and wall of Hadleigh Castle sit next door and are accessible by road (not through the park). Then there are the multiple seaside amusements of Southend including the longest pier in world.

Where can you eat?
Try the family-friendly Broker at Leigh-on-Sea which has a garden, or the Liberty Bell in Southend, which has a children's area and menu plus a garden with toys (10 Marine Parade).

 OS Landranger Map 178

JORDANS OVER 8s

128 Hainault Forest country park

Why should you go?
For a hearty dose of undulating countryside – with links to nearby Havering Forest country park for the adventurous.

Where is it?
On the London-Essex border south of the M11/M25 junction. There are car parks on the Chigwell Row-Lambourne End road, and entrances on the A1112. The nearest train station is Hainault (on the Central Line). Bikes are permitted via Woodford on to the Leyton-to-Epping section, and to Newbury Park.

Where can you ride?
Help yourself to the signposted

tracks shown on the maps at the car parks – but be warned, they are muddy after rain and the horses were here first. There is a circuit of the main area, plus a signposted path over to the horse tracks of wooded Havering country park (one-and-a-half miles) and on to Bedfords Park (three miles).

What else can you do?
Pat hides and admire horns at the rare breeds farm at the visitor centre, or if it rains, zip over to Fairlop Waters country park (one mile away) where there is an indoor children's activity centre.

Where can you eat?
There is a kiosk for snacks at the western car park.

 OS Landranger Map 177

JORDANS ALL AGES

129 Langdon Hills country park tracks

Why should you go?
Children are particularly welcome. The park organises children's events and guided cycle rides, with more than 18 miles of cycle paths in lovely flat Essex countryside to explore.

Where is it?
West of Basildon in Essex. Park at One Tree Hill or at Westley Heights, or nearby Langdon nature reserve.

Where can you ride?
On 18 miles of signposted tracks shared with horses. Or, if you prefer, at One Tree Hill you can work out you own route from either the information boards or by using the detailed map of cycle paths from the office (01268

542066). There are two bike shops in Basildon, Cycle King (01268 727110) and Cycle UK (01268 286072).

What else can you do?
Kite-making is one of the more popular activities. Or else you can join the park's playschemes or go bird-spotting at Langdon nature reserve at Westley Heights.

Where can you eat?
The Crown pub has a wacky children's playhouse. You'll find it at the Westley Heights entrance off the B1007.

 OS Landranger Map 178

JORDANS ALL AGES

130 Weald country park

Why should you go?
For easy riding on a firm track – and teddy bears picnics!

Where is it?
West of Brentwood, Essex. Use the cricket ground car park on Weald Park Way on the east side of the park.

Where can you ride?
On two-and-a-half miles of firm, sloping tracks on the bridleway within the park.

What else can you do?
The visitor centre organises children's fun events like Easter egg hunts and teddy bear picnics (01277 261343). The kids will love getting up close with the cows, sheep and horses at Old MacDonald's children's farm, one-and-a-half miles away.

Where can you eat?
At the visitor centre.

 OS Landranger Map 177

JORDANS
ALL AGES

131 Thorndon country park

Why should you go?
For easy riding in lovely countryside and children's events.

Where is it?
South of Brentwood, Essex. Two car parks lie en route, off The Avenue, Brentwood and the nearest station is Brentwood, one-and-a-half miles away.

Where can you ride?
On one signposted track (four miles in total) that can survive most bad weather. Get your free map at the visitor centre (01277 211250). There are also cycle paths into Hart's Wood (en route from the station) and to St George's playing fields which has swings and refreshments.

What else can you do?
Sign up the children for pond-dipping or welly walks, bug hunts or games days. The visitor centre also has interactive displays for children of five and over and an ancient breed of feral goats. There is a ski slope and go-karting at Brentwood Park half a mile away.

Where can you eat?
There is a cafe and a fenced picnic area at the visitor centre.

 OS Landranger Map 177

JORDANS
ALL AGES

132 Flitch Way rail trail

Why should you go?
Because it's easy family riding – and you can't get lost!

Where is it?
Braintree, Essex. Park at the station at Braintree.

Where can you ride?
From the east the trail starts at Braintree station and runs for seven miles via Rayne to Little Dunmow. The trail forms part of the long-distance National Cycle Route 16, which uses cycle paths and quiet roads.

What else can you do?
Chances are the kids will love the House on the Hill Museum Adventure, a toy, film and theatre museum near Stansted.

Where can you eat?
Head four miles southwest for the White Horse at Pleshey, which has a children's room and menu. From the trail, a lane leads to the general pub in Little Dunmow, which should be fine in emergencies although it has no listed children's facilities.

 OS Landranger Map 167

JORDANS
ALL AGES

133 Valley Walk rail trail

Why should you go?
Because the walk makes a smooth flat trail as it runs alongside the beautiful River Stour.

Where is it?
Sudbury, northwest of Colchester. Parking for the trail is signposted opposite the main entrance to Sudbury leisure pool, which also has a car park.

Where can you ride?
Pick up the route at Sudbury station (the trail is the old continuation of the line) and ride three miles to Rodbridge, which is on the B1064 west of Rodbridge Corner.

What else can you do?
A children's guide brings the Elizabethan manor at Melford Hall to life. You will find it two miles to the north.

Where can you eat?
Head for Long Melford (two miles north) for the Bull Hotel, which has a garden and children's menu, and the Crown Hotel for games, a garden and family food. Sudbury is a busy little town with a choice of eateries.

 OS Landranger Map 155

JORDANS
OVER 8s

134 Alton Water circuit

Why should you go?
Because you love the countryside. The circuit is an undulating tour of a watery nature haven.

Where is it?
South of Ipswich. Head for the visitor centre off the B1080, three miles east of the A137 Colchester-Ipswich road. The nearest station is Manningtree.

Where can you ride?
The eight-mile circuit starts and finishes at the visitor centre near Stutton. There are some lanes and wet-weather diversions. You can hire bikes in the spring and summer (Alton Water Cycle Hire, Holbrook Road, Stutton, 01473 328873).

What else can you do?
Try water sports on the reservoir (01473 328268) or hire a boat over in Dedham Vale at Flatford. (Bridge Cottage there was painted by Constable.) Enjoy river views

East of England

and go boating at Pin Mill, four miles north on the River Orwell.

Where can you eat?
At the visitor centre cafe and in general pubs at Tattingstone and Holbrook, or you can try the child-friendly Sun Hotel pub at Dedham eight miles west, with its family room and garden toys.

 OS Landranger Map 169

JORDANS OVER 12s

135 The Three Forests Trail

Why should you go?
For a taste of tranquil road-and-forest riding along the coastline.

Where is it?
Northeast of Ipswich. One place to park is the Forest Enterprise park at Tangham House in Rendlesham Forest. Nearest stations are Woodbridge, Wickham Market, Saxmundham and Yoxford.

Where can you ride?
The main start point is at the Forest Enterprise office in Rendlesham Forest, and the trail continues for some 25 miles through Butley, Chillesford, Tunstall Forest, Snape, Aldeburgh, Aldringham, Eastbridge and Dunwich. Or you can ride short forest trails in each. A leaflet is available from Forest Enterprise, Tangham IP12 3NF (01394 450164).

What else can you do?
Along the the coast find Sutton Hoo, the Anglo-Saxon longship burial ground with new visitor facilities. Also Woodbridge and Letheringham watermills, Orford Castle (which has a children's activity sheet), Orford Ness

(children's spy trail), and Snape Maltings (a classical music venue with shops and cafes). Kids can ride battery-operated tractors at Easton Farm Park near Wickham Market (01728 746475).

Where can you eat?
In cafes and pubs along the way.

 OS Landranger Map 156, 169

JORDANS OVER 12s

136 Suffolk Coastal road tour

Why should you go?
To rediscover the kind of English countryside road riding you thought was lost forever.

Where is it?
The full tour is a 75-mile circuit of idyllic lanes around Suffolk.

Where can you ride?
Choose the distance and venue, riding either way around a circuit of signposted lanes via Felixstowe, Woodbridge, Letheringham, Framlingham, Snape, Orford, Hollesley and Bawdsey. Ride in sections or make a weekend of the whole tour. A leaflet detailing routes, cycle shops and accommodation is available from Suffolk CC, Economic Development Unit, St Edmund House, County Hall, Ipswich IP4 1LZ (01473 583400). There are offroad riding opportunities in Tangham and Tunstall Forests and a foot-ferry at Old Felixstowe.

What else can you do?
For details, see the previous entry for the Three Forests Trail.

Where can you eat?
Children are welcome in the dining room at Ye Olde Bell &

Steelyard in Woodbridge (*below*), and in the conservatory at the Seckford Arms. At Dennington,

two miles north of Framlingham, the Queen's Head has a family area and garden toys. At Dunwich, on the northern extension of the route, the Ship Inn has a garden and changing facilities. Pubs and cafes en route are marked on the tour leaflet.

 OS Landranger Map 156, 169

JORDANS OVER 8s

137 Thetford Forest open tracks

Why should you go?
Because Thetford is East Anglia's best offroad venue, offering a huge choice of open riding among the scented pines.

Where is it?
Thetford, Norfolk. The nearest station is Brandon.

Where can you ride?
Wherever you like on the forest tracks (but not on the military land), or on the easier six-mile family High Lodge Loop. For the latter, start at High Lodge Forest Centre on the forest drive off the B1107 east of Brandon and follow the green signs. The slightly harder Brandon Park Loop is six miles (blue signs) and starts at Mayday Farm car park off the B1106.

What else can you do?
Family events include night cycling and treasure hunts. Details from the Forest District office, Santon Downham IP27 0TJ (01842 810271) or High Lodge Forest Centre (01842 815434), where there is bike hire. Both stock trail maps of the forest.

Where can you eat?
At High Lodge Forest Centre. There are also pubs in Brandon and Thetford.

 OS Landranger Map 143, 144

JORDANS
OVER 8s

138 Marriotts Way rail trail

Why should you go?
For gentle countryside riding capped by a steam train ride.

Where is it?
Between Norwich and Aylsham.

Where can you ride?
Between Norwich, Drayton, Themelthorpe, Reepham and Aylsham. At Norwich, ride from the roundabout junction of Barn Rd/St Crispins Rd at the River Wensum; at Drayton, start at the A1067 Drayton-Taverham road; at Reepham, at the old railway station half a mile north of the centre on the B1145; at Aylsham, at the Bure Valley railway station. Hire bikes at Reepham station, also in Aylsham at Le Bon Bon (Red Lion Street, 01263 732935, summer only) and from Huff & Puff cycle hire at Bure Valley railway station (wintertime only). You can get a leaflet from Dept of Planning, County Hall, Martineau Lane, Norwich NR1 2SG (01603 222230).

What else can you do?
How about combining your ride with a trip on the Bure Valley steam railway? (01263 733858)

Where can you eat?
Try the family pub, the Marsham Arms, at Hevingham four miles south of Aylsham. There is plenty of choice in Aylsham, Reepham and Norwich, and the Bure Valley railway restaurant at Aylsham.

 OS Landranger Map 133, 134

JORDANS
ALL AGES

139 Weavers Way rail trail

Why should you go?
For gentle countryside pedalling on an old railway line, and a trip on the Bure Valley steam railway from Aylsham to Wroxham.

Where is it?
North of Norwich, between Aylsham in the west and North Walsham in the east. At North Walsham use the car park on Station Road, half a mile west of the station, and at Aylsham park at the Bure Valley railway station.

Where can you ride?
For 12 miles there and back between Aylsham and North Walsham. Get the leaflet from Planning Dept, Norfolk CC, County Hall, Martineau Lane, Norwich NR1 2DH. Hire bikes in Aylsham at Le Bon Bon (Red Lion Street, 01263 732935, summertime only) and at Huff & Puff cycle hire at Bure Valley railway station (winter only).

What else can you do?
After that bike and train ride, what more could you want?

Where can you eat?
Try the restaurant at the steam railway station.

 OS Landranger Map 133

JORDANS
OVER 12s

140 Fulbourn Roman Road track

Why should you go?
For a taste of Roman engineering

East of England

on the road that linked Colchester, Cambridge and Godmanchester.

Where is it?

Southeast of Cambridge. Park at the western end near Fulbourn.

Where can you ride?

Ride in either direction. In the northwest, start at the minor road south-west of Fulbourn, continue to the A11 at Worsted Lodge and on to the B1052 to Balsham. The Roman paving is long gone and the track becomes impassable after wet weather.

What else can you do?

See animals at Linton Zoo (two miles off the western end on the B1052, 01223 891308), racehorses at Newmarket Horseracing Museum (01638 667333), and historic aircraft at the Imperial War Museum at Duxford (two miles southwest of the route, 01223 835000).

Where can you eat?

Try the Pear Tree pub at Hildersham, one-and-a-half miles off the route near the eastern end. It has a children's menu and a garden with an aviary.

 OS Landranger Map 154

JORDANS
OVER 8s

141
Grafham Water

Why should you go?

To wear out the teens while keeping an eye on any smaller children. The good-looking ten-mile reservoir circuit is a challenge for older ones while youngsters will be fine on a short out-and-back trip.

Where is it?

West of Huntingdon. Use the car

parks at Mander Park, Plummer Park or Marlow Park.

Where can you ride?

Go anticlockwise round the reservoir from the start/finish point at West Perry on the B661. Hire bikes and pick up a map at Grafham Water Cycling in Marlow Park (01480 812500).

What else can you do?

Children can get their hands on working models at Houghton Mill on an island in the Great Ouse (three miles east of

Huntingdon, 01480 301494).

Where can you eat?

At cafes at Mander Park and Marlow Park, or in the garden at the family-friendly Black Bull Inn in Post Street, Godmanchester.

 OS Landranger Map 153

JORDANS
ALL AGES

142 Priory Country Park path & trail

Why should you go?

For pretty parkland riding plus an extra piece of easy rail trail for the older ones.

Where is it?

East of Bedford. Park at Priory Country Park signposted off the A421 St Neots road.

Where can you ride?

For the little ones there is a short ride (under two miles) beside the park's lake. For older ones, there is an extra four-mile trip on the old Bedford-to-Sandy line, now called the Countryway, past Willington through woods and fields towards Sandy.

What else can you do?

Visit 16th-century Willington Dovecote & Stables, four miles east of Bedford north of the A603 Sandy road (01494 528051). It has nesting boxes for some 1500 pigeons but is only open by arrangement.

Where can you eat?

Head back to the Priory Marina pub at the start.

 OS Landranger Map 153

JORDANS
ALL AGES

143 Ayot Greenway rail trail

Why should you go?

To have fun spotting nature along an old railway line where it's impossible to get lost.

Where is it?

Wheathampstead, Hertfordshire. Use the car park on East Street, then follow the bridleway from the river bridge to Waterend. The nearest stations are Harpenden and Welwyn North.

Where can you ride?

From the west, ride from Wheathampstead for three miles to the minor road south of Welwyn.

What else can you do?

Head for Knebworth House, for an adventure playground, miniature railway, maze and the house itself (01438 812661).

Where can you eat?
Wheathampstead & Welwyn pubs.

 OS Landranger Map 166

JORDANS ALL AGES
144 The Cole Greenway rail trail

Why should you go?
To experience a tranquil rural rail trail between two towns.
Where is it?
West of Hertford. Start on the southeast edge of Welwyn GC and go right off B195 signposted for the QE2 Hospital. Park in Holwell Hyde Lane or Holwell Hyde. At Cole Green, park in the Greenway car park beyond the Cowper Arms. In Hertford use Hertford Town FC car park. Stations are Welwyn Garden City and Hertford.
Where can you ride?
From the western end, for four miles between Welwyn Garden City, Cole Green and Hertford.
Where can you eat?
Welwyn town centre has all usual facilities, but for a family meal head for the White Horse pub in Hertford's Castle Street, which has a garden, and The Cowper Arms at Cole Green.

 OS Landranger Map 166

JORDANS ALL AGES
145 The Albanway rail trail

Why should you go?
For peace and quiet on an old line linking two towns.
Where is it?
Hertfordshire, between St Albans and Hatfield. For parking near St Albans Abbey station turn left before the station into Prospect Road then right at the T-junction to park near the shops. Then for the start of the trail follow the road for 300m, cross the railway bridge, go right and stay right. At Hatfield, use the Galleria shopping centre car park. The trail starts on the far side of the decorative brick wall.
Where can you ride?
For a total of four miles between the two endpoints.
What else can you do?
Take the children to the magnificent nave of medieval St Albans Abbey on the hilltop. The Verulamium Museum in the park below displays precious artefacts of Roman life and mosaics (01727 751810).
Where can you eat?
St Albans town centre has plenty of tea shops and cafes, as does the Galleria shopping centre on the A1 in Hatfield.

 OS Landranger Map 166

JORDANS OVER 8s
146 The Nicky Line rail trail

Why should you go?
Because the safety and prettiness of old railway lines is hard to beat, whatever the season – and you don't need a map.
Where is it?
Between Hemel Hempstead and Harpenden. Park at Park Hill in Harpenden, and the Eastman Way trading estate in Hemel. The best stations are Hemel Hempstead and Harpenden.

Where can you ride?
From Hemel, ride five miles from the Eastman Way trading estate to the B487/A5185 roundabout at Harpenden (Park Hill). There are slopes, and you should watch out on three busy road crossings.
What else can you do?
Whipsnade Wild Animal Park is one of the best in the country and is home to some 2500 beasts. It's on the Chilterns ridge eight miles north of Hemel (0990 200123).
Where can you eat?
Both Hemel and Harpenden have tea rooms and cafes.

 OS Landranger Map 166

JORDANS ALL AGES
147 Hatfield Forest trails

Why should you go?
To ride good tracks in an ancient forest run by the National Trust.
Where is it?
Takeley near Bishop's Stortford, Essex (not near Hatfield town). Hatfield Forest lies four miles east of Bishop's Stortford off the A120. Park at the entrance. The best station is Bishop's Stortford.
Where can you ride?
Roam where you will on the forest trails, using the signboards. Be prepared for mud after rain.
What else can you do?
The Trust organises family events in the forest throughout the year.
Where can you eat?
Get light refreshments near the lake (where the toilets have baby changing) otherwise pack a family picnic.

 OS Landranger Map 167

South West

Holidaymakers throng to the classic rail trails of the West Country. The Tarka, the Camel and Plym Valley lines used to haul minerals from the mines to the ports and today give family cyclists a great day out. For a 60-mile view, ride the Okehampton to Lake trail on the northwest scarp of Dartmoor. Down in Cornwall, pedal around the old tram network near Redruth. Meanwhile, canals have been resurrected in Somerset, and the Kennet & Avon in Wessex is re-emerging as a complete system.

Where to cycle when you visit

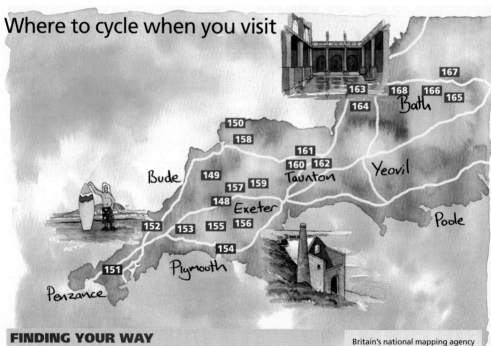

FINDING YOUR WAY

OS Landranger maps covering these areas:
172/173/174/180/181/182/190/191/193/200/201/203/204

www.britainonview.com

PLACES TO SEE

The Eden Project, St Austell, Cornwall (01726 811911)
Discover the world's biggest, most spectacular greenhouse, a creation dubbed the 'Eighth wonder of the world'. Designed within futuristic domes, thousands of different plant species have been included to show the world's differing climates, with birds, insects and reptiles added to control pests. Though hard walking in places, on-site restaurants offer the chance to refuel.

Cheddar Showcaves and Gorge, Cheddar (01934 742343)
Entertainment for children and grown-ups alike. Cox's Cave – with numerous small, winding passages – is perfect for kids, so too Crystal Quest, a journey on which they'll encounter wizards, goblins and a fire-breathing dragon.

MAIN EVENTS

• International Beach Kite Festival
Competitors come from around the world to Weymouth Beach for this two-day festival of aerial expertise. Take the kids and marvel at musical stunt kite displays, giant 150ft kites, fighting kites and, to maintain the theme, kite-powered buggy racing. There are also free children's workshops, competitions, stalls and fireworks. From 5th to 6th May.

WHAT ELSE IS ON?
• Somerton Summer Festival
A fun-packed festival of music, art and drama, featuring market and craft fayres and a special family fun day. From 12th to 20th July.
• Stockland Country Fair
Honiton's annual country fair features more than 50 stalls and sideshows, country dancing, demonstrations of local crafts, clay pigeon shooting and, for burly menfolk, a tug-of-war (3rd June).
• Old Harbour Oyster Festival
Weymouth's unique and fun-filled oyster fest also boasts live music, competitions and sideshows. Unmissable (2nd June).

CONTACT

• South West Tourism Tel: 0870 4420830; website: www.westcountrynow.com; email: info@westcountryholidays.com

South West

JORDANS ALL AGES

148 Okehampton to Lake Viaduct rail trail

Why should you go?

Children will love this ride traversing the north-west flanks of Dartmoor. Billed the most spectacular in the South West and converted at a cost of £750,000, the trail has a 60-mile view over north Devon into Cornwall and its own special railway service.

Where is it?

On the north side of Dartmoor. Park at Okehampton railway station and take the special train to the dramatic start of the trail (bikes go free).

Where can you ride?

Catch the tourist train from Okehampton station to the start of the trail at the wonderful Meldon Viaduct (it's 154ft tall and one of only two high metal viaducts still existing in the country). Follow the high rail trail for three miles southwest as far as the superb granite viaduct at the village of Lake. By 2005 the trail, which lies on National Route 27, will run for eight miles between Okehampton and Lydford. Meantime, from Lake you can jump on to the interim route (which runs parallel to the extension) at Bridestowe to Lydford. To return, either ride back the way you came or make up a circular route using country lanes. You can find more information on the 'Making Tracks' pages on Devon County Council's website: www.devon.gov.uk

What else can you do?

Chill out at Meldon reservoir, or head for highland Dartmoor.

Where can you eat?

There are places at Okehampton and at the start of the trail at Meldon, as well as pubs at Okehampton, Sourton and Lake.

 OS Landranger Map 191

JORDANS ALL AGES

149 Holsworthy Corkscrew

Why should you go?

It may only be a mile long, but the Corkscrew is well worth a diversion. Built at a cost of £500,000 as part of National Cycle Route 3, the structure waltzes down off the viaduct (the first one built from concrete in the country), spins through more than 360 degrees and under one of the huge arches on a 1:16 gradient.

Where is it?

Holsworthy, west Devon. Start in Station Road.

Where can you ride?

For that single, intoxicating mile. The route connects to what will eventually be the Bude-Holsworthy rail trail, which, when completed in 2005, will link via Hatherleigh with the Tarka Trail (**158**) and the Okehampton-Lydford rail trail (NCN27). A second viaduct on the east side of Holsworthy is also due for conversion.

What else can you do?

Head for the coast – particularly if the sun is shining.

Where can you eat?

It's best to pack your own snacks, though you can also find refreshments in Holsworthy.

OS Landranger Map 190

JORDANS ALL AGES

150 Ilfracombe rail trail

Why should you go?

Children of all ages can enjoy this short and relatively sloping rail trail, especially if they get a lift to the top at the Lee Bridge end. You can then ride down to the harbourside in Ilfracombe for an ice cream reward.

Where is it?

On the coast of north Devon. Park in Ilfracombe. The nearest train station is Barnstaple ten miles to the south.

Where can you ride?

For a mere but memorable two miles, from Lee Bridge to Ilfracombe. The 1:42 gradient might have been tough on the trains but it's not too stiff for even little legs, so you could do the climb, and consider the descent your reward.

What else can you do?

Enjoy the seaside delights of Ilfracombe and the north Devon coastline (*above*).

Where can you eat?

There's everything you would expect in Ilfracombe, and there

are plenty of picturesque spots
ideal for a picnic.

 OS Landranger Map 180

*• Summer cycling: The
South West is the perfect
destination during the
school holidays.*

JORDANS
ALL AGES

151 Redruth and Chacewater railway paths

Why should you go?
To ride around a piece of Cornish
history. The paths form a
signposted network along former
mining tramlines and railways.

Where is it?
A good place to start is the
Mineral Tramways Discovery
Centre at Old Cowlins Mill,
Penhallick, Carn Brea, Redruth
(01209 613978), south of the
A3047 on the Pool-Four Lanes
road. The station is Redruth.

Where can you ride?
For up to 30 miles around what is
a growing network of paths,
starting from the Discovery
Centre. Work out your own route
from the map available at the
Discovery Centre.

What else can you do?
See the patients at the seal
sanctuary at Gweek (it's eight
miles south) or visit Pendennis
Castle, Cornwall's mightiest
fortress, ten miles south near
Falmouth (01326 316594).
Trebah Garden, a sub-tropical
ravine paradise with children's
activities and play area, is
situated on Helford River near
Falmouth (01326 250448).

Where can you eat?
At a children-friendly real ale
pub, The Fox & Hounds, with
its garden and children's menu,
at Comford on the A373, two

South West

miles southeast of Redruth near Gwennap.

 OS Landranger Map 203, 204

JORDANS ALL AGES

152
The Camel Trail

Why should you go?
One of Britain's best-known and loved tracks, this disused railway follows the course of the River Camel steadily down from its source on Bodmin Moor via Wadebridge at the head of the estuary to Padstow. It's very popular in the holiday months, and you won't be stuck for ice cream, bike hire or views.

Where is it?
Wadebridge, Cornwall. Start at the quay at Padstow, or Wadebridge centre, or at Bodmin jail in the town centre. The nearest train station is Bodmin Parkway station five miles southeast of Bodmin along hilly roads.

Where can you ride?
For up to 17 miles between Padstow and Poley's Bridge. The most popular stretch is along the estuary between Padstow and Wadebridge (six miles one way). Heading inland, the trail remains low-lying as far as Bodmin (six miles from Wadebridge). The turn-off for the uppermost stretch lies one mile northwest of Bodmin centre. Much quieter, this seven-mile ride features a steady 200ft climb as far as Poley's Bridge near Blisland. Hire bikes from: Bridge Bike Hire (01208 813050), Bridge Cycle Hire (01208 814545), Camel Trail Cycle Hire

(01208 814104), Brinham Cycle Hire (01841 532594), Park & Ride (01208 814303) and Padstow Cycle Hire (01841 533533).

What else can you do?
Visit the huge Norman keep of Restormel Castle (a mile-and-a-half north of Lostwithiel, 01208 872687). Or see the fascinating Victorian Lanhydrock House, which has a children's adventure playground. It's three miles south of Bodmin (01208 73320). Otherwise, head for the Jamaica Inn Museums on the A30 at Bolventor in the middle of Bodmin Moor.

 Chris Juden

Where can you eat?
There's lots of choice in Bodmin, Wadebridge and Padstow, or take your patronage to Jamaica Inn, made famous by the Daphne Du Maurier novel, atop Bodmin Moor on the A30 (01566 86250).

 OS Landranger Map 200

JORDANS OVER 8s

153
Cardinham Woods

Why should you go?
For an easy family-friendly forest trail in picturesque woods.

Where is it?
The woods lie not far from

Bodmin or the Camel Trail (152) in Cornwall. Follow the A38, the Plymouth road, for two miles, then a quarter of a mile beyond the roundabout turn left for Cardinham. After another half a mile turn left to the forest car park. The nearest train station is Bodmin Parkway.

Where can you ride?
For four miles, around a signposted forest circuit. For bikes head for Glynn Valley Cycle Hire in Cardinham Woods (01208 74244).

What else can you do?
Visit Restormel Castle with its huge Norman keep, one mile north of Lostwithiel (01208 872687). There is a children's adventure playground at Lanhydrock House, three miles south of Bodmin (01208 73320) or you can relive the age of smugglers at the Jamaica Inn Museums on the A30 at Bolventor. The Carnglaze slate caverns lie four miles east near Ley, while Dobwalls Adventure Park is six miles away.

Where can you eat?
Callywith Cottage next to the car park does good teas. It's also worth trying Jamaica Inn itself on the A30 (01566 86250), while in Lostwithiel the Royal Oak Inn has a good family room (Duke Street).

 OS Landranger Map 200

JORDANS ALL AGES

154
Plym Valley Trail

Why should you go?
For easy riding on a popular rail

trail that gradually climbs up and over a number of splendid viaducts up the River Plym toward Dartmoor.

Where is it?
Plymouth. At the southerly end, Laira Bridge is where the A379 crosses the Plym estuary. You can park at Point Cottage, at the entrance of Saltram House, Plym Bridge and Clearbrook. The nearest train station is Plymouth.

Where can you ride?
For nine miles, from Laira Bridge to Goodameavy.

What else can you do?
Visit the Plymouth Dome on the Hoe, and learn the story of the town from which Drake, Cook, Darwin and the Pilgrim Fathers set sail (01752 600608). Or visit Morwellham Quay, an historic riverside village with a one-mile train ride into 18th-century copper mines. It's six miles west of Clearbrook via the A390 through Tavistock. The Georgian mansion at Saltram has magnificent interiors, plus a children's guide and kids' menu at the cafe (Plympton, 01752 336546). The Upper Plym Valley contains scores of ancient and medieval sites over six square miles (National Trust). Meanwhile, Merrivale Prehistoric Settlement, the remains of a Bronze Age village, displays two impressive rows of standing stones. It's two miles northwest of Princetown.

Where can you eat?
In Plymouth at the Millbridge Inn, which welcomes children in the back bar and serves real ale (Molesworth Road, Stoke, 01752 563056). There's also a general pub in Clearbrook.

 OS Landranger Map 201

155
Princetown rail trail

Why should you go?
To let the children blast 600ft down off Dartmoor on a remote disused railway that once served the moorland mines. Formerly a section of the Yelverton to Princetown line, the trail begins close to bleak Dartmoor jail, built originally to house French and American POWs.

Where is it?

On Dartmoor (*above*). The trail is signposted next to Princetown fire station, and there is a car park in Princetown.

Where can you ride?
For six miles, from Princetown southwestward to near the B3212. The best thing to do is ride to the first stile which you reach just before the B3212.

What else can you do?
You can visit the High Moorland visitor centre at Princetown, or perhaps the open air Merrivale Prehistoric Settlement.

Where can you eat?
At the top of the trail, the Plume of Feathers Inn at Princetown has a family room, garden toys and a children's menu. There is also the Alpine Bunkhouse in the Square in Princetown (01822 890240). Near the bottom end of the trail on the B3212 near Dousland, The Burrator Inn has playground toys and a children's menu (01822 853121). And for a fabulous cream tea, go northeast of Princetown to the Two Bridges Hotel, where you will also find a garden and children's menu (Two Bridges, 01822 890581).

 OS Landranger Map 191, 201, 202

156 Bellever Forest

Why should you go?
To enjoy a short and hilly circuit around a forest high on the moor.

Where is it?
Dartmoor. Park at Bellever Forest six miles northeast of Princetown off the B3212.

Where can you ride?
For five miles, on a round-forest route starting from the forest car park.

What else can you do?
Visit the High Moorland visitor centre at Princetown, or the remains of 24 Bronze Age huts dramatically sited at Grimspound, east of the minor road that comes due south off the B3212 eight miles northeast of Two Bridges.

Where can you eat?
Six miles southwest at Princetown are two child-friendly pubs: the Plume of Feathers Inn, which has a family room, garden toys and children's menu, and the Alpine Bunkhouse, which is at The

South West

Square (01822 890240). The Two Bridges Hotel at Two Bridges has a garden and children's menu and does great cream teas (01822 890581).

 OS Landranger Map 191

JORDANS
OVER 8s

157 Abbeyford Woods

Why should you go?
To discover a true woodland trail. The route runs through forests off the northern edge of Dartmoor and is well within the capabilities of stronger children as long as they can slog up a few slopes.

Where is it?
North of Okehampton, Devon. Start at the car park in Abbeyford Woods. To find it, take the B3217 from Okehampton towards Exbourne and after one mile turn left. Half a mile after entering the woods the car park is on the right.

Where can you ride?
The circuit twists and turns for four miles – just watch out for those hills.

What else can you do?
There is a beautiful picnic area at Okehampton Castle, the ruins of the largest fortress in Devon (01837 52844). Or there is the Dartmoor Life Museum in Okehampton and the Museum of Waterpower, with its fascinating 19th-century forge powered by three waterwheels, at Sticklepath, three miles east of Okehampton.

Where can you eat?
At the Plymouth Inn at Okehampton, which boasts board games, a garden and

offers children's food (West Street, 01837 53633). Otherwise, you could try the cafe at the Museum of Waterpower.

 OS Landranger Map 191

JORDANS
ALL AGES

158 The Tarka Trail

Why should you go?
To enjoy one of the country's best-known and earliest railway line conversions as it runs inland through peaceful countryside.

Where is it?
Barnstaple, Devon. You can start at Meeth, Petrockstowe, East Yarde, Torrington, East-the-Water, Instow, Barnstaple or Braunton. The nearest train station is Barnstaple.

Where can you ride?

Chris Juden

For anything up to 33 miles inland from Meeth to Braunton. You can tackle a section and return under your own steam or arrange to get picked up. The busiest and most accessible section is on the estuaries between Bideford, Barnstaple and Braunton. You can get laminated routes cards from the Barnstaple Tourist Information Centre (01271 375000).

What else can you do?
Visit the Pixie Kiln & Gnome

Reserve near West Putford, ten miles west of Great Torrington, or the North Devon Farm Park (four miles southeast of Barnstaple off the A361 near Swimbridge). The Barnstaple Heritage Centre has interactive exhibits housed in a Grade I listed historic building on the quayside (Queen Anne's Walk, 01271 373003). Or take a horse-drawn carriage ride and be astonished at the rooms full of models, costumes and shells at neo-Classical Arlington Court.

Where can you eat?
In Bideford East-the-Water the Ship On Launch pub welcomes children except in the Old Bar. It also has baby-changing facilities and does bicycle hire, as well as having a garden and children's menu (01237 472426). There is also plenty of choice in Bideford and Barnstaple.

 OS Landranger Map 180, 191

JORDANS
OVER 8s

159 Eggesford Forest

Why should you go?
Because if there's a better way to tire out energetic ten-year-olds, we haven't yet found it. This slightly challenging circuit winds through a forest in deepest, darkest Devon, and at six miles is a good distance for fitter, stronger children.

Where is it?
Northwest of Exeter. Park at Eggesford Garden Centre, on the A377 Exeter-Barnstaple road, near Chulmleigh. Eggesford is the nearest train station.

Where can you ride?

For six miles, on a signposted forest circuit. There is a leaflet available from Forest Enterprise, Bullers Hill, Kennford, Devon EX6 7XR (01392 832262) and bike hire at Eggesford Country Cycle Hire (01769 580250).

What else can you do?

The nearest attractions are in Barnstaple and Exeter.

Where can you eat?

Either by visiting the garden centre or, again, head for Barnstaple or Exeter.

 OS Landranger Map 180, 191

JORDANS OVER 8s

160 Grand Western Canal

Why should you go?

To ride a pleasant mix of canal towpath and rail trail, though you'll need good bike control.

Where is it?

Tiverton, Devon. For the western end, start on the eastern side of Tiverton at Blundells Road/ Western Way junction. You can also start at Halberton, Sampford Peverell, Westleigh and Whipcott. There is a train station at Tiverton Junction six miles east of Tiverton.

Where can you ride?

For ten miles between Tiverton eastward via Halberton, Sampford Peverell and Westleigh to Whipcott (five miles west of Wellington). The route forms part of the long distance West Country Way between Padstow and Bristol. The West Country Way map is available from Sustrans (see p8).

What else can you do?

See the grandeur of Knightshayes Court, a work of Victorian romanticism which has a children's quiz on the house and garden plus cycle parking; it's one mile north of Tiverton at Bolham (01884 254665). Or visit the castle and museum in Tiverton, or the Coldharbour working wool museum at Uffculme, four miles southeast of Sampford Peverell. The Devon railway centre is located at Bickleigh, which is four miles south of Tiverton.

Chris Juden

Where can you eat?

There are pubs in Tiverton, Halberton and Sampford Peverell, and the Exeter Inn, a family-friendly pub at Bampton, six miles north of Tiverton (Tiverton Road, 01398 331345).

 OS Landranger Map 181

JORDANS OVER 12s

161 The Quantock Hills mountain bike trails

Why should you go?

For a family challenge. Cycling the steep-sided, flat-topped Quantock Hills is tough and the trails are best suited to older children with some mountain bike experience.

Where are they?

North Somerset. There is a car park on the top, east of West Bagborough, ten miles west of Bridgwater on the Durleigh-Enmore-Timberscombe-Bishops Lydeard road. The nearest train stations are Taunton (six miles south with a steep climb) and Bridgwater (ten miles east with a steep climb).

Where can you ride?

For up to seven miles, along the unsigned bridleway across the top of the hills. The other possibility is making up circuits using the rewarding bridleway network. If you really love climbing and descending, start in one of the villages below the hills.

What else can you do?

Visit the nature reserve and have a picnic or tea at the Quantocks visitor centre at Fyne Court, Broomfield (at the southeastern end of The Quantocks, 01823 451587). Of general interest is Cleeve Abbey, a 13th-century monastic site rare for its complete cloisters. You'll find it at Washford, northwest of the hills (01984 640377).

Where can you eat?

At Triscombe, down on the western side of the Quantock Hills, is the Blue Ball Inn, which welcomes children in the conservatory and has a garden and a children's menu. The Inn also serves real cider, a speciality of the region (off the A358, 01984 618242).

 OS Landranger Map 181

South West

162 Bridgwater & Taunton Canal

Why should you go?
To ride a peaceful piece of canal towpath on the western edge of the Somerset levels.

Where is it?
In Somerset. At the western end, at Taunton, use the Coal Orchard car park. At the eastern end, at Bridgwater (Binford Place/Town Bridge), use the Market Street car park. The nearest train stations are Taunton and Bridgwater.

Where can you ride?
For 15 miles, from Bridgwater, via Huntworth, North Newton, Creech St Michael and Bathpool to the county cricket ground at Taunton. The towpath lies on the West Country Way cycle route. For a map and route details contact Sustrans (see p8 for details).

What else can you do?
Cricket fans can visit the Somerset Cricket Museum in Taunton, while halfway along is the Bridgwater & Taunton Canal Museum (near Hedging). Bridgwater, meanwhile, is home to the Blake Museum, commemorating the life and works of the hallucinating poet.

Where can you eat?
There is a family-friendly real ale pub, the Malt Shovel Inn, at Cannington, four miles northwest of Bridgwater, which offers games and a children's menu (01278 653432).

 OS Landranger Map 182, 193

163 Bristol-Pill riverside path

Why should you go?
Because all children can enjoy this easy, highly scenic trail.

Where is it?
The trail runs along the bottom of the spectacular Avon Gorge. From Bristol city centre the path starts opposite 78 Cumberland Road (car parking is beyond on the left, heading away from the city centre). From the Arnolfini art gallery (which has a fine cafe) in the docks cross Prince Street Bridge past the Lifeboat Museum, and at the roundabout go right on to Cumberland Road. Or, for an alternative countrified place to pick up the path at Leigh Woods, cross Clifton Suspension Bridge to the far side of Clifton and go first right into North Road, past three left turns then turn right through the wooden gates into the woods. The best station is the main Bristol station, Temple Meads, in the city centre.

Where can you ride?
The path runs for five miles from the centre of Bristol (Cumberland Road), passing below Isambard Kingdom Brunel's Clifton Suspension Bridge and on to Pill, two miles short of the sea.

What else can you do?
The regenerated Bristol docklands area is a thriving centre of arts and good for eating out. It's also the home of Brunel's pioneering steamship, the SS Great Britain. Otherwise, you can head for Bristol Zoo on the downs above Clifton on the northeastern side

of the gorge (0117 973 8951).

Where can you eat?
There are plenty of cafes and facilities in the docklands. Mud Dock, behind the Arnolfini, is a trendy bike shop-cum-cafe.

 OS Landranger Map 172

164 Bristol & Bath railway path

Why should you go?
Wide and flat with a tarmac surface, this rail trail follows the roundabout railway line that lost out to the direct Great Western route between Bristol and Bath. Graded very easy, you can ride as far as you wish. Features along the way include the old steam trains at Bitton Station, disused station platforms and sculptures installed by Bristol-based Sustrans (*pictured below*).

Chris Juden

Where is it?
Between Bristol and Bath. There are signposted cycling links from each city centre: in Bristol from Bristol Bridge to the rail trail at Midland Road, St Philips (near Gardiner Haskins); and in the

centre of Bath from the Avon riverside to the rail trail at Brassmills Trading Estate. The nearest stations are Bristol Temple Meads and Bath.

Where can you ride?
For anything up to 13 miles. Send for a route leaflet from Bristol City Council, Fourth Floor, Wilder House, Wilder Street, Bristol BS2 8BH. If you are feeling fit and particularly adventurous, the Kennet & Avon Canal continues from Bath (for a total of 56 miles) to Hungerford and Newbury.

What else can you do?
Central Bristol is rich in regenerated dockland attractions, including the Watershed and Arnolfini art galleries and the historic SS Great Britain. In Bath find the luxurious 2,000-year-old Roman Baths (01225 477785), also the oldest bunhouse in town, Sally Lunn's refreshment house and museum (4 North Parade Passage, 01225 461634). Or see fashion since 1600 in the Museum of Costume in the basement of the restored Assembly Rooms (Bennett Street, 01225 477785), while Number 1 Royal Crescent is a preserved Georgian house from the late 18th-century (01225 428126).

Where can you eat?
Very near the trail five miles west of Bath at Saltford is the Riverside Inn which welcomes children in the upstairs bar and restaurant. The inn also has games, garden toys and a kids' menu. There is a pub in Bitton and a wide choice of eateries in the city centres.

 OS Landranger Map 172

Tom Bailey

JORDAN'S OVER 8s

165 Kennet & Avon Canal

Why should you go?
To give children a taste of calm in the 21st-century on one of the longest rideable towpaths in the country. The canal stretches through some of England's most glorious countryside and passes splendid viaducts at Avoncliff and Dundas as well as the spectacular 16-lock staircase at Caen Hill near Devizes.

Where is it?
Between Bath and Thatcham (east of Newbury). The towpath runs from behind the main railway station in Bath, but parking is much easier if you head for Bathampton or Bradford-on-Avon. The best train stations are Bath, Freshford, Bradford-on-Avon, Pewsey, Great Bedwyn, Hungerford and Newbury.

Where can you ride?
You are free to ride anywhere for 56 miles from the centre of Bath in the west, through Bradford-on-Avon, Devizes, Pewsey, Hungerford, Newbury and Thatcham Bridge. Pick a section, say between Bradford-on-Avon and Devizes, and either ride in one direction and get picked up at the far end, return by bike or catch the train.

Make sure children can control the bike before letting them tackle the towpath (and the fishing rods that lie across it). You may have

Stockfile

South West

to walk in places where the towpath gets crowded or too rough and narrow, and you should find out beforehand if any sections are closed (for weir-building and the like). Ride carefully and observe the Waterways Code.

What else can you do?
Visit the Canal Centre at Devizes. An authoritative map of the canal can be bought from GEOprojects, 9 Southern Court, South Street, Reading RG1 4QS (0118 939 3567). And if you want to make a weekend of it, leaflets about accommodation and rideable sections are available from the canal centre.

Where can you eat?
You're spoilt for choice. At Freshford, three miles west of Bradford-on-Avon, is The Inn, with a garden and children's menu (01225 722250). On the canal at Seend Cleeve, five miles west of Devizes, is the family-friendly Barge Inn (01580 828230). On the canal at Devizes, is the Black Horse (above the flight of locks at Caen Hill) with a garden and children's menu (01380 723930). Also on the canal at Alton Priors, eight miles east of Devizes, is another Barge Inn, with games, a garden and children's menu (01672 851705). Near the canal at Little Bedwyn, four miles west of Hungerford, is the Harrow Inn with a garden and children's menu (01672 870781). On the canal at Kintbury, four miles east of Hungerford, is the Dundas Arms with a patio and children's menu (01488 658263). Also on

the canal, at Aldermaston Wharf two miles northeast of Aldermaston, is the Butt Inn with garden toys and kids grub (0118 971 2129).

 OS Landranger Map 172, 173, 174

166
Marlborough to Chiseldon rail trail

Why should you go?
Because you're looking for a slice of none too taxing cycling. The children can spin along the old Midland & Southwest Junction railway where it cuts through the Marlborough Downs.

Where is it?
In Marlborough, park at the Figgins Lane car park by the River Kennet then follow the pavement along the A4 east. After the old railway bridge, turn left into Barnfield. In Chiseldon use the car park off the A346 south of town. Stations are Swindon (four miles north of Chiseldon) and Great Bedwyn (seven miles southeast of Marlborough).

Tom Bailey

Where can you ride?
For a total of eight miles, between Marlborough at the southerly end, and Ogbourne St Andrew, Ogbourne St George and Chiseldon. Extensions will link with the River Ray Parkway (167) at Swindon and the Kennet & Avon Canal (165) near Pewsey.

What else can you do?
Visit the steam trains at the GWR Museum in Swindon, or Avebury stone circle, which lies six miles west of Marlborough. Silbury Hill, south of Avebury, is a great grassy cone whose purpose baffles experts.

Where can you eat?
Head into Chiseldon and you'll find the Patriots Arms. It boasts a family room, garden toys and a children's menu (01793 740331).

 OS Landranger Map 173, 174

167
River Ray Parkway

Why should you go?
To cycle alongside an easy riverside route which runs between two country parks.

Where is it?
Swindon. Start at Coate Water country park, off the A4259, two miles northwest of the M4 J15. The nearest station to use is Swindon.

Where can you ride?
For eight miles, from Coate Water Country Park via Old Town and Mannington Recreation Ground to Mouldon Hill Country Park.

What else can you do?

This is train land. Visit the GWR Museum in Swindon and take a trip on the Swindon & Cricklade steam railway.

Where can you eat?

Three miles east of Coate Water at Wanborough is the child-friendly Shepherds Rest, with a restaurant, garden toys and camping (01793 790266).

 OS Landranger Map 173

168 Chippenham & Calne rail trail

Why should you go?

For easy riding along an old branchline over a magnificent arched Millennium Bridge.

Where is it?

Between the southeastern edge of Chippenham and the western edge of Calne in Wiltshire.

Where can you ride?

For six miles along a flat rail trail.

What else can you do?

There is a children's guide at Lacock Abbey, a converted 16th-century country house used as a film location for the BBC TV's Pride & Prejudice and Moll Flanders. It's four miles south of Chippenham (01249 730227). Children will love the massive adventure playground at Bowood House & Gardens at Calne (01249 812102).

Where can you eat?

There is a good choice of eateries at the end towns, but it's advisable to carry your own snacks en route.

 OS Landranger Map 173

Chris Juden

• *The Plym Valley trail climbs up to Dartmoor via a series of viaducts and here, the Shaugh Tunnel.*

Southern England

Much of the landscape of southern England is attractively gentle, with a few more remote and adventurous-feeling areas, such as the Ridgeway and upland Hampshire.

Among the best runs in the region are the forest trails of Queen Elizabeth Country Park to the north of Portsmouth and the 100 miles of open track in the New Forest. To the west of London lie the country parks of Denham, Black Park and Langley, while towpath lovers can take a trip to the Basingstoke canal, or strike out towards the Midlands on the Oxford Canal, one of the lesser-known traffic-free gems of the country.

A smattering of low-lying disused railway lines are easy to get to, with no need for a map to navigate.

Where to cycle when you visit

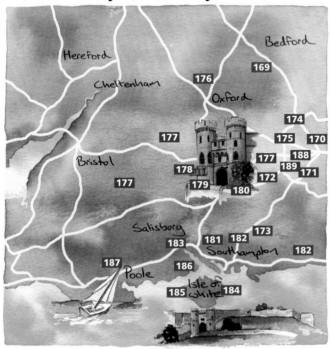

OS Landranger maps covering these areas:
57/151/152/164/165/173/174/176/175/176/185/186/195/196

FINDING YOUR WAY

Britain's national mapping agency

 **Ordnance Survey**®

www.ordnancesurvey.gov.uk

Really get to know an area with **Landranger** The all purpose map

www.britainonview.com

PLACES TO SEE

Naval ships at Portsmouth (02392 861512)
As you'd expect from the world's leading maritime heritage centre, the historic Naval Dockyard is packed with attractions. First port of call for most visitors are the historic ships – HMS Victory, the Mary Rose and HMS Warrior (1860). There's also the Royal Navy Museum, dockyard trails and the Children's Playship to make an afternoon of it.

Roald Dahl Children's Gallery (01296 33141)
Willy Wonka, the BFG and Fantastic Mr Fox await in an imaginative interactive environment aimed at teaching kids (and parents) through investigation and discovery.

MAIN EVENTS

• The Salisbury Festival
A fortnight of family-friendly festivals held throughout the city and featuring more than 100 events. The onus here is firmly on music – from prestigious cathedral concerts to street entertainment in a variety of forms. Excellent entertainment for all ages. Runs 24th May-9th June.

WHAT ELSE IS ON?
• New Forest & Hampshire County Show
Visit one of the country's finest agricultural and equestrian shows, a three-day event held during the final week of July which attracts more than 100,000 visitors each year. Expect farmyard animals galore on the show farm, a flower show, craft marquees and exhibitions plus birds, rabbits and bees.

• Journey Into Middle Earth
Celebrating the life and times of author JRR Tolkien, this unique and fascinating exhibition includes a wide variety of original photographs, sketches, letters and artefacts. It's held annually at the Museum of Oxford and is suitable for the whole family. From 7th December to 31st March.

CONTACT
• Southern Tourist Board Tel: 02380 625400;
website: www.southerntb.co.uk

Southern England

169 Milton Keynes Redway

Why should you go?
Because you can get anywhere you like peacefully in Milton Keynes on its visionary car-free cycle network, constructed as part of the new town.

Where is it?
Milton Keynes, Buckinghamshire. Car parks are at Willen Lakes (J14 off M1), North Loughton Valley Park, and in linear parks down either side of the city. Nearest train stations are Milton Keynes Central and Wolverton.

Where can you ride?
Choose from 200 miles of car-free tarmac around town, across expansive parkland and round numerous lake and canal towpaths. The comprehensive Redway map, which covers numerous rides, is available from Milton Keynes Tourist Centre, 890 Midsummer Boulevard (0870 1201269).

What else can you do?
Xscape in the town centre is an indoor ski dome with real snow, amusements, cinema and bowling (01908 230260). Gullivers Land theme park at nearby Newlands is good for younger children (01908 200010), while Woburn Safari Park (three miles from the M1 off J13, 01525 290407) provides a brush with big game.

Where can you eat?
You can try the cafe at Willen Lakes Watersports Centre or The Gifford – a family-friendly pub at Gifford Park (01908 210025). Otherwise take your pick from various eateries in the centre of Milton Keynes.

 OS Landranger Map 152

170 Denham Country Park trails

Why should you go?
For flat riding on tracks and towpaths in a beautiful corner of the Colne Valley.

Where is it?
Buckinghamshire. Park at the Colne Valley visitor centre in Denham Country Park, off the Denham roundabout at the M40/A40 junction. Cycle in on the canal towpath at Denham village or at Denham Green near Denham train station.

Where can you ride?
For three miles, on shared tracks with walkers, on the link to Denham station and on links to the Grand Union Canal towpath. For a cycle path leaflet, call the visitor centre on 01895 833375.

What else can you do?
The country park hosts numerous children's events, including a cycling picnic and cycling proficiency, and boasts a Coot Trail (with map, 01895 833375) and birdwatching for kingfishers and herons. Alternatively, Bekonscot Model Village is six miles away at J2 on the M40.

Where can you eat?
At the area's prettiest cafe – Fran's Tea Rooms, Denham Lock – the visitor centre, or at the family-friendly Horse & Barge in Moorhall Road.

 OS Landranger Map 176

171 Slough Arm of Grand Union Canal

Why should you go?
For easy riding from the outskirts of London to Slough, on a narrow, straight towpath.

Where is it?
East of Slough at Cowley Peachey. The canal can be picked up at 12 points. Cowley Peachey junction is three miles south of Uxbridge on the A408, the terminus on the B416 Stoke Poges road north of Slough station. Stations are West Drayton, Iver, Langley and Slough.

Where can you ride?
For five miles on the towpath, from Slough centre in the east to Langley, Iver and Cowley Peachey junction, from where you can take the Grand Union Canal into London, or northwards.

What else can you do?
Take a dray ride at the Courage Shire Horse Centre at Cherry Garden Lane, Maidenhead Thicket (01628 824848), seven miles west of Slough.

Where can you eat?
A short walk from the towpath on Thorney Lane at Iver, the family-friendly Fox & Pheasant boasts a garden, ball pond and entertainment.

 OS Landranger Map 176

172 Windsor Great Park estate roads

Why should you go?
For the opportunity to cruise the

smooth tarmac of the attractive Royal parkland estate.

Where is it?

South of Windsor, west of London. There are several entrance points including Bishopsgate (on the east side, two miles south of Old Windsor, off the A328, which links with the A30 and A308), at Virginia Water (on the south side, off the A30), and Blacknest (on the south side, off the A329). The nearest stations are Windsor and Sunningdale.

Stockfile/Steven Behr

Where can you ride?

Anywhere on 20 miles of excellent estate roads. Maps of the park are available from the ticket office at Savill Gardens (south of Bishopsgate), and by calling Windsor Roller Rink & Cycle Hire at Alexandra Gardens (0468 452531).

What else can you do?

Legoland Windsor has models and rides (08705 040404) and Windsor Royal Castle is open daily (01753 869898).

Where can you eat?

The Watermans Arms, which has a conservatory, is well worth

● Cycling in the New Forest. For details see entry No.186.

Chris Juden

149

Southern England

a visit – you'll find it in Brocas Street, Eton.

 OS Landranger Map 175

JORDANS OVER 8s

173 Queen Elizabeth Country Park forest trails

Why should you go?
For the chance to ride lovely forest trails in prime off-road biking country.

Where is it?
Near Petersfield, Hampshire.

Where can you ride?
For seven miles, either on the easy family trail with its gentle hills, or on the more technically demanding MTB trail. You can also pick up the 100-mile South Downs Way to go east or west. A ride guide, priced 75p, is available from the visitor centre.

What else can you do?
Children's events are held at the country park (02392 595040). Or visit nearby Uppark, a 17th-century house restored after a fire in 1989, where there's an exhibition (01730 825857).

Where can you eat?
At either the cafe at the country park's visitor centre, or, at the family-friendly pub in nearby Catherington, The Farmer.

 OS Landranger Map 57

JORDANS OVER 8s

174 Ashridge Forest

Why should you go?
For easy, pleasant riding through woodlands above the picturesque Chilterns escarpment.

Where is it?
On the Chilterns, close to Hemel Hempstead. Park at the visitor centre off the B4506, three miles north of Berkhamsted. The closest train stations are Tring (two miles) and Berkhamsted (three miles).

Where can you ride?
On forest bridleways and estate roads for up to nine scenic miles. A comprehensive map/cyclists' guide to the estate can be purchased at the visitor centre or from the National Trust (01442 842488).

What else can you do?
See thousands of wild animals at Whipsnade Wild Animal Park (four miles to the north, 0990 200123) or visit Whipsnade Tree Cathedral which, as the name suggests, is a curious cathedral created from trees. Alternatively, you can fly kites and model aeroplanes at Ivinghoe Beacon, north of Ashridge.

Where can you eat?
There's a kiosk at the visitor centre, or head for the Cock & Bottle pub in nearby Aldbury.

 OS Landranger Map 165

JORDANS OVER 12s

175 Aston Hill Woods trail

Why should you go?
To race the kids to the top of this short but extremely steep circuit up the sides of the Chiltern escarpment. If they can ride it comfortably, give the national mountain bike coach a call!

If it proves just too tough, visit Wendover Woods for a few easier alternatives.

Where is it?
North of Wendover in leafy Buckinghamshire. There's a car park at the top of Aston Hill on the road from the A4011 towards St Leonards. The nearest train stations are Wendover (two miles away) and Tring (four miles).

Where can you ride?
On the three-mile signposted circuit from the car park. With the Ridgeway & Icknield Way (177) running along the Chiltern ridge and boasting long bridleway sections, this is truly great riding terrain. For the more adventurous, use the OS map to design your own off-road route.

What else can you do?
With its Giant Peach and Great Glass Elevator, there's quirky fun to be found at the Roald Dahl Children's Gallery at Buckinghamshire County Museum in Aylesbury (01296 331441). Alternatively, visit the billies and nannies at Bucks Goat Centre at Stoke Mandeville.

Where can you eat?
At the family-friendly Red Lion Hotel in the High Street, Wendover (01296 622266).

 OS Landranger Map 165

JORDANS OVER 12s

176 Oxford Canal

Why should you go?
To give children with good bike control get the chance to explore the canal and its surroundings.

Where is it?
In the heart of Oxfordshire. The nearest train stations are at Oxford, Tackley, Heyford, Kings Sutton and Banbury.

Where can you ride?
From central Oxford up to and through Kidlington, Lower Heyford, Banbury and Cropredy, finishing up at Fenny Compton. It's 38 miles in all, and the surface can be rough in places.

What else can you do?
There's a maze and butterflies at majestic Blenheim Palace. You'll find it at Woodstock, two miles west of the canal from the A4095 (01993 811325).

Where can you eat?
Try one of Oxford's many child-friendly pubs, the Turf Tavern, for example (Bath Place, 01865 243235). The Rock of Gibraltar – ten miles north of Oxford, where the canal crosses the A4095 north of Oxford Kidlington airport – is great for garden toys and pasties. Call 01869 331223.

OS *Landranger Map 151, 164*

JORDANS OVER 12s

177 Ridgeway & Icknield Way

Why should you go?
For lovely riding on an ancient road over low hills with exceptional views. Highlights, of which there are many, include Avebury, the village inside a stone circle, Barbury Castle, the White Horse of Uffington, the gallops and nags of Lambourn Downs, the Thames crossing at Goring & Streatley and the beechwood escarpment of the Chilterns.

Chris Juden

Where is it?
It's a long-distance bridleway running between West Kennett in Wiltshire and Chinnor on the Chilterns along the Buckinghamshire border. The trail is called the Ridgeway in the west, doubling up with the Icknield Way where the route heads northeast at Goring Gap. Parking is available at West Kennett, Ogbourne St George, Uffington, Goring, Wallingford, Watlington and Chinnor. The most convenient train stations are Pewsey, Didcot, Goring and Princes Risborough.

Where can you ride?
For up to 70 miles over variable terrain. The flattest, most open stretch lies between White Horse Hill near Uffington and the top of the scarp before Goring. This is punctuated by minor roads which are ideal for being dropped off. In good weather open sections can be negotiated on any tough bike, but a mountain bike is recommended and becomes essential in mixed weather or for distance riding.

What else can you do?
Ancient monuments abound in the western half, including the mysterious mound at Silbury Hill, the wooded burial site at Wayland's Smithy, historic Barbury Castle, and the White Horse of Uffington.

Where can you eat?
Carry water and snacks with you, as sections are quite remote for southern England. All pubs are off route. The best family pubs can be found at Avebury (The Red Lion) and Chiseldon (The Patriot's Arms), two miles north of the path near Barbury. At Goring, The Catherine Wheel allows children at the Forge Bar and has a garden, while The Crown at Lower Basildon, just south of Goring, has garden toys. The Crown, this time at Nuffield, has a family room and garden (on the main A4130 Henley-Wallingford road), while at Lewknor, Ye Olde Leathern Bottel welcomes children in the snug and lounge bar and has garden toys.

OS *Landranger Map 165, 173, 174, 175*

JORDANS OVER 12s

178 Wayfarer's Walk westerly section

Why should you go?
To ride a long-distance trail along remote downs in a beautiful part of the country.

Southern England

Where is it?

South of Newbury. Park at the White Hill car park on the B3051, two miles south of Kingsclere, or at Walbury Hill and Inkpen Hill above Inkpen. The nearest stations are Great Bedwyn, four miles north of the western end, and Thatcham, five miles north of White Hill.

Where can you ride?

Sturdy mountain bikes are needed for the 18-mile route, which runs from White Hill (off the B3051 south of Kingsclere) through Watership Down, the A34, Ashmansworth, Walbury Hill, Inkpen Hill, Ham Hill and Botley Down. Long sections follow wide tracks or lanes, the easiest section being the ten miles from Botley Hill in the west via Ham Hill, Inkpen Hill and Walbury Hill to the A343 near Ashmansworth. The eastern section to White Hill is harder. For full trail details call 01962 846045.

What else can you do?

The unmissable stone circle of Stonehenge is 15 miles southwest, close to Amesbury.

Where can you eat?

At the Harrow Inn at Little Bedwyn, four miles from Ham Hill.

 OS Landranger Map 174

JORDANS OVER 12s

179 Wayfarer's Walk southerly section

Why should you go?

For some mountain biking through fine farmland and empty trails and lanes.

Where is it?

In Hampshire. Park at the steam railway station in New Alresford, or on the street in either Dummer or Brown Candover. Your nearest stations are Basingstoke (four miles north of Dummer) and Winchester (eight miles west of New Alresford).

Chris Juden

Where can you ride?

For 13 miles on the gentler bridleway section of this long-distance trail, running from north to south between Dummer (south of Basingstoke), Brown Candover and New Alresford (east of Winchester).

What else can you do?

Climb aboard the Mid-Hants-Watercress Line steam railway from New Alresford to Alton. Alternatively, Northington Grange, a stately home and park, lies four miles north of New Alresford (01962 846924) and Jane Austen's house is preserved at Chawton, eight miles east of New Alresford (01420 83262).

Where can you eat?

The Sun Inn, boasting garden toys and a children's menu, is at North Waltham, a mile-and-a-half west of Dummer.

 OS Landranger Map 185

JORDANS OVER 8s

180 Basingstoke Canal

Why should you go?

Children with good control can enjoy this easy ride through the heart of leafy Hampshire. For those with real stamina, it can become a car-free connection all the way into London.

Where is it?

Through Hampshire and Surrey. Park at a choice of Odiham Wharf car park in Odiham (east of Greywell), Fleet (off the B3013), Basingstoke Canal Centre at Mytchett near Farnborough, or at the Brewery Road car park in Woking. The nearest train stations are Hook, Fleet, Aldershot, Farnborough, Woking, West Byfleet, Weybridge and Byfleet and New Haw.

Where can you ride?

For 32 miles in all. From Greywell – one mile south of Hook – the route runs through Fleet, Aldershot, Ash, Woking and Weybridge (the Thames). The central section, around Aldershot, is easier to ride than the westerly section in Hampshire, with the highlight coming between Ash and Woking. From Weybridge, the Wey Navigation runs southerly to Guildford and Godalming, while the Thames Towpath (**122**) heads east to Putney Bridge and west towards Reading. A canal map is available to order by calling 0118 9393567.

What else can you do?

Visit the Basingstoke Canal Centre at Mytchett, and the Spirit of Brooklands at Weybridge to see the famous banked car race track and automobile collection (01932 857381).

Where can you eat?
There's plenty of choice along the way. For families, the Dover Arms at Ash has a garden and children's menu (31 Guildford Rd), while the Robin Hood Inn near Woking allocates part of its bar to families. It's one mile off the route at 88 Robin Hood Road, Knaphill. The Old Crown at Weybridge welcomes children in the lounge bar and has games and a garden to keep them entertained.

 OS Landranger Map 176, 186

 JORDANS
ALL AGES

181 Meon Valley rail trail

Why should you go?
Visiting the lovely Meon Valley is a double pleasure – an easy rail trail with no risk of getting lost.

Where is it?
North of Fareham, Hampshire. Park in West Meon, in the car park at Droxford near the church. At Wickham follow the 'free parking' signs from the centre towards the A32. The nearest station, Fareham, lies four miles south of Wickham.

Where can you ride?
The route runs for ten miles, between West Meon, Droxford, Soberton and Wickham. The South Downs Way bridleway (**198**) crosses the route one mile south of West Meon.

What else can you do?
See 200 species of animal at Marwell Zoo Park, with lots

more to keep children entertained. It's at Colden Common, seven miles west of Droxford (01962 943163). In Portsmouth harbour is Porchester Castle, a great walled compound and keep, while the Mary Rose, HMS Victory and HMS Warrior are all stationed in Portsmouth's historic dockyard at HM Naval Base, seven miles south of Wickham (02392 861533).

Where can you eat?
The family-friendly White Horse Inn at Droxford, on the A32, is worth a visit, boasting table football, a garden and a children's menu (01489 877490). There are a number of other pubs worth visiting at West Meon, Droxford, Soberton and Wickham.

 OS Landranger Map 185, 196

JORDANS
OVER 8s

182 West Walk Forest trail

Why should you go?
Because this picturesque circular trail through the Forest of Bere is ideal for adults and kids alike.

Where is it?
Northwest of Portsmouth. Park at West Walk Forest car park on the minor road towards Soberton heath, off the A32 Fareham-Alton road, three miles north of Wickham. The nearest train stations are Fareham and Botley.

Where can you ride?
For three miles on a signposted forest circuit, outlined in a leaflet available to order from Forest Enterprise (01420 23666).

What else can you do?
See Meon Valley (**181**).

Where can you eat?
Try the pub in nearby Wickham.

 OS Landranger Map 196

JORDANS
ALL AGES

183 The Test Way rail trail

Why should you go?
For an easy and enjoyable ride along an old railway line which runs beside the River Test.

Where is it?
In Stockbridge, Hampshire. The northern end starts from Stockbridge, the southern end at Mottisfont, where you'll also find the trail's closest station.

Where can you ride?
For five miles, along the Test Valley between Stockbridge and Horsebridge and on to the A3057 at Stonymarsh.

What else can you do?
There's a children's quiz on offer at the 12th-century Mottisfont Abbey on the river. The Abbey is a picturesque private house converted by the National Trust and famous for its fabulous interiors and its rose garden (01794 340757).

Where can you eat?
For a limited choice of refreshments try Stockbridge.

 OS Landranger Map 185

JORDANS
ALL AGES

184 Cowes to Newport cycleway

Why should you go?
For the chance to pedal along a picturesque rail trail down

Southern England

the Medina Valley – running from the top to the middle of the Isle of Wight.

Where is it?

Parking is available at the northerly end of the route at Cowes Hotel, located on Arctic Road. There's also parking on the southwest edge of Cowes and, alternatively, at the southerly end at the industrial park, on the north side of Newport.

Where can you ride?

The route runs for four miles from Cowes, via the River Medina, to Newport. The Isle of Wight has a great cycle network generally, on lanes and bridleways. For full details you can ring for the map from Isle of Wight Council (01983 821000).

What else can you do?

The island, of course, is a holiday destination, so you will be spoiled for choice. Head for the resorts of Ventnor and Shanklin for Shanklin Chine, a historic gorge and attractions (01983 866432). Medieval Carisbrooke Castle has a donkey-driven waterwheel (01983 522107). Osborne House, Queen Victoria's Italianate retreat, features the Swiss Cottage built for her children – you'll find it one mile southeast of Cowes (01983 200022).

Where can you eat?

Try the Traveller's Joy in Northwood, for garden toys and pétanque, while the Wheatsheaf Hotel, at St Thomas Square in Newport, is family-friendly, with games and a children's menu. Cowes also offers a variety of good places to eat.

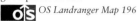 *OS Landranger Map 196*

 JORDANS ALL AGES

185 Yarmouth to Freshwater cycleway

Why should you go?

For the pleasure of riding an easy trail along the scenic Yar Estuary from the little port of Yarmouth to the cliffs of Freshwater Bay.

Chris Juden

Where is it?

On the Isle of Wight. Park in Yarmouth at the large car park on the southeast edge, ride east along the A3054 and take the second right turning.

Where can you ride?

For threeextremely scenic miles from south Yarmouth up the estuary to Freshwater. Offshore Sports offer bike hire and accessories (Shooters Hill, Cowes, 01983 291914).

What else can you do?

Visit the glassworks at Alum Bay, admire the surge at Needles Point and the spectacularly-situated fort at the Needles Old Battery, which has its own children's exhibition and guide.

Where can you eat?

Children are welcome in the Harbour Lounge and conservatory at the Wheatsheaf Inn in Yarmouth, where there are also games and a garden to

entertain them (Bridge Road, 01983 760456), and there's a choice of eateries in Yarmouth and Freshwater Bay.

OS Landranger Map 196

JORDANS OVER 8s

186 The New Forest

Why should you go?

To take your pick of over 100 miles of signposted sandy trails – and the chance to spot wild ponies as you go.

Where is it?

Hampshire. Tracks start close to each of the 140 car parks. The most convenient train station is Brockenhurst.

Where can you ride?

Anywhere you like on the vast signposted forest network. A valuable companion for riders is the 'Cycling in the Forest – a Network Map' from Forest Enterprise (02380 28314) or Lyndhurst Tourist Information, (02380 282269). The New Forest Cycle Experience (01590 624204) offers cycle hire and accessories.

Chris Juden

What else can you do?

See the vintage cars and ride the monorail and minibikes at nearby Beaulieu House and National Motor Museum (01590 612123).

Where can you eat?

Family-friendly pubs in the area include the White Hart at Cadnam (northeast of the forest), which has a garden and children's menu (Old Romsey Road, 02380 812277), and the Chequers Inn at Lymington (Lower Woodside, 01590 673415).

 OS Landranger Map 196

JORDANS
ALL AGES

187
Castleman rail trail

Why should you go?
Because you want a nice run along an old railway line where the pedalling is low-effort and the chance of getting lost is zero.

Where is it?
Wimborne Minster, Dorset. Park at Moors Valley Country Park, off the minor road heading west from the A338/A31 roundabout to west of Ringwood. Alternatively, try the Willet Arms pub (but ask permission first) at Merley, south of Wimborne, just off the most southerly of two roundabouts near the A31/A349 junction or at Upton Country Park off the A35 east of Upton.

Where can you ride?
The trail is split into halves by a new building. So, for four miles from Moors Valley Country Park (Ashley Heath, west of Ringwood) to West Moors, and for four miles from Merley (south of Wimborne Minster) to Upton Country Park.

What else can you do?
Bournemouth with its seafront and myriad attractions lies just eight miles further southeast.

Where can you eat?

At the visitor centres in both Moors Valley Country Park and Upton Country Park.

 OS Landranger Map 195

JORDANS
ALL AGES

188 Black Park Country Park trails

Why should you go?
For the chance to ride the rugged woodland tracks which sit adjacent to Pinewood Studios, the setting for James Bond's many films.

Where is it?
Buckinghamshire. Park off Black Park Road signposted from the A412, five miles from J1 of the M40. The nearest train stations are at Langley, 2.5 miles to the south, and Denham, two-and-a-half miles to the north.

Where can you ride?
Wherever you desire over 15 miles of woodland trails except, of course, where signs tell you otherwise.

What else can you do?
Pay a visit to the park's adventure playground or see the moving models and gauge 1 railway at Bekonscot Model Village – eight miles northwest near J2 of the M40. For more thrills and spills, head for Legoland Windsor (08705 040404) which has rides and models and sits ten miles southwest off the B3022 southwest of Windsor.

Where can you eat?
At the visitor centres (01753 511060). Good family pubs can be found a couple of miles east

---

at Iver. The Fox & Pheasant (Thorney Lane, near the Slough arm of the Grand Union Canal) has an excellent selection of garden toys for kids, while The Swan Inn, on Iver's High Street, has a garden and children's menu.

 OS Landranger Map 176

JORDANS
OVER 8s

189 Langley Park Country Park trails

Why should you go?
Because the trail offers families the chance to enjoy peaceful, easy-riding woodland tracks in an historic and picturesque parkland estate.

Where is it?
It's Black Park's smaller neighbour in Buckinghamshire (so see Black Park for details), though weighing in at 130 acres, it's still sizeable. It's best to park off Billet Lane (south off the A412 Uxbridge-Slough road), which is 500m west off the Crooked Billet roundabout. The nearest and most convenient train stations are Langley (two miles south) and Denham (four miles north).

Where can you ride?
Across several clearly marked trails over several miles of parkland previously inhabited by herds of deer.

What else can you do?
See Black Park (**188**).

Where can you eat?
See Black Park (**188**).

 OS Landranger 176

South East England

England's right-hand corner is a memorable mix of long trails and gorgeous short hops, many of them on old railway lines, all of them rural. For example, you may choose to ride all the bridleway sections of the inland North Downs, or perhaps much of the glorious, mostly coastal South Downs.

Alternatively, lying between the two is the long, easy Downs Link, while The Cuckoo Trail, a middle distance route, passes through beautiful countryside. As you'll quickly discover, your options are almost endless.

Where to cycle when you visit

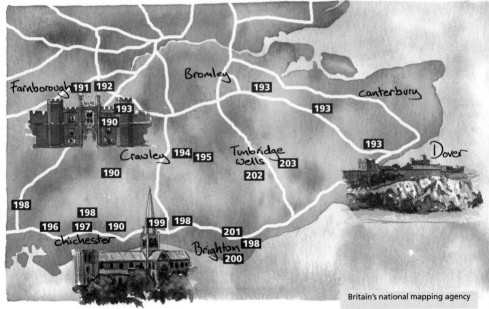

FINDING YOUR WAY

190	Downs Link rail trail	p158
191	Alice Holt Forest	p158
192	Wey Navigation	p159
193	North Downs Way	p160
194	Worth Way rail trail	p160
195	Forest Way rail trail	p160
196	Centurion Way rail trail	p161
197	Houghton Forest	p161
198	The South Downs Way	p162
199	The Dyke rail trail	p163

200	Friston Forest	p163
201	The Cuckoo Trail	p164
202	Bewl Water	p164
203	Bedgebury Forest	p165

OS Landranger maps covering these areas:
176/178/185/186/187/188 /189/197/198/199

www.britainonview.com

PLACES TO SEE

Weald and Downland Open Air Museum, Chichester (01243 811348)
Set in 50 acres of beautiful parkland, these historic buildings – more than 40 in all – tell the story of British architecture and construction. Kids can explore the houses and gardens, plus discover the workshops and the working flour mill of traditional craftsmen.

Groombridge Place Gardens and the Enchanted Forest, Royal Tunbridge Wells (01892 861444)
You may fancy exploring acres of gardens and woodland, or a relaxing canal boat ride. However, mere mention of Jurassic Valley, The Mystic Pool, Serpent's Lair, Dinosaur's Nest or Smugglers Lookout will have your kids dragging you there instead in a flash.

MAIN EVENTS

• Selsey Fireworks
Featuring a funfair, live entertainment, food and drink, a bonfire and, most dramatically, a spectacular fireworks display set to music, here's the perfect way to wind down after a day in the saddle. Held in Chichester and scheduled for 19th October this year, should bad weather intervene, a fall back date has been set for a week later.

WHAT ELSE IS ON?

• Brighton Festival
England's biggest annual arts festival rolls into Brighton every May, bringing with it an exceptional array of musical merriment from opera to jazz, and mixing theatre and dance to dazzling effect.

• Apple Day
Head to West Dean to celebrate the humble English apple. Promising more than 100 apple varieties on display, a range of 'appley' events, including tastings and apple-bobbing, and tours of the lovely walled gardens, Apple Day is an excellent family attraction.

USEFUL ADDRESS & NUMBERS

• South East England Tourist Board
Tel: 01892 540766; website: www.southeastengland.uk.com

South East

190 Downs Link rail trail

Why should you go?
For easy pedalling for as far as you like on an old railway line which runs through countryside between the two main ridgelines of southern England.

Where is it?
North-south through Surrey and West Sussex, between Bramley (south of Guildford) and Bramber (north of Shoreham-on-Sea). At the northern end use the car park at Bramley and Wonersh Old Station (from the roundabout at the A281/B2128, Wonersh exit, go left after 80m, signposted 'Station'). Or park at Cranleigh at the far corner of the main car park off the High Street near the NatWest bank. Starting from the southern end, park at Southwater Country Park. Close train stations are Guildford (three miles on main roads), Shalford (one mile), Christ's Hospital (half a mile) and Shoreham (four miles on backroads).

Chris Juden

Where can you ride?
North-south for up to 27 miles from Bramley (on the A281 south of Guildford) through Cranleigh, Rudgwick, Slinfold, Southwater, Partridge Green and Henfield to Bramber (on the A283 north of Shoreham-on-Sea). Note, there is one climb south of the Thurlow Arms at Baynards (just south of Cranleigh).

What else can you do?
Visit the Doll's House Museum at Petworth – there are 100 inhabited houses on display. You'll find it ten miles west of Christ's Hospital.

Where can you eat?
Family-friendly pubs come at intervals. At the northern end, the Jolly Farmer (Shalford Road, Millbrook) has a terrace, garden and kids' menu. The Parrot Inn (Broadford Road, Shalford) has a garden and also offers kids' meals. Halfway down and virtually en route is the Bax Castle (Two Mile Ash, near Horsham), with its family room, garden toys and children's menu. At the southern end is the highly recommended Star Inn (130 High Street, Steyning), which has a family room and toys, children's toilets, a quaint garden and nappy changing facilities.

 OS Landranger Map 186 (north section), 187 (middle), 198 (south)

191 Alice Holt Forest

Why should you go?
Because the kids won't get stuck in the mud on this signposted forest ride, as the sandy soil drains well throughout the year.

Where is it?
West of Farnham, Surrey. Park at

• *The South Downs Way (198) runs for 100 miles on chalk ridgeland and is perfect for fit families.*

Alf Alderson

the visitor centre, four miles southwest of Farnham off the A325 Petersfield road at Bucks Horn Oak. The nearest train station, Bentley, is one mile to the northeast.

Where can you ride?
For four miles on the signposted circular route that starts and finishes at the visitor centre.

What else can you do?
Birdworld, including Underwater World with its alligator swamp, is on the A325, three miles south of Farnham (01420 22140). Alternatively, Farnham Castle (01737 223000) – the remains

of a motte and bailey – stands just north of Farnham centre.

Where can you eat?
Pack a picnic for a day out, or head for pretty Tilford, five miles east, where the riverside pub attracts families in the summer.

 OS Landranger Map 186

JORDANS
OVER 12s

192
Wey Navigation

Why should you go?
To explore this canal that shadows the River Wey from Godalming through the Surrey countryside and Guildford to join the Thames towpath at Weybridge on the outskirts of London. The whole canal is now under the wing of the National Trust, including historic Dapdune Wharf at Guildford. At West Byfleet, three miles before Weybridge, the route is joined by the Basingstoke Canal.

Where is it?
Surrey. There are car parks off the A281 near Shalford and on the B367 between Ripley and West Byfleet. The nearest stations are Godalming, Guildford, Woking, West Byfleet, Brooklands and Weybridge.

Where can you ride?
For up to 20 miles, of which all bar the five-mile section south of Weybridge is demanding, from Godalming in the southwest to Guildford, Byfleet and as far as Weybridge and the confluence with the Thames.

What else can you do?
At Dapdune Wharf (01483 561389) lies the Reliance, a restored Wey barge that houses an exhibition about the canal. Also, starting from Guildford

South East

Boat House at Dapdune Wharf, you can take boat trips along the River Wey. Southwest of Guildford is Loseley Park, a fine stately home with a children's playground (01483 304440). Or visit the race car collection at the Spirit of Brooklands at the famous banked track at Weybridge (01932 857381).

Where can you eat?
There are several good family pubs. At the northern end, the Jolly Farmer (Shalford Road, Millbrook) boasts a terrace, garden and kid's menu. The Parrot Inn is nearby (Broadford Road, Shalford), offering a garden and children's meals. The Old Crown, on the old course of the Wey at Weybridge, allows children into the lounge bar and has a patio and garden. Godalming, Guildford, Byfleet and Weybridge are busy towns, with plenty of choice.

 OS Landranger Map 176, 186, 187

JORDANS
OVER 12s

193
North Downs Way

Why should you go?
For your first taste of offroad riding – rarely easy and frequently tough – through some lovely hilly countryside.

Where is it?
On a hilly, long-distance walking trail through Surrey and Kent, between Farnham and Dover. There are three shorter bridleway sections that can be cycled. Nearby stations are Guildford and Dorking (for section one),

and Borough Green and Rochester (section two).

Where can you ride?
On three sections of bridleway. From Puttenham (west of Guildford) to Guildford and Dorking. From Wrotham (J2 on the M20) to Rochester and Blue Bell Hill, and from Hollingbourne (east of Maidstone) to Dunn Street (north of Ashford).

What else can you do?
For attractions at the western end, see Wey Navigation (**192**).

Where can you eat?
For family-friendly pubs near Guildford, see the 'Wey Navigation' (**192**).

 OS Landranger Map 186, 187 (Puttenham-Guilford), 178, 188 (Wrotham-Blue Bell Hill), 188, 189 (Hollingbourne-Dunn Street)

JORDANS
ALL AGES

194 Worth Way
rail trail

Why should you go?
For nice, easy riding along an old railway line in fine countryside.

Where is it?
West of East Grinstead, West Sussex. Park at East Grinstead station. The nearest stations are East Grinstead and Crawley.

Where can you ride?
For six miles from East Grinstead station at the eastern end, to Crawley Down and Worth on the eastern edge of Crawley.

What else can you do?
See meerkats, among other beasties, at Gatwick Zoo. It lies six miles northeast of Worth, at Russ Hill, Charlwood (call 01293 862312).

Where can you eat?
Try the Star Inn at Lingfield, it's a real ale pub with excellent children's facilities and is situated on Church Road, four miles north of East Grinstead.

 OS Landranger Map 187

JORDANS
ALL AGES

195 Forest Way
rail trail

Why should you go?
To take it easy on a disused railway line through the countryside that inspired AA Milne's 'Winnie the Pooh'.

Where is it?
East of East Grinstead, into East Sussex. At East Grinstead use the car park on College Lane/De La Warr Road on the town centre side of the roundabout on the A22. On the bike, return to De La Warr Road and go right, at the T-junction with College Lane go right again. After 100m go left downhill by a stone wall, and at the end of Old Road, cross to the opposite pavement, turn left, then right through the fence on to the path. At the next road Forest Way goes straight ahead. The nearest train stations are East Grinstead and Groombridge.

Where can you ride?
For nine miles, from East Grinstead in the west (at the College Lane/A22 roundabout), via Forest Row and Hartfield, to the B2110 (one mile west of Groombridge).

What else can you do?
There are numerous attractions within ten miles of the trail. With kids in mind, Hever Castle has a

maze and adventure playground (01732 865224), Penshurst Place, a 14th-century manor house, has a good adventure playground (01892 870307), and the children's farm at Godstone includes big play areas (01883 742546). Alternatively, Penshurst Vineyard mixes wine-tasting and wallabies, while the idyllic Chiddingstone village is mostly National Trust-owned.

Where can you eat?

Try the Anchor Inn in Hartfield, a real ale pub which has garden toys and a children's menu. It lies 500m south of the trail.

 OS Landranger Map 187, 188

The South East is studded with wonderful medieval and Saxon castles.

South East England TB

196 Centurion Way rail trail

Why should you go?

For the chance to see trail sculptures without working up too much of a sweat.

Where is it?

Chichester. The southern end starts at Westgate (on the west of Chichester), the northern end starts at Warble Heath Close in Mid Lavant, off the A286 north of Chichester. The nearest train station is Chichester.

Where can you ride?

For two miles, from the west of Chichester at Westgate, north to Mid Lavant. A route leaflet is available from Local Transport Planning (01243 777353).

What else can you do?

Children will enjoy the walkways above the mosaic floors at Fishbourne Roman Palace,

a mile-and-a-half west of Chichester (01243 785859). One attraction of general interest is the Weald & Downland Open Air Museum, whose preserved buildings include a working water wheel and medieval farmstead. It's at Singleton, six miles north of Chichester (01243 811349).

Where can you eat?

The family-friendly Earl of March pub at Mid Lavant (on the A286) is worth visiting. It boasts a garden for the kids to play in, great views and real ale. Chichester has a bustling city centre offering plenty of alternatives.

 OS Landranger Map 197

197 Houghton Forest

Why should you go?

To give the kids some exceptional views on a short, signposted forest trail high on the South

Downs. Bear in mind, however, that several sections of this hilly route are quite demanding.

Where is it?

North of Arundel, West Sussex. Park off the A29/A284 Whiteways roundabout at Houghton Forest, three miles north of Arundel. The nearest train stations are Amberley (one-and-a-half miles away) and Arundel (three miles away).

Where can you ride?

For three miles, following the green cycle signs around hilly Houghton Forest.

What else can you do?

Visit magnificent Arundel Castle, or head 12 miles north to the Doll's House Museum at Petworth, which boasts 100 inhabited doll's houses.

Where can you eat?

Drinks and snacks are available from the kiosk at the forest entrance, or you can head for the cafe and pub – with garden – near Amberley Station, just one mile to the east.

 OS Landranger Map 197

South East

198 THE SOUTH DOWNS WAY

JORDANS
OVER 12s

Why should you go?

Because it's the queen of offroad riding in southern England. The wide track is quite easy to follow, and most of it is rideable during summer months. Stronger children with good bike skills will love the long climbs – and the equally long descents.

Where is it?

The 100-mile bridleway runs between Winchester and Eastbourne. Detailed here are six flatter sections for fit families.

Wheely Down

Ten miles on rolling downland which start from the car park on Telegraph Hill (on the A272 east of Winchester) and run all the way to Warnford (on the A32).

 OS Landranger Map 185

Matthew Roberts

Petersfield

A three-mile run near Petersfield, from above Buriton to the B2146 above South Harting. It's more suitable for strong children, due to the steep climb from the car park in Queen Elizabeth Country Park and rollercoaster slopes on Harting Downs.

 OS Landranger Map 197

Midhurst

Ideal for stronger children who can cope with major slopes at the start and finish, this is a five-mile forest section over high ground near Midhurst.

Go eastward from above Cocking (the climb) to the A285 Petworth road (the descent) near East Lavington.

 OS Landranger Map 197

Rackham Hill

Start from the car park at the top of the minor road off the B2139, two miles southwest of Storrington. Try the five-mile stretch which runs along Rackham Hill, south of Storrington, to the A24 Worthing road. The ascents and descents at either end are steep and will test children and adults alike.

 OS Landranger Map 197, 198

Brighton

A high, smooth four-mile run from near Brighton, downhill into Lewes, heading eastwards from the car park at Ditchling Beacon.

 OS Landranger Map 198

Newhaven

This option offers a two-mile stretch with excellent views

199
The Dyke rail trail

Why should you go?
For the chance to climb the Downs the civilised way – up the steady incline of an old railway line.

Where is it?
Hove, West Sussex. There's a car park at the top, at the Devil's Dyke off the A27/A23 north of Hove. Hove is also your closest, most convenient station.

Where can you ride?
For two miles, from Hangleton on the north side of Hove up 230ft on a steady gradient to the Devil's Dyke on the South Downs Way (198).

What else can you do?
Visit a working Victorian pumping station packed full of real and model engines at the British Engineerium in Hove (off Nevill Road, 01273 559583).

Where can you eat?
Hove provides the best options, numerous and varied. Alternatively, you may encounter the occasional ice cream van on the top of the hills.

 OS Landranger Map 198

---

suitable for young children above West Firle, north of Newhaven. Park at the car park and ride for about a mile in either direction, but stay high unless you want to climb back up again!

 OS Landranger Map 198

What else can you do?
Take your pick. The animals of Marwell Zoo live to the southeast of Winchester, Petersfield boasts the Bear Museum, and the interesting Downland Museum sits to the north of Chichester. Arundel

Castle is a vast and magnificent medieval structure, while Brighton's numerous and varied delights lie close by and can entertain even the choosiest of visitors. An equally-entertaining alternative is a trip into Eastbourne, located at the eastern terminus of the route.

Where can you eat?
Because there's no water on the ridge, pack drinks (and snacks) before you depart. Child-friendly pubs lie at South Harting (the White Hart), East Dean (the Hurdlemakers), Steyning (the Star Inn), Firle (the Ram Inn) and Alfriston (the Sussex Ox).

200 Friston Forest

Why should you go?
Because you're up for riding in beautiful and breathtaking Downland in the Seven Sisters Country Park, where the Cuckmere River slices its

South East

way through a line of hills to the sea.

Where is it?
West of Eastbourne, West Sussex. Park at Exceat on the A259, seven miles west of Eastbourne. The nearest stations are Berwick (four miles north of Exceat) and Polegate (seven miles northeast of Exceat).

Where can you ride?
The two-mile riverside route is particularly good for smaller, less capable children, following the Cuckmere from Exceat southward to the seaside at Cuckmere Haven and back. For the more demanding four-mile forest ride – better suited to stronger children – follow the signed forest circuit going east, north then southwest from the car park at Exceat through Friston Forest.

What else can you do?
Pull silly faces and make odd noises at the animals at Drusilla's Zoo Park, where there's also an excellent Toddler's Village. It's three miles north at Berwick (01323 870234). Of general interest is Alfriston Clery House, a 14th-century thatched hall house, the first property bought by the National Trust (01323 870001).

Where can you eat?
You'll find an exceptional family pub at Alfriston – the Sussex Ox. It's located two miles north of Exceat, reached by crossing the river on the footbridge at Litlington. The Berwick Inn, another good family pub, is situated three miles north, close to Berwick station.

 OS Landranger Map 199

201
The Cuckoo Trail

Why should you go?
To enjoy sublime countryside on an easy rail trail which you and the kids can ride in full or shorter sections. The disused line runs north-south through gorgeous parts of inland Sussex, with easy access at four towns.

Where is it?
Between Hailsham and Polegate, East Sussex. There are car parks near the trail in all four towns – Polegate, Hailsham, Horam and Heathfield – and the A267 road plots the same course as the trail. The most convenient station is Polegate.

Where can you ride?
For 11 miles, from Heathfield at the northern end, via Horam and Hailsham to Polegate. The trail drops 300ft from north to south.

What else can you do?

Chris Juden

See the animals and head for the Toddler's Village at Drusilla's Zoo (01323 870234). Your best bet is to park at Berwick – four miles west of Polegate. Then again, you may be more taken by the historic charms of Pevensey Castle (01323 762704), a great

moated Saxon defence, located just off the A259.

Where can you eat?
Take your pick from the wide variety that you'll sail past in the four towns en route.

 OS Landranger Map 199

---

202 Bewl Water

Why should you go?
Because you're inspired by the fact that this circuit skirts the largest expanse of water in southeast England and provides the perfect run for older, more adept children. The trail closes in winter, however, due to excess mud, so you're best to avoid riding here after a wet spell.

Where is it?
Near Lamberhurst, Kent. Park at the Bewl Water visitor centre, near Lamberhurst off the A21 Hastings road. The most convenient station to arrive at or depart from is Wadhurst.

Where can you ride?
On a 12-mile circuit, starting from the visitor centre on the north side of the lake. Bear in mind that the 'Round Water Route' signs are rather patchy, so you'll need to watch closely for them on the lane junctions. The route leaves the water's edge on the south side.

What else can you do?
Visit romantic Scotney Castle Gardens (01892 891081), or see, hear and smell a recreation of 17th-century Tunbridge Wells at 'A Day at the Wells'. It's on show at the Pantiles, Royal Tunbridge Wells (01892 546545).

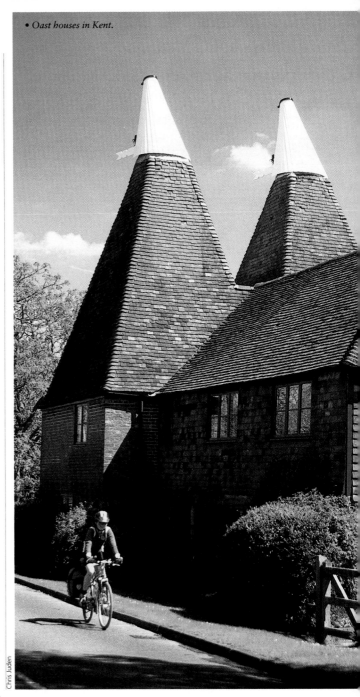
• *Oast houses in Kent.*

Where can you eat?
You may fancy the cafe at Bewl's visitor centre, though your kids may prefer you to drop in at the Brown Trout pub at Lamberhurst Down – entertainment in the shape of trampolines and swings awaits them. Alternatively, there's The Bull pub at Three Leg Cross, located – rather conveniently – halfway round the route.

 OS Landranger Map 188

JORDANS
OVER 8s

203
Bedgebury Forest

Why should you go?
To enjoy the woodland sights and smells on a signposted forest route in the High Weald.

Where is it?
Hawkhurst, Kent. Park near Louisa Lodge, on Park Lane, a minor road west of the main A229 Hawkhurst-Cranbrook road. The train station is Etchingham, four miles southwest of Hawkhurst.

Where can you ride?
For three miles. The woodland circuit starts at Louisa Lodge on the eastern side of the forest.

What else can you do?
Of general interest, Bedgebury Pinetum houses Europe's finest collection of coniferous trees (01580 211044). Or you can head for the 14th-century ruined castle at Scotney Castle Gardens (01892 891081).

Where can you eat?
Head to the west of the forest and refuel at Bedgebury Pinetum.

 OS Landranger Map 188

Chris Juden

Scotland

Scotland is a wonderful place for a holiday of day trips or for full-length bike journeys because routes can be found in both the wilderness and the populated areas. A combination of forest trails in the Highlands and a number of cycle routes linking the towns have multiplied the choice three-fold in recent years. Well-served by long and short routes on the national cycle network, this is the perfect destination for cyclists of all ages.

Where to cycle when you visit

OS Landranger maps covering these areas:
10/11/16/17/19/20/21/26/28/29/30/34/35 /36/37/38/41/44/45/48/49/50/55/56/57/62 /63/64/65/66/68/73/76/77/78/79/83/84

Britain's national mapping agency

Ordnance Survey®
www.ordnancesurvey.gov.uk

Really get to know an area with

Landranger™
The all purpose map

www.britainonview.com

The Big Idea Inventor Centre, Irvine (08708 404030)
This living laboratory is an essential stop-off for budding inventors. With a host of hands-on activities – including the Flutterbug, a battery-powered bug that jumps around at random – a visit makes you question why and how inventions work – and will maybe even inspire you to invent something yourself.

Storybook Glen, Aberdeenshire (01224 732941)
Great for younger kids, this beautiful 20-acre site is home to an abundance of storybook and nursery rhyme characters. Old Macdonald's Farmhouse is here, for example, and houses goats and Highland cattle. Elsewhere, local wildlife abounds, making it ideal as an easy introduction to nature.

• Hebridean Maritime Festival
For a series of exciting water-based events suitable for participants and spectators of all ages, Stornoway Harbour on Isle Of Lewis is worth a visit. Events on offer include long distance sailing, a sailing challenge, windsurfing, rafting, rescue displays, stalls, exhibitions and plenty more to keep you entertained. Held between 1st and 3rd of August.

WHAT ELSE IS ON?
• Inverness Tattoo
In which military and pipe bands are joined by display teams plus country and Highland dancing teams for this annual extravaganza. Held at the Northern Meeting Park from 22nd to 27th July.
• Traquair Fair
Held in Innerleithen in August, Traquair Fair is an excellent family weekend packed with entertainment including music, street performers, workshops, crafts and contemporary medicine. Held on 3rd and 4th August.
• Highland Games
Cowal hosts the world's largest, most spectacular Highland games every August, featuring a vast array of bands, bagpipes and shinty.

• Scotland Tourist Board via website only

Scotland

JORDANS
ALL AGES

204 Johnstone to Greenock rail trail

Why should you go?
For great views over the Clyde, and to see Sustrans' signature sculptures on an old railway line.

Where is it?
West of Glasgow. Start in Johnstone where Old Road goes under the railway off the B789 (Main Road), one mile west of the B789/A761 roundabout. Also in Bridge of Weir, Kilmacolm, Port Glasgow and Greenock. The nearest stations are Johnstone, Whinhill and Greenock Central.

Where can you ride?
It's a 13-mile route between Johnstone, Bridge of Weir, Kilmacolm, Port Glasgow and Greenock (Lady Octavia Recreation Centre). This is part of the Clyde-Forth route (NCN75), which continues eastward into Glasgow along more traffic-free routes. Another rail trail runs south out of Johnstone to Kilbirnie.

    A map and details of NCN75 are available from Sustrans (0117 9290888).

What else can you do?
Visit the McLean Museum and Art Gallery. It's free to enter and full of local history regarding James Watt and engines (15 Kelly St, Greenock, 01475 715624).

Where can you eat?
There is plenty of choice in the towns you pass through along the way.

 OS Landranger Map 63, 64

JORDANS
ALL AGES

205 Johnstone to Kilbirnie rail trail

Why should you go?
Because you're looking for easy riding on a rail trail which runs past three lochs and a country park.

Where is it?
Southwest of Glasgow. Start in Johnstone where Old Road goes under the railway, off the B789 (Main Road) one mile west of the B789/A761 roundabout. It's also accessible at the Castle Semple visitor centre at Lochwinnoch. The nearest train stations are Johnstone, Lochwinnoch and Glengarnock.

Where can you ride?
For 11 miles, from the northeast, between Johnstone, Lochwinnoch and Kilbirnie. From Johnstone, the long-distance cycle route, the Clyde-Forth (NCN75), continues on short stretches of road and rail trail for ten miles via Paisley into central Glasgow. A map with details of NCN75 is available from Sustrans (0117 9290888).

What else can you do?
Visit Castle Semple country park visitor centre, or the RSPB reserve.

Where can you eat?
Throughout Johnstone, or at the Castle Semple visitor centre.

 OS Landranger Map 63, 64

JORDANS
ALL AGES

206 Glasgow to Loch Lomond

Why should you go?
To ride from the heart of Glasgow

– virtually car-free – to beautiful Loch Lomond on a rail trail along Clydeside, the towpath of the Forth & Clyde Canal and the Leven riverside path.

Where is it?
Between Glasgow and Loch Lomond. Start anywhere en route, perhaps making use of the train links – 15 stations lie nearby between Glasgow Central and Balloch.

Where can you ride?
For 20 miles between Glasgow Central station, the Scottish

• Scotland offers some of the pick of the UK's traffic-free cycle paths.

Exhibition Centre, Whiteinch, Yoker (Renfrew ferry), Mountblow, Bowling, Dumbarton, Alexandria and Balloch. This green escape route forms part of the long-distance Lochs & Glens cycle route from Carlisle to Inverness.

A useful Glasgow cycle map detailing numerous routes is available from CycleCity (01373 453533), while a map with details of the Clyde-Forth (NCN75) route is available from Sustrans (0117 9290888).

What else can you do?
Glasgow has eight proud museums for you to explore, including Fossil Grove and the People's Palace (0141 287 4350). Along the route, you'll also have the opportunity to stop off at Dumbarton Castle and Balloch Castle country park.

Where can you eat?
There are plenty of options to suit all tastes along the way. At Old Kilpatrick, for example, at the western end (off the A82 beside Erskine Bridge), you'll find the

Ettrick Bar boasts an excellent garden and children's menu (159 Dumbarton Rd, 01389 872821). Balloch is also worth a visit for its two family-friendly real ale haunts, the Balloch Hotel, with a river terrace and children's menu (01389 752579), and the Tullichewan Hotel, offering games and a children's menu (01388 752052). Alternatively, why not try the cafe at the end of the canal at Bowling?

 OS Landranger Map 63, 64

Scotland

207 BORDERS FOREST TRAILS IN THE TWEED VALLEY

Why should you go?
For peace and pinewoods in the glorious Borders country, including a route which runs around the lovely River Tweed.

Where are they?
East of Peebles. Contact Peebles Tourist Information Centre (01721 720138) for details.

Where can you ride?
On one or more of the following signposted trails in the forests of Glentress, Cardrona, Elibank and Traquair:

JORDANS OVER 8s

The Anderson trail
This lies in Glentress Forest. Start at Falla Brae car park, off the A72 east of Peebles, and follow the red signs. At three miles long, the trail is suitable for fit kids.

JORDANS OVER 12s

The Highlandshiels and Wallace's Hill trails
Lying in Cardrona Forest the Highlandshiels trail is an easy five-mile route that can be picked up at Kirkburn car park, off the B7602, southeast of Peebles. Follow the red signs. The green-signposted Wallace's Hill trail is three miles longer and slightly more arduous. It's best for stronger children.

JORDANS OVER 8s

The Touring and Cheesewell trails
Find them in the Elibank and Traquair forests. The 12-mile Touring trail (yellow signs) begins at the Plora Entrance car

park, off the minor road parallel with the A72, east of Innerleithen. From the same starting point pick up the nine-mile Cheesewell trail (green signs) for stronger children.

What else can you do?
The main towns nearby are Peebles and Innerleithen. The main local places of interest are the romantic Traquair House (near Innerleithen, 01896 830323), and Melrose Abbey, a uniquely elegant 14th-century ruin off the A7 (01896 822562).

Where can you eat?
If you're looking for a family-friendly pub, the Traquair Arms at Innerleithen has a garden, children's menu and brewhouse (01896 830229).

 OS Landranger Map 73

JORDANS ALL AGES

208 Airdrie to Bathgate rail trail

Why should you go?
For gentle pedalling along an old railway line. Good train connections allow a choice of ways to complete the trip.

Where is it?
Between Airdrie and Bathgate. Start at Craigneuk on Airdrie's eastern edge, off the A89 east of the junction with the A73. Or at Whiteside, southwest of Bathgate, off the B7002. Both Airdrie and Bathgate have stations, but they are on unconnected lines.

Where can you ride?
For 14 miles between, from the west, Airdrie, Caldercruix, Blackridge (south of Armadale) and Bathgate. A map with details of the Clyde-Forth route (NCN75) is available from Sustrans (0117 9290888).

What else can you do?
There are a number of historic sights worth visiting dotted around the route, including the Summerlee Heritage Centre (at Coatbridge), the Weavers Cottages Museum (Airdrie) and the Bennie Museum (Bathgate).

Where can you eat?
Although there's plenty of choice in the towns en route, it's wise to pack your own snacks as there are no services for the eight

miles between Caldercruix and Armadale.

 OS Landranger Map 64, 65

JORDANS ALL AGES

209 Dalkeith and Penicuik rail trail

Why should you go?
For the enjoyment of following an easy path through wooded embankments and beside the rushing North Esk River.

Where is it?
South of Edinburgh. Start at Eskbank Post Office in Lasswade Road on the southwest edge of Dalkeith (off the A768/A6094 roundabout), or in Penicuik on

the southeast edge at the octagonal church on the junction of the A701/B6372. The nearest train station is Musselburgh (three miles north).

Where can you ride?
For eight miles, starting in the northeast, between Eskbank (on the southwest edge of Dalkeith), Bonnyrigg and Lasswade, south of Roslin and Penicuik. The NCN1 connects at Dalkeith. A cycling map of Midlothian is available from SPOKES (0131 3132114), a map with details of NCN1 can be obtained from Sustrans (0117 9290888).

What else can you do?
In Penicuik you'll find the sparkly Edinburgh Crystal Centre, offering a factory tour and a film

history (01968 675128).

Where can you eat?
Dalkeith and Penicuik offer a number of good options.

 OS Landranger Map 66

JORDANS
ALL AGES

210 Loch Katrine lakeside ride

Why should you go?
To sample a wonderful journey along the north and south banks of Loch Katrine (*above*).

Where is it?
In the Trossachs, north of Glasgow. Park at the Trossachs Pier car park, at the eastern end of Loch Katrine, at the end of the

A821 west of Callander and north of Aberfolyle, 30 miles north of Glasgow.

Where can you ride?
For ten miles around the loch. All but the southeastern end of the loch is open to biking and there's a pier complex at the eastern end for parking and refreshments. The ride can be extended between the southern shore and Loch Lomond on a minor road which runs past Stronachlachar (20 miles return), which is where you'll find the Inversnaid Hotel.

What else can you do?
See the SS Sir Walter Scott on the loch, stop off at the Trossachs Discovery Centre (four miles south at Aberfoyle), or visit Dunaverig Farmlife Centre, ten

Scotland

miles southeast, just before Thornhill on the A873.

Where can you eat?
At the Captain's Rest cafe at the start. The Inversnaid Hotel (on the east shore of Loch Lomond) lies along a quiet road five miles west of Stronachlachar (along the southern shore) adding ten miles (return) to the ride. You'll also find the Byre Inn, which boasts a good garden, a children's menu and nappy changing facilities (01877 376292). It's at Brig O'Turk, two miles east of the visitor centre along the A821 to Callander,

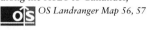 OS Landranger Map 56, 57

JORDANS ALL AGES

211 Callander to Balquhidder rail trail

Why should you go?
For the chance to ride on a superb rail and forest trail through the Pass of Leny – dubbed 'The Entrance to the Highlands' – past the Falls of Leny and Loch Lubnaig, and below the impressively towering Ben Ledi.

Where is it?
Northwest of Stirling. Park in Callander, on the western edge of town on the A84 Crianlarich road. It's past the end of the shops, turn left and go downhill to the river. Park also at the Falls of Leny, at Strathyre, and at Balquhidder. The nearest station is Dunblane ten miles east.

Where can you ride?
For 13 miles at least between, from the south, Callander, the Falls of Leny, Loch Lubnaig's

west shore, Strathyre and Balquhidder. From Strathyre the route follows a quiet road to Balquhidder and the eastern tip of Loch Voil. At Balquhidder you can continue on the NCN7 for another two miles to pick up another traffic-free former military road and trails north-eastward towards Lochearnhead. The trip can also be extended in the south using the Callander-Brig o'Turk route south along the shores of Loch Venachar (212).

A map and details of NCN7 (Glasgow-Inverness) are available from Sustrans (0117 9290888).

What else can you do?
Attractions in Callander include the Rob Roy & the Trossachs visitor centre, plus the Hamilton Toy Collection, while Bracklin Falls lie up the hill in the same direction. Rob Roy's grave lies in Balquhidder. Meanwhile, ten miles east of Callander is Blair Drummond Safari Park (Blair Drummond, near Stirling, M9/A84 J10, 01786 741456).

Where can you eat?
Callander boasts a good choice of eateries. The Byre Inn at Brig o'Turk, six miles west of Callander off the A821, has a kid's menu and nappy changing facilities (01877 376292).

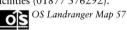 OS Landranger Map 57

JORDANS ALL AGES

212 Callander and Brig o'Turk – via Loch Venachar

Why should you go?
To savour a glorious lochside run through the Trossachs, from

Callander, along the southern shores of Loch Venachar, to the village of Brig o'Turk.

Where is it?

Northwest of Stirling. Start in Callander at the riverside car park, ride across the river (the busy A81 Bridge Street) and look for cycle signs to go right. If starting in Aberfoyle, follow the A821 east for half a mile, go left at the sign for 'Dounans Centre' and right through the car park and past the golf course. At the T-junction with the forest track, go left following signs. The nearest train station is Dunblane, ten miles east of Callander.

Where can you ride?
For eight miles between, from the east, Callander, Loch Venachar's southern shore and Brig o'Turk. For an extra dose of fine forestry riding, but with two major slopes, continue six miles southwards on zig-zagging forest trails from the western tip of the loch through Achray Forest to Aberfoyle, which is a good centre for touring the area. This route is part of Sustrans' long-distance NCN7 Lochs & Glens Cycle Route.

A leaflet detailing the forest section can be purchased (£1) from Forest Enterprise, Aberfoyle (01877 382383), and a map and details of NCN7 from Sustrans (0117 9290888).

What else can you do?

For attractions in Callander, see Callander to Balquhidder (211). At Aberfoyle there's the Scottish Wool Centre and the Trossachs Discovery Centre.

Where can you eat?

The Byre Inn at Brig o'Turk has a garden, kid's menu and nappy changing (01877 376292). You have a choice in Callander.

 OS Landranger Map 57

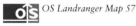

213 Formartine & Buchan Way rail trail

Why should you go?

For the chance to chug along a long rail trail adapted from the Great North of Scotland railway, which ran from 1861 to 1979.

Where is it?

Branching out from Dyce, northeast of Aberdeen, to Fraserburgh and Peterhead. Park in Dyce at the station, in Newmachar on the northeastern edge at the bridge over the B979, at Ellon on the A920 on the southeast edge of town, at Auchnagatt off the A948 in the town centre and at Maud off the B9029 in the town centre. At Mintlaw park north of town at the crossing of the A952, at Peterhead park near the A90, at Strichen park near the river crossing, and in Fraserburgh head for the town centre. The only nearby station is Dyce.

Where can you ride?

For 25 miles from Dyce (six miles north of Aberdeen), through Newmachar, Udny

Station, Ellon and Auchnagatt to Maud. At this, the 25-mile point, the trail divides and heads northward via Strichen to Fraserburgh (15 miles) and eastward via Mintlaw and Longside to Peterhead (13 miles). In places the Way is part of the NCN1 (Aberdeen to John O'Groats). Aberdeen Tourist Information produces a trail leaflet (01224 632727), a map with details of NCN1 is available from Sustrans (0117 9290888).

What else can you do?

You can visit Maud Railway Museum, or the Aberdeenshire Farming Museum (at Old Deer, west of Mintlaw). There's the Strichen stone circle (to the southwest of the trail), while Peterhead offers the Maritime Museum and Ugie Salmon Fish House. In Fraserburgh visit the Heritage Museum and Museum of Scottish Lighthouses, which includes a tour to the top of Kinnaird Head Lighthouse, built in 1787 (01346 511022).

Where can you eat?

West of Mintlaw, at the cafe at Aden Country Park.

 OS Landranger Map 30, 38

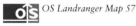

214 Queen Elizabeth Forest Park trails

Why should you go?

Because you want to choose a signposted route that will take you through the forests of this exceptional park.

Where is it?

The Trossachs. There's parking

at Aberfoyle Tourist Centre (on the A81), the Queen Elizabeth Forest Park visitor centre (on the A821 north of Aberfoyle) and Strathyre Information Centre (on the A84 north of Callander).

Where can you ride?

From the starting points, ride the forest roads in Strathyre Forest, Achray Forest and Loch Ard Forest. A handy leaflet on the forest section can be purchased (£1) from Forest Enterprise, Aberfoyle (01877 382383).

What else can you do?

Aberfoyle boasts the Trossachs Discovery Centre and the Scottish Wool Centre. Callander has the Rob Roy and Trossachs visitor centre, and the Dunaverig Farmlife Centre lies six miles east of Aberfoyle on the A873 Stirling road.

Where can you eat?

The aforementioned visitor centres offer your best opportunity to refuel.

 OS Landranger 56, 57

Scotland

215 SOUTHWEST FOREST TRAILS OF GALLOWAY FOREST PARK

Why should you go?

To explore a great area of pine forests riddled with good on-road and off-road routes.

Where is it?

In Dumfries and Galloway. See below for start points.

Where can you ride?

The new edition of the OS Explorer map (1:25,000) for Galloway Forest Park is recommended as it shows cycle routes in the forests, and allows you to devise your own.

JORDANS OVER 8s

Windy Hill Trail & Upper Ae Trail

Head for the Forest of Ae (eight miles north of Dumfries, free maps from the Forestry office in Ae village, 01387 860247). The moderate ten-mile Windy Hill trail starts from the Glen Ae car park on the A701 north of Dumfries. Follow the green signs. The Upper Ae Trail is equally moderate, and starts from the same point, but it runs for 15 miles. Follow the red signs.

JORDANS ALL AGES

Around Loch Bradan Loop & Tairlaw Forest Loop

These are in Carrick Forest. The longer of two moderate trails, the metalled ten-mile Around Loch Bradan Loop starts at Stinchar Bridge car park at the south of Straiton, and features extensive views across the loch. Follow the green signs. The four-mile

Tairlaw Forest Loop starts at Stinchar Bridge and runs through the forest and along the north side of Loch Bradan. Both trails have links with Barr-Loch Doon.

JORDANS ALL AGES

Clatteringshaws Loch circuit & Craignell Hill Trail

Clatteringshaws Loch is six miles west of New Galloway (visitor centre: 01644 420285). The easy-riding 14-mile loch circuit follows the bike map and uses numbered junction posts. Start at Clatteringshaws Forest Wildlife Centre, on the A712, six miles west of New Galloway. The equally moderate 15-mile Craignell Hill Trail uses the same navigation method and starts from the same point.

JORDANS ALL AGES

Moyle Hill trail & Ironhash Hill trail

Find them in Dalbeattie Forest, two miles south of Dalbeattie (01671 402420). Both trails – the easy seven-mile Moyle Hill Trail (following the green signs) and the moderate Ironhash Hill Trail (following purple signs) – start at Richorn car park, found on the A711 south of Dalbeattie.

JORDANS OVER 12s

Palgowan Trail & Caldons & Water of Minnoch Trail

Find these two trails in Glentrool Forest (lying ten miles northwest of Newton Stewart, 01671

840302). The Palgowan Trail is an eight-mile route, while the Caldons & Water of Minnoch Trail is two miles longer, and thus suitable for stronger children in the mood for a memorable ride. Both routes offer moderate riding and, despite also including sections of road open to traffic, they are relatively quiet. Both the trails follow the bike routes on the OS Explorer map, so use the numbered junction posts for navigating and start at Glentrool visitor centre on the A714, ten miles north of Newton Stewart.

JORDANS
OVER 12s

Larg Hill Trail & Dallash Trail

Kirroughtree Forest lies three miles east of Newton Stewart at Palnure. Devise your own route or follow the markings (little red bicycles on the OS map, a free map is available from the visitor centre) and numbered junction posts for the two set trails. Both set routes are moderate and start at the Kirroughtree visitor centre (signed left off the A75, three miles east of Newton Stewart at Palnure). Larg Hill is seven miles long, Dallash is 11.

JORDANS
ALL AGES

Woodhead trail, Craigend Hill trail & Lochbank trail

Mabie Forest sits five miles south of Dumfries (01387 860247). The easy four-mile Woodhead Trail (following the green signs), the moderate eight-mile Craigend Hill Trail (purple signs) and the ten-mile Lochbank Trail (blue signs) all start at the Old Quarry, on the A710 south of Dumfries.

What else can you do?
Take your time and go with the tracks' flow. The area needs no extra attractions.

Where can you eat?
Several of the forest visitor centres have their own cafe. Or venture into Minnigaff, just outside Newton Stewart, and you'll find the family-friendly Creebridge House Hotel. It has a garden and children's menu (01671 402121). Dumfries and Girvan are the closest stations.

OS *OS Landranger Map 76, 77, 78, 83, 84*

Scotland

JORDANS ALL AGES

216 Strathblane & Kirkintilloch rail trail (Strathkelvin Walkway)

Why should you go?
For the chance to escort the high Campside Fells on their east-west march on an easy-going former railway line.

Where is it?
North of Glasgow. Strathblane is ten miles north of the city on the A81, just east of the A81/A891 junction. Kirkintilloch lies eight miles northeast of Glasgow on the A803. At this end start on the north side of town on the B757 towards Milton. The nearest train stations are Milngavie (three miles south of Strathblane) and Auchinloch (two miles south of Kirkintilloch).

Where can you ride?
For eight miles between Strathblane, Lennoxtown, Milton of Campside and Kirkintilloch.

What else can you do?
Parents may enjoy visiting the Glengoyne Distillery. It's just north of Strathblane on the A81.

Where can you eat?
In the towns en route.

OS Landranger Map 64

JORDANS OVER 8s

217 Forth & Clyde Canal

Why should you go?
Because the route allows easy, traffic-free travelling on one of two routes between Scotland's two biggest cities.

Where is it?
Between Glasgow and Edinburgh. In the west the canal starts at the Clyde, off the A82 between Clydebank and Dumbarton, one mile west of the Erskine Bridge. The eastern end lies between Falkirk and Grangemouth, west of J6 of the M9. The Glasgow Central-Linlithgow line runs parallel to the canal.

Where can you ride?
For up to 42 miles between Bowling, Clydebank, north Glasgow, Kirkintilloch, Kilsyth, Bonnybridge, Falkirk and Grangemouth.

What else can you do?
Glasgow's many attractions include eight proud museums. Of those, Fossil Grove and the People's Palace (0141 2874350) are well worth a visit.

Where can you eat?
Near the western end of the route in Old Kilpatrick (off the A82 beside Erskine Bridge), you'll find the Ettrick Bar. It boasts a good garden and children's menu (159 Dumbarton Rd, 01389 872821).

 OS Landranger Map 64, 65

JORDANS OVER 8s

218 Forth Road Bridge

Why should you go?
Because if the opportunity to cycle across the great bridge that spans the dramatic Forth River doesn't send your heart racing, the fabulous views and choice of circuits and connections certainly will.

Where is it?
Eight miles west of Edinburgh. The route runs eastward to Burntisland (north bank) and southward to Newbridge. The most convenient parking is in Queensferry, Newbridge and North Queensferry. The nearest train stations are Dalmeny and North Queensferry.

Where can you ride?
Cycle paths run either side of the bridge, between Queensferry and North Queensferry.

A choice of two cycle routes, one traffic-free, run from near Dalmeny station on the south bank to the start of the road bridge. The circuit runs from Queensferry, north across the bridge, and back either on the far cycle path or by train from North Queensferry station over the railway bridge.

The eight-mile route east to Edinburgh centre (on the south bank, NCN1) includes three miles of car-free riding on rail trails. A car-free route diverges en route at Cramond Bridge along the River Almond and the shoreline to Cramond and Granton (north Edinburgh).

The North Queensferry (on the north bank) option is a nine-mile shoreline route through Dalgety and Aberdour (Silver Sands beach) to Burntisland, including a four-mile stretch of excellent car-free riding.

It's also possible to pick up the rail trail that continues south from Queensferry for five miles to Newbridge. An extensive cycling map which covers Midlothian and Edinburgh is available from SPOKES, call (0131 313 2114) to order.

Why should you go?
To explore a variety of trails in the beautiful Highlands, many within a stone's throw of the glassy lochs.

Where are they?
They run between Fort William and Inverness.

Where can you ride?
There are a number of trails (listed below) which offer varying degrees of difficulty.

JORDANS OVER 12s

Glen Loy Forest Trails
Glen Loy Forest lies off the B8004 at Strone, five miles northeast of Fort William at the southerly end of the Glen. Take your pick from the numerous unmarked forest tracks.

What else can you do?
Savour the great bridges. The railway crossing, built in 1890,

is painted with 7,000 gallons of paint. The road bridge (above) replaced an 800-year-old ferry, and there's a museum on the

JORDANS OVER 8s

Inchnacardoch Forest Trails
Inchnacardoch Forest sits on slopes above the Caledonian Canal, adjacent to Fort Augustus. Parking is in Fort Augustus, and you can choose from a number of scenic tracks.

JORDANS OVER 8s

Farigaig Forest Routes
Farigaig Forest grows on the lapping southern shores of Loch Ness at Inverfarigaig and Loch Mhor. Park at the visitor centre at Inverfarigaig, and cycle on quiet roads and forest tracks to view the forest's spectacular 80ft waterfall.

north bank. Visit Aberdour Castle or the Edwardian Fair Museum at Burntisland, while Edinburgh's delights are plentiful and diverse.

Where can you eat?
Beside the rail bridge on the south bank is the famous family-friendly Hawes Inn. It boasts real ale, garden toys, a children's menu and nappy changing and is worth a stop off (0131 3311990).

o¦s *OS Landranger Map 65*

JORDANS ALL AGES

220 The Innocent rail trail

Why should you go?
To sample a pleasant, car-free cruise from the imposing Arthur's

JORDANS OVER 8s

Glenurquhart & Cannich Trails
Glenurquhart & Cannich lies west of Drumnadrochit and offers a good choice of road and off-road trails. Parking is in Drumnadrochit and, to the east, at Urquhart Castle.

What else can you do?
It's worth visiting the atmospheric Urquhart Castle. It sits on the shores of mystical Loch Ness.

Where can you eat?
Pack a picnic, or grab a snack at the odd café dotted around.

o¦s *OS Landranger Map (in order) 41, 34, 26 (&35), 26*

Seat in the centre of Edinburgh to Musselburgh, passing through an illuminated tunnel on the way.

Where is it?
On the eastern approaches to Edinburgh. You can park at St Leonard's Bank in Newington (near the Commonwealth Pool, on the southwest edge of Holyrood Park). The nearest train stations are Edinburgh Waverley, Musselburgh and the newly-built Brunstane.

Where can you ride?
For four miles between, from the west, St Leonard's Bank, Duddingston Loch, Bingham, Brunstane and Musselburgh station (on the southern edge of town). The route lies on the long-distance NCN1 which runs from Newcastle to Aberdeen and

Scotland

221 FOREST TRAILS IN NORTHEAST SCOTLAND

Why should you go?
To select a route from a dozen forest trails, all of which run for no more than 12 miles.

Where is it?
Between Inverness and Aberdeen. For trains, the Aberdeen-Inverness line has stations at Elgin, Huntly, Insch and Dyce.

Where can you ride?
On a variety of easy-to-moderate trails. Choose from…

JORDANS ALL AGES
Bunzeach Forest Trails
Bunzeach Forest is in Strathdon, 40 miles west of Aberdeen, near the junction of the A944/A939. All three trails can start at either Bellabeg village car park or Semeil car park near Strathdon. The green and blue trails (four and five miles respectively) are both easy riding, the red trail, at eight miles, is slightly harder and more suited to stronger children.

JORDANS ALL AGES
Pitfichie Forest Trails
Pitfichie Forest lies 16 miles west of Aberdeen, near the junction of the B993/A944 at Monymusk. Both trails start at Pitfichie car park, southwest of Monymusk. The blue route lasts nine miles, the four miles of the red route are a far harder proposition suited to mountain bikers only.

JORDANS ALL AGES
Gartly Moor trails
Gartly Moor is six miles southwest of Huntly, off the A96.

All three trails here share the same start at Gartly Moor car park (on a minor road south of the A96 towards Insch). The easy six-mile route uses brown signposts, while the moderate blue and red routes run for three and five miles respectively.

JORDANS OVER 12s
Kirkhill Forest Trails
Kirkhill Forest is six miles west of Aberdeen on the A96, at the junction with the B979. The five-mile red trail (moderate) begins at Mountjoy car park and follows the white markers up the hill to meet the trail proper around Tyrebagger Hill. Hill of Marcus, a moderate four-miler, starts from East Woodlands car park and follows the white markers to the red trail, then retraces its steps.

JORDANS OVER 12s
Durris Forest Trails
Durris Forest sits 15 miles southwest of Aberdeen, on the A967, south of the junction with A93. The moderate eight-mile white trail starts at Inchloan car park (on a minor road towards Inchloan, off the A957); the more arduous red-signed trail runs for one mile from the Slug Road car park on the A957.

JORDANS ALL AGES
Blackhall Forest Trails
Blackhall Forest is 16 miles west of Aberdeen, just west of Banchory on the A93. There you

will find the easy, six-mile white trail that starts at Shooting Greens car park on the minor road between Potarch (on the A93, west of Banchory) and Walkmill (on the B796, west of Strachan). The equally easy, seven-mile red trail starts at Banchory, west of Aberdeen.

JORDANS OVER 12s
Drumtochty Forest Trail
Drumtochty Forest lies 25 miles southwest of Aberdeen. The 12-mile white trail is located off a minor road between the B794 Banchory-Montrose road and the village of Auchenblae, starting at Drumtochty Glen car park.

JORDANS ALL AGES
Fetteresso Forest Trails
Fetteresso Forest sits 16 miles southwest of Aberdeen on the A957, northwest of Stonehaven and contains three trails. The nine-mile blue trail starts at Swanley car park on the minor road to the village of Kirktown of Fetteresso, going northwest to the A957. The easy seven-mile yellow trail starts at the Slug Road car park on the A957, and the moderate six-mile red trail starts at Quithel car park on the minor road southwest of Kirktown of Fetteresso.

JORDANS OVER 12s
Whiteash & Wood of Ordiquish Trails
Whiteash & Wood of Ordiquish is ten miles east of Elgin on the

A96, south of Fochabers. There are three moderate trails that inter-connect to create a 20-mile circuit. The eight-mile orange trail starts from the Winding Walks car park a mile east of Fochabers on the A98. The six-mile blue trail connects at two points on the orange trail and links to the red trail, a six-mile route which starts from the Slorachs Wood car park on the minor road south from Fochabers, parallel with the River Spey, or from the start of the blue trail. The most convenient station is Elgin.

JORDANS
OVER 12s
Ben Aigan trails
Ben Aigan lies 12 miles southeast of Elgin on the A95, southwest of Mulben. The two trails here together form a circuit that contours around the slopes of Ben Aigan, meeting on the far side from the start point at Arndilly, where the Speyside Way comes in. You can retrace your steps the way you've come, turn on to the Speyside Way, or tackle the trail you haven't yet completed. The five-mile red trail starts at Ben Aigan car park and finishes at the Speyside Way, the six-mile blue trail is harder, steeper and rougher, suited only to dedicated mountain bikers.

JORDANS
OVER 12s
Culbin Forest trails
The Culbin Forest trails run through a low-lying pine forest between Nairn and Forres on the Moray Firth, 15 miles from Inverness, along the A96. The nine-mile red trail starts at Nairn's East Beach car park, the 11-mile yellow trail starts at the same point and covers much of the same route. There are links to Cloddymoss car park, nearer the Forres end of the forest.

JORDANS
OVER 8s
Kirkhill Forest Trailquest
Kirkhill Forest is just west of Aberdeen on the A96 to Inverurie. The Trailquest is a permanent bicycle orienteering course, suitable for older, stronger children, open 365 days a year and free to ride. Navigate your way round the forest via checkpoints (which are changed regularly). The course takes up to four hours to complete in its entirety, and you can send off for a certificate on completion. Request the Trailquest leaflet, with map and instructions, from Kincardine Forest District, Kirkton of Durris, Banchory AB31 6BP, 01330 844537.

What else can you do?
Chill out among the conifers in this remote and beautiful part of the world. When you've finished cycling, head for a wee dram in one of the region's famous whisky distilleries.

Where can you eat?
Pack a picnic. There's only a small choice in the area's towns and villages.

OS *OS Landranger Map 28, 29, 30, 37, 38, 44, 45*

onward. The Edinburgh City cycling map is available from SPOKES (0131 313 2114), and details of the NCN route can be obtained from Sustrans (see p8).

What else can you do?
Visit the Dynamic Earth exhibition (near Holyrood Park), or the Abbey and Palace of Holyrood House. The Royal Yacht Britannia is now permanently moored at the Port of Leith – and there's always historic Edinburgh Castle.

Where can you eat?
Take your pick in the city centre.

OS *OS Landranger Map 66*

JORDANS
ALL AGES
222 Pencaitland Walk rail trail

Why should you go?
To enjoy the rural landscape east of Edinburgh on an old railway line that doesn't demand you get up much steam.

Where is it?
East of Edinburgh. Park at Pencaitland (mid-route) at the car park off the A6093. The nearest train station is Wallyford (three miles north).

Where can you ride?
It's a six-mile run between Crossgatehall, Ormiston, Pencaitland and West Saltoun. The Edinburgh City cycle map is available from SPOKES (0131 313 2114).

What else can you do?
Parents will almost certainly enjoy visiting Glenkinchie Distillery. It can be found at Peaston Bank, one mile south of Pencaitland.

Scotland

Where can you eat?
Take your pick en route.

 OS Landranger Map 65

JORDANS
OVER 8s

223 The Water of Leith and Union Canal path

Why should you go?
To indulge in carefree riding along Edinburgh's waterways on a route taking you in or out of the city.

Where is it?
On the western approach to Edinburgh. Start in Balerno (off the A70 on the north side of the village), or at the joining of the river and the canal at Union Canal Bridge on the A70 east of Kingsknowe station. The nearest stations are Curriehill, Wester Hailes, Kingsknowe, Slateford, Haymarket and Waverley.

Where can you ride?
For seven miles between Balerno, Currie, Colinton, Kingsknowe (Union Canal Bridge), Morningside and The Meadows. The path follows the Water of Leith riverpath between Balerno and Kingsknowe, and the Union Canal towpath into the city centre. You need lights for the tunnel at Colinton. In the city centre, you can follow a mile of cycle-signed roadway north (via Waverley station) to pick up the rail trail that follows the last mile of the Water of Leith to its mouth at Leith Harbour (and the Royal Yacht Britannia) on the Firth of Forth. On the Union Canal route heading out west is a one-mile break in the towpath after Kingsknowe, after which it can be picked up again at Wester Hailes near the junction of the Calder Road-A720 city ring road. The route lies on NCN75 (Clyde to Forth). The Edinburgh City cycle map, providing further route information, is available from SPOKES (0131 313 2114), a map and details of NCN75 can be obtained from Sustrans (0117 9290888).

What else can you do?
Edinburgh offers plenty, see 'The Innocent rail trail' for details (220).

Where can you eat?
With its family room and garden, the family-friendly Johnsburn House pub in Balerno is well worth a visit (0131 4493847).

 OS Landranger Map 65, 66

JORDANS
OVER 8s

224 Union Canal

Why should you go?
So children with good waterside bike control can cycle a peaceful towpath along the old waterway.

Where is it?
West of Edinburgh, between Falkirk and the city centre.

Where can you ride?
For up to 30 miles between South of Falkirk (Glen Village), Linlithgow, Broxbourn, Ratho and Edinburgh. At the Edinburgh end, you need a street map of Edinburgh to navigate the missing section of towpath between Wester Hailes and Kingsknowe. The Edinburgh City cycling map, providing further route details, is available from SPOKES (0131 3132114).

What else can you do?
Visit the Edinburgh Canal Centre at Ratho. For Edinburgh's many attractions, see the Innocent rail trail (220).

Where can you eat?
At the family-friendly Four Marys pub in Linlithgow, where children have their own menu in the dining area (67 High St, 01506 842171). Alternatives are available en route.

 OS Landranger Map 65, 66

JORDANS
OVER 8s

225 Haddington to Longniddry rail trail

Why should you go?
Because you're looking for an undemanding trail which runs along a pleasant stretch of old railway line.

Where is it?
To the east of Edinburgh. In Haddington, the route begins on Alderston Road on the west side of town (from the centre follow signs for Edinburgh). If starting from Longniddry, pick the route up close to the railway station – the most convenient rail link.

Where can you ride?
For five miles between, from the west, Longniddry station and the west side of Haddington.

What else can you do?
The Chesters Fort ancient monument – three miles north of Haddington – is worth visiting.

Where can you eat?
There are a variety of good options at both Longniddry and Haddington.

 OS Landranger Map 66

Why should you go?

For the chance to experience wide skies and remote lands in northern Scotland's forests.

Where are they?

In the forestry areas north of a line drawn across Scotland between Inverness and Ullapool.

Where can you ride?

Most of the forest's trails are suitable for stronger children. A more comprehensive list appears in the Forestry Commission's 'Cycling in the Forest – North Scotland', available from Forest Enterprise North Scotland, 01463 232811.

JORDANS
OVER 12s

Glen Sgiach Trail

Head for Torrachilty 20 miles northwest of Inverness on the A835 north of Garve for a moderate 16-mile trail, starting from the Contin car park.

JORDANS
OVER 12s

Truderscraig Trail

The Truderscraig Trail runs for 13 moderate miles, starting from Rosal village car park. It is in Truderscraig, 35 miles southwest of Thurso, at the junction of the B871/B873.

JORDANS
OVER 12s

Borgie Forest Trail

This is a moderate nine-mile route that starts from a car park on the A836. It is in Borgie, 30 miles west of Thurso on the A836, west of the junction with the B871.

JORDANS
OVER 12s

Morangie Hill Trail

Head for Ardross, 35 miles north of Inverness, off the A9 to the west of Tain. The trail is a moderate ride running for 14 miles. It starts at Lamington car park, southwest of Tain.

JORDANS
OVER 12s

Military Road

This one's at Black Isle, ten miles north of Inverness on the minor road parallel to the A832, near Mount Eagle Mast on the Munlochy-Culbokie road. A moderate journey over ten miles, you start from the aforementioned minor road, close to Mount Eagle Mast.

JORDANS
OVER 12s

Camster Forest Trail

Head for Camster, 12 miles southwest of Wick, on the minor road north from the A99, starting just east of Lybster. The Camster Forest Trail runs along 14 moderate miles, starting from the aforementioned minor road east of Lybster.

JORDANS
ALL AGES

Riverside Trails

Choose from an easy-riding four-mile trail, or the more arduous eight-mile red trail, only suitable for teenagers. Both routes begin at Lael, which you'll reach seven miles south of Ullapool on the A835, near Inverlael village.

JORDANS
OVER 12s

Beinn Donuill Trail

This moderately testing trail begins its journey at Achormlarie, 50 miles north of Inverness. Eight miles long in its entirety, your best bet is to start at the car park at Loch Buidhe. It's on the minor road west of the A9.

OS *OS Landranger Map 10, 11, 16, 17, 19, 20, 21, 26*

Scotland

227 Livingston cycle paths

Why should you go?
To ride a peaceful network taking in the River Almond and the River Murieston along the way.
Where is it?
West of Edinburgh. Using the Livingston map – Harvey Maps (01786 841202) – you can pick up the route wherever you like. Nearest stations are Livingston North, Livingston South and Uphall.
Where can you ride?
For up to 200 miles, wherever you wish on the network. The dedicated map holds the key to the cycle paths. The Clyde-Forth cycle route (NCN75) – running through the middle of town, en route from Glasgow to Edinburgh – can also be picked up.
What else can you do?
Visit Almond Valley Heritage Centre (in Livingston village), or Almondell & Calder Wood (to the northeast of town).
Where can you eat?
Livingston offers a choice.

 OS Landranger Map 65

228 Borders forest trails in Craik Forest

Why should you go?
So you can choose from three good tracks in the pinewoods of Craik Forest, reaching a 1,500ft high point in Dumfries and Galloway.

Where is it?
Southwest of Hawick. All the trails start from the hamlet of Craik (off the B711 Hawick-Ettrick road), six miles west of Hawick.

Where can you ride?
For reasonably fit children, the four-mile easy trail (following the blue signs) is best. Stronger children have a choice between two intermediate routes, the seven-mile trail (follow the green signs), or the nine-mile alternative (follow the purple signs). It's advisable to pick up a map of the forest from the Forest District Manager before you set off. To obtain one call 01750 721120.
What else can you do?
Because there are few other places of interest in these parts, just slow down, relax and enjoy the smell of pine resin.
Where can you eat?
Hawick is the nearest town and provides a number of options.

 OS Landranger 79

229 Gatehouse to Glen Trool forest route in Galloway Forest Park

Why should you go?
For a dramatic ride on a long track through a great expanse of Scottish wilderness. Highlights include views of Loch Trool and Loch Dee, and long slopes along the way. Suitable for strong children.
Where is it?
Dumfries and Galloway. Park at either Murray Centre in Cally Woods (Gatehouse of Fleet), Clatteringshaws on the A712 (Craigenchallie, west of Clatteringshaws Loch), or at the Glen Trool visitor centre. The nearest train stations are Stranraer and Dumfries.
Where can you ride?
Between Dumfries and Glen Trool the long-distance Lochs & Glens Cycle Route NCN7 divides into two parallel routes, one on quiet roads, the other, described here, a remote 30-mile forest route through the magnificent Galloway Forest Park via four lochs. For a dramatic ride, suitable for strong children, head north then northwest from the village of Gatehouse of Fleet (ten miles west of Kirkcudbright) to Glen Trool. The route falls into two natural halves, between Gatehouse and Clatteringshaws (16 miles one way) and between Clatteringshaws and Glen Trool (14 miles one way). The route *(continued on p186)*

Why should you go?
Because the route will afford you some excellent Highland riding broken down into sections (ranging from easy to demanding).

Where is it?
The route lies between Aviemore and Buckie on the Moray Firth. The most convenient train stations are Aviemore and Keith (seven miles east of Fochabers).

Where can you ride?
The 65-mile-long Speyside Way tracks the Spey from Aviemore, below the Cairngorms to close to its mouth at Buckie on the Moray Firth. Two sections cannot be ridden; the stretch between Buckie and Fochabers (where you can divert on minor roads) and the run between Ballindalloch and Nethy Bridge (where the route has to detour over hills). The Way is new, and a further section, Aviemore-Newtonbridge, is due for

completion during 2002. At present, the four cycleable sections listed below run for a total of 36 miles.

The official Speyside Way map (from Harvey Maps, 01786 841202) and a leaflet from the Speyside Way Rangers (01340 881266) provide further details.

JORDANS OVER 12s

Fochabers-Boat o'Brig Trail
This runs for five miles between Fochabers (on the A96 east of Elgin) and Boat o'Brig (on the B9103). Along the way, there's a great viewpoint two miles south of Fochabers.

JORDANS OVER 12s

Boat o'Brig-Craigellachie Trail
This eight-mile route runs between Boat o'Brig (see above) and Craigellachie (on the A95 northeast of Charlestown) along a demanding rail trail with a one-mile, 300ft slope south of Boat o'Brig. The slope, which you'll almost certainly have to walk up, climbs the sides of Ben Aigan. The section also uses rutted farm tracks and is only suitable for tough teens and adults.

JORDANS ALL AGES

Craigellachie-Ballindalloch Trail
This is an easy-riding 12-mile run stretching between Craigellachie (see above) and

Ballindalloch (on the A95/B9008 junction). Because it runs along a relatively flat rail trail, it's the most suitable route for small children. Includes car parking at both ends.

JORDANS OVER 12s

Nethy Bridge-Boat of Garten-Aviemore Trail
This 11-mile route runs between Nethy Bridge (on the B970 southwest of Grantown-on-Spey), Boat of Garten and Aviemore (on the A9). Featuring quiet roadway, forestry and several slopes, the trail runs near the RSPB reserve at Loch Garten, and, between Boat of Garten and Aviemore (233), on a route shared with the Sustrans NCN7.

What else can you do?
Visit Fochabers Folk Museum or Carrbridge Landmark Heritage and Adventure Park (Carrbridge lies five miles northwest of Boat of Garten) or take a ride on the Strathspey vintage railway (between Boat of Garten and Aviemore). The Cairngorm Reindeer Centre is by Loch Morlich, five miles east of Aviemore. Adults can take their pick of nearby whisky distilleries at Cardhu, Glenfarclas, Glen Grant and Glenfiddich.

Where can you eat?
There's a choice at Aviemore, and the towns en route.

 OS Landranger Maps 28, 36 and OS Outdoor Leisure 3 The Cairngorms

Scotland

231 WEST OF SCOTLAND FOREST TRAILS, HIGHLANDS AND A

Why should you go?
To explore Highlands forests on a fine collection of cycle trails designed for different abilities.

Where are they?
Up and down western Scotland in great areas of harvested pine forest on lochs, shores and isles.

Where can you ride?
See below for each route. For further details send for the leaflet 'West of Scotland – Cycling in the Forest' (01397 702184).

JORDANS ALL AGES
Faery Isles Trail
The easy six-mile Faery Isles trail (simply follow the red signs) starts at the car park at Druim-an-Duin, which lies off the B8025 Tayvallich road, 20 miles south of Oban.

JORDANS ALL AGES
Kilmory-Carrick Trail
This is a nice easy-riding trail, which follows blue signs and runs for six miles. Pick it up at the start at the car park at Kilmory Castle near Lochgilphead, 25 miles south of Oban, and south of the A816/A83 junction.

JORDANS ALL AGES
Loch Glashan (Ardcastle) Trail
Starting at Ardcastle car park on the A83 north of Lochgilphead, this easy-riding route runs for a good nine miles, via a series of easy-to-follow purple and red signs.

JORDANS OVER 12s
Ormaig Trail
This runs along a fairly moderate track which lasts for nine miles. If you are driving here, your best bet is to park at Carnasseries Castle car park on the A816, 15 miles south of Oban. When cycling the route, follow the purple signs.

JORDANS ALL AGES
Two Lochs Trail
This easy route follows green signs for nine miles and starts at Barnaline car park, on the minor road on the west side of Loch Awe, at the road junction east of Loch Avich (southeast of Oban).

JORDANS ALL AGES
Fearnoch & Glen Lonan Trail
This easy trail starts at the quarry car park in the forest east of Fearnoch village, on the A85 between Connel and Taynuilt (northeast of Oban). On the trails, follow the red and green signposts for five miles.

JORDANS ALL AGES
Mill Farm & Barcaldine Trail
Starting at the forest car park (one mile south of Barcaldine on the A828 northeast of Oban), this easy-riding route follows the red and purple signs and runs for eight miles.

JORDANS ALL AGES
Glen Dubh Trails
A five-mile, easy-riding trail (blue signs) from Sutherlands Grove car park, half-a-mile northeast of Barcaldine on the A828 (northeast of Oban). A more arduous eight-mile trail (green signs) starts at the same place.

JORDANS ALL AGES
Glenachulish & St Johns Trail
This route begins at the car park in Glenachulish, a few hundred

JORDANS
OVER 12s

Head of Loch Aline & Savary Trail

Starting at Lochaline at the end of the A884, 40 miles southwest of Fort William, this moderate trail runs for nine miles and follows red signposts.

JORDANS
ALL AGES

Head of Loch Aline & Arienas Trail

This easy route runs for four miles from Loch Arienas, off the A884, four miles north of Lochaline (40 miles southwest of Fort William).

JORDANS
ALL AGES

Isle of Mull Trails

Both of these easy trails start from the Aros Forest office on the A848, ten miles southeast of Tobermory at Lettermore and Loch Frisa. The five-mile route follows blue signs, the 16-mile alternative follows the red ones.

JORDANS
ALL AGES

Ardmore & Glengorm Trail

Starting at the forest car park two miles along the minor road between Tobermory and Glengorm, this easy trail runs for four miles using red signposts.

 OS Landranger Map 41, 47, 48, 49, 50, 55, 56, 62, 68

---

yards west of Ballachulish Bridge on the A82 Oban road (east of the A82/A828 junction). It runs over easy terrain for six miles, following blue and red signposts as it goes.

JORDANS
ALL AGES

Leanachan Forest Trails

This is a chance to visit one of the UK's only biking venues that can boast a chairlift ride to transport you up the mountain.

All of the trails in Leanachan Forest start at the Aonach Mor ski station, six miles north of Fort William, watched over by Ben Nevis.

Choose your own route along the forest's tracks, or choose one from the forest's route leaflet (available from Lochaber Forest Enterprise, order on 01397 702184/5).

Whichever route you take, you have an excuse to use the gondola lift that carries skiers in winter and walkers in summer to the top of the mountain and the start of the mountain bike downhill course. The permanent bicycle orienteering Trailquest course also starts here.

Scotland

runs through, from the south, Cally Woods, Gatehouse of Fleet, Loch Grannoch, over Queensway on the A712, western Clatteringshaws Loch, Loch Dee, Loch Trool and Bruce's Stone to the Glen Trool visitor centre.

A cycle map of the Clatteringshaws-Glen Trool section is available from Clatteringshaws visitor centre (01644 420285), Glen Trool visitor centre (01671 840302) and Kirroughtree visitor centre (01671 402165). Several shops in the area hire bikes, including Rick's Bike Shed (Dumfries, 01387 270275), Ace Cycles (Castle Douglas, 01556 504542) and Da Prato & Sons (Newton Stewart, 01671 402656).

What else can you do?
Visit the Red Deer Range, three miles west of Clatteringshaws along the A712. Guided tours meet at the car park on Tuesdays, Thursdays (both 11am and 2pm) and Sundays (2.30pm).

Where can you eat?
The Murray Arms Hotel in Gatehouse has a garden and children's menu (01557 814207). Alternatively, you could try Clatteringshaws visitor centre and Glen Trool visitor centre (open April-October).

 OS Landranger Map 77, 83 & Explorer new editions

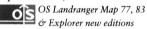

232 The Great Glen cycle route

Why should you go?
Because it's the classic cross-Scotland route.

Where is it?
The Great Glen bisects the Highlands between Fort William and Inverness. There are train stations at both.

Where can you ride?
For a total of 80 miles along the Great Glen, a massive geological depression along the old Continental faultline. Ride between Fort William, Gairlochy, Clunes, Loch Lochy, Invergarry, Loch Oich, Fort Augustus, Loch Ness, Drumnadrochit and Inverness. The signposted route runs along the Caledonian Canal and Loch Ness, and through forests. The child-friendly sections of the trail are: Fort William-Clunes (14 miles), Clunes-Laggan (nine miles), Oich Bridge-Fort Augustus (four miles), Fort Augustus Invermoriston (eight miles) and Bark Sheds-Drumnadrochit (three miles). More cycle routes exist in forests along the journey, detailed in 'Great Glen – Cycling in the Forest' (available by calling 01320 366322).

What else can you do?
You can't visit this part of the world and not snatch a view of Ben Nevis, Britain's tallest peak (at Fort William). There's also Neptune's Staircase locks, Tor Castle, the Clan Cameron Museum (at Gairlochy), Laggan Locks, the Clansman Centre (at Fort Augustus), the Falls of Moriston (at Invermoriston), Urquhart Castle (at Strone), the Loch Ness Monster exhibitions (at Drumnadrochit) and the Castle Garrison Encounter (at Inverness). If that's not enough, make a note to watch for red deer and golden eagles on the

northern slopes between Clunes and Laggan.

Where can you eat?
There are numerous options in Fort William and Inverness, and it's worth stopping off at the family-friendly Clachnaharry Inn (17 High St, Clachnaharry), which boasts a garden and a children's menu. There's also a good choice in the towns en route, and the youth hostels – at Glen Nevis, Loch Ness and Inverness – are also an option.

 OS Landranger Map 26, 34, 41

JORDANS ALL AGES

233 Aviemore to Boat of Garten

Why should you go?
For the chance to pedal through fine, peaceful mountain surrounds on the outward journey, and to rest your legs by hopping aboard a steam train for the journey back.

Where is it?
Below the Cairngorm Mountains between Aviemore and Boat of Garten. Aviemore station at the start of the route provides train connections.

Where can you ride?
It's a four-mile route which runs from Aviemore (at the southern end) to Boat of Garten. The route lies on the Speyside Way (230) and the Lochs & Glens Cycle Route (from Inverness to Glasgow).

What else can you do?
Feeling particularly active? Why not go skiing and walking in the mountains at Aviemore.

Where can you eat?

Aviemore has numerous options for hungry cyclists.

 OS Landranger Map 36

---

234 Argyll Forest Park trails – the Cowal Peninsula

Why should you go?

For lovely riding routes on forest and lochside trails. But be aware that the ever-popular trails sometimes close for upgrading.

Where is it?

The Cowal Peninsula lies over the Firth of Clyde (west of Glasgow). Catch a ferry from Gourock to Dunoon, or head down the A82 and A83 via Arrochar.

Where can you ride?

On one tough, two easy and two moderate trails. Both easy routes – the eight-mile Glenshellish Loop (blue signs) and the nine-mile Loch Eck Shore trail (green signs) – start from Glenbranter on the A815 south of Loch Fyne (right). The moderate routes – the five-mile Cat Craig Loop (green signs) and the seven-mile Ardgartan Shore route (blue signs) – begin at the Ardgartan visitor centre. The hard trail – the six-mile Glenbranter Splash – also starts from Glenbranter.

What else can you do?

Visit the Younger Botanic Garden at the southern end of Loch Eck.

Where can you eat?

Pack a picnic, or try the Ardgartan visitor centre.

 *OS Landranger Map 56*

Northern Ireland

A famously beautiful place and now a target for Sustrans' National Cycle Network, Northern Ireland boasts headline examples of traffic-free riding. There's no better way to approach the spectacular Giant's Causeway on the magnificent Antrim shoreline than by bike from Portstewart. Inland, by contrast, the Newry to Portadown Canal, a 20-mile stretch of newly-reclaimed towpath, is proving enormously popular. When it comes to tackling Belfast, you can cut through the centre from the Lough to Lisburn on sweet cycle tracks virtually the whole way.

The small population and gentle pace of life make Northern Ireland a good holiday destination, especially if combined with a tour of the Republic.

Where to cycle when you visit

Britain's national mapping agency

Ordnance Survey®
www.ordnancesurvey.gov.uk

Really get to know an area with
Landranger®
The all purpose map

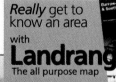

www.britainonview.com

PLACES TO SEE

Giant's Causeway (028 20731159)
Having stood as a rampart against the ferocious Atlantic storms for millions of years, Giant's Causeway is arguably Ireland's most dramatic attraction and has to be seen to be truly appreciated. There's also a visitor centre, a National Trust shop and a tea-room in which you can reflect on the beauty of it all.

Belfast Zoo (028 90776277)
The place many of the world's rarest and most beautiful animals call home. There are elephants and bears, monkeys and cockatoos, all of which will keep the kids entertained and enthralled. And if you want to aid the zoo's exceptional work and adopt a new pet in the process, there's also a sponsor-an-animal scheme available.

MAIN EVENTS

• Shoreline Festival
A family-friendly event – held in Jordanstown Park (in Newtownabbey, County Antrim) each year – the Shoreline Festival includes colourful band concerts, circus performers, stalls, a puppet show and a family fun day. You can sample it between 1st August and 30th September 2002, and annually.

WHAT ELSE IS ON?
• Children's Fun Day
If you are wondering how to keep the kids entertained for an afternoon, you won't regret heading for the Crom Estate in Newtownbutler, County Fermanagh. If you do, watch as the numerous games, races and bouncy castle bring a smile to their little faces. 21st July only.
• Londonderry Walled City Festival
Held annually, and this year between the 7th and 9th June, this excellent festival takes place within the historic city walls and includes parades, carnivals, costumed dancers, samba and steel bands, floats, marching bands and vintage vehicles. Excellent family fun.

USEFUL ADDRESS & NUMBERS
• Northern Ireland Tourism
Tel: 028 90231221; website: www.discovernorthernireland.com/

Northern Ireland

• *The magical Giant's Causeway awaits you and the kids along Northern Ireland's National Cycling Network.*

Chris Juden

JORDANS
ALL AGES

235 Lisburn to Whiteabbey

Why should you go?
Because there's so much to see over 19 easy-to-ride miles through the heart of the capital.

Where is it?
Via the Lagan River, Belfast Docks and Belfast Lough, the route winds from Lisburn through central Belfast to Waterfront Hall and on to Whiteabbey. Park in Lisburn at The Island, in Belfast at Waterfront Hall and in Whiteabbey on the Lough's edge.

Where can you ride?
From the southwest, start at Lisburn and you'll ride via Ballyskeagh, Lagan Valley Park, Stranmillis, the Belfast riverside, the Belfast dockside and Greencastle, ending your journey at Whiteabbey.

What else can you do?
How about visiting The Island in Lisburn, the Giants Ring Earthworks, Minnowburn Beeches or the Botanic Gardens in Belfast?

Where can you eat?
In Lisburn there's a cafe at The Island, you've a choice in Belfast centre, and Whiteabbey offers several tea rooms.

OS *OS NI Discoverer 20*

JORDANS
OVER 8s

236 Giant's Causeway ride

Why should you go?
Because there's no finer way reach

the Giant's Causeway than cycling along the spectacular Antrim coast.

Where is it?
On the northern coast of Ireland. If you're coming by car, you can park in Portstewart, Portrush at West Strand, Bushmills and the Giant's Causeway visitor centre. The nearest railway stations are in Coleraine, Dhu Varren and Portrush.

Where can you ride?
For nine miles eastwards along the National Cycle Network, from Portstewart to Portrush, along a high lane to Bushmills and a rail trail to the Giant's Causeway visitor centre. Contact Sustrans for a map and further route details (0117 9290888).

What else can you do?
Walk to the Giant's Causeway from the visitor centre to view the 40,000 hexagonal basalt columns cast down by giant Finn MacCool. The rest of the time will probably be spent trying to drag Dad away from nearby Bushmills whiskey distillery. It's the world's oldest.

Where can you eat?
You've a choice in Portrush and Portstewart, and there's always the Giant's Causeway visitor centre for hungry peckings.

 OS NI Discoverer 4, 5

JORDANS
OVER 8s

237 Ballypatrick Forest Park circuit

Why should you go?
Because you can pedal at your own pace round a peaceful, spectacular five-mile circuit, with

options to ride connecting paths and forest roads where traffic is slow and minimal.

Where is it?
Near Ballycastle, North Antrim. The forest and car park are signposted off the A2, five miles from Ballycastle.

Where can you ride?
On several circuits in the forest, and a stretch of the National

Cycle Network (NCN93).
Contact Sustrans for a map and
further route details (see p8).
What else can you do?
There's little else in the area, so
take your time on the trails.
Where can you eat?
At a choice of places in
Ballycastle and Cushendall.

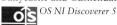 *OS NI Discoverer 5*

238 Oxford Island to Portadown (via Craigavon Lakes)

Why should you go?
To sample one of the first sections
of the National Cycling Network
created in Northern Ireland. This
is an easy six-mile journey
through woods and wetland.
Where is it?
Armagh. Park and start at the
Lough Neagh Discovery Centre.
Where can you ride?
For six miles via Oxford Island to
Craigavon Lakes and Portadown.
For details of riding a complete
circuit on the NCN94 contact
Sustrans on 0117 9290888.

Northern Ireland

What else can you do?
The Oxford Island Nature Reserve will keep the kids entertained for hours.
Where can you eat?
There's a tea room at the Discovery Centre.

 OS NI Discoverer 20

 JORDANS OVER 8s

239 Rathlin Island

Why should you go?
Because this remote, traffic-free island – Northern Ireland's only inhabited rock – boasts excellent bird and sealife. Bike hire is also available (call 02820 763954).
Where is it?
North Antrim. Catch a ferry from Ballycastle to Church Bay.
Where can you ride?
Starting at Church Bay, ride across the island on empty lanes, encountering one minor slope along the way. Then ride back.
What else can you do?
Savour the abundant wildlife and both lighthouses on your journey – and make a trip of it by staying overnight at the island's hostel (call 02820 763954).
Where can you eat?
The pub at Church Bay is your only option.

OS NI Discoverer 5

JORDANS ALL AGES

240 Castle Archdale Country Park forest trails

Why should you go?
Because it's great lakeside riding.

Where is it?
On the eastern shores of Lower Lough Earne, Fermanagh. The park is signposted from Lisnarrick. Park at the hostel, 50m from the route.
Where can you ride?
On three miles of signposted forest trails.
What else can you do?
Make a holiday of it. A caravan site, marina and hostel provide accommodation around the lough and there are good bus services (that carry bikes free at the driver's discretion) from nearby Enniskillen to Belfast and Dublin.
Where can you eat?
There's a cafe in the park, plus pubs in Lisnarrick and Kesh.

 OS NI Discoverer 17

JORDANS OVER 8s

241 Newry to Portadown canal towpath

Why should you go?
To ride a lovely waterside route on a newly-constructed towpath. Particularly impressive are the Scarva-Poyntz Pass and the Steenson-Newry route. Sculptures dot the path, bike parking has been provided at the villages en route and there are good transport links.
Where is it?
Between Newry and Portadown. Park at Moneypenny's Lock, Scarva, Lough Shark, Poyntz Pass and Steenson's Bridge. The nearest train stations are Portadown and Newry.
Where can you ride?
For 20 miles alongside the canal, from Portadown Bann Boulevard finishing off at the Newry Canal Quay/Town Hall.
What else can you do?
Visit the Moneypenny's Lock centre and museum, drop in at Scarva, which recently won a Village in Bloom competition, and tour the visitor centre at Lough Shark.
Where can you eat?
At one of several tea rooms at Scarva and Lough Shark visitor centres, or at a choice of eateries in Portadown and Newry.

 OS NI Discoverer 20, 29

JORDANS ALL AGES

242 Foyle Valley cycleway

Why should you go?
For the satisfaction of riding a six-mile scenic, car-free route along the Foyle through the heart of the city of Londonderry.
Where is it?
In Derry. Park at either the Quay Side shopping centre, the Foyle embankment or on Foyle Street. Your nearest station is Waterside.
Where can you ride?
Start at Sainsbury's supermarket and head for the Foyle quayside to Craigavon Bridge, then on beside the steam railway line to the end of the new path just short of Carrigans.
What else can you do?
Of the numerous attractions in historic Derry, The Tower Museum – which chronicles the history of the city through to the present day – is well worth a visit.
Where can you eat?
You've a wide choice in Derry.

 OS NI Discoverer 7

• Always take care on the roads. For how to choose your cycling helmet turn to p28.

Wales

The demise of coalmining has seen the creation of new routes from old in the industrial lands of South Wales. Several of the valleys now carry dedicated cycle routes along canals or disused railways which rise inland past greening slag heaps. Southern forestry lands also have specially laid-out cycle routes which attract many riders.

The Lon Las Cymru, the Welsh national route, is an excellent, demanding test, crossing three mountain ranges en route between Cardiff in the south and Anglesey in the north.

Clusters of easier though equally impressive cycling are found around Swansea and Llanelli, and Bangor and Caernarfon, much of it based on disused railway lines.

Not to be missed, however, are the specialist mountain bike trails of Coed Y Brenin and the spectacular and easy estuary trail inland of Barmouth.

Where to cycle when you visit

OS Landranger maps covering these areas:
115/116/124/146/147/159/160/161/170/171

Britain's national mapping agency

Ordnance Survey®

www.ordnancesurvey.gov.uk

Really get to know an area

with

Landranger™

The all purpose map

www.britainonview.com

PLACES TO SEE

**Folly Farm, Kilgetty
(01834 812731)**
Folly Farm's diverse attractions appeal to all ages; from the farm animals and pet centre, to the unmissable trip-back-in-time experience of the vintage funfair. Time your visit right, and you'll also be able to bottle-feed the younger animals or milk the friendly goats and cows.

The National Showcaves Centre for Wales, near Swansea (01639 730284)
There's far more to discover here than just the award-winning showcaves. If, for example, the biggest dinosaur park in northern Europe, the Shire Horse Centre, the Iron Age Village, farm and museum don't excite the kids, Barney Owl's Playground certainly should.

MAIN EVENTS

• The Celtic Festival of Wales
This brilliant, fun-packed weekend of family fun combines concerts, dances, storytelling and a wide variety of Celtic arts and crafts. Hosted annually, the weekend is ideal for all the family. Held in Porthcawl on the 1st and 2nd of March.

WHAT ELSE IS ON?
• Treasure Hunt
A really excellent opportunity to let the kids run free, following their treasure maps (and noses), picking up clues en route to their hidden prize. Big kids – otherwise known as dads – can also take part. The event is held in Llanwrda, Carmarthenshire between 29th March and 1st April 2002.

• Eggstravaganza
A variation on the Treasure Hunt should you be in Mold at Easter. Designed to be a fun day for families, you're challenged to follow a trail left by Squirrel Nutley that should help you unearth his secret stash of easter eggs (30th March).

USEFUL ADDRESS & NUMBERS
• **Wales Tourist Board** Tel: 029 20499909;
website: www.visitwales.com

Wales

243 Newport to Pontypool Canal towpath

Why should you go?
The kids will love this north-south towpath forming a green corridor through a built-up area.

Where is it?
South Wales, on the more northerly of two canals which run out of Newport. Start on the Malpas Road (A4042) in Newport. From J26 of the M4, take this road south, park in one of the side streets on the right then follow Malpas Road for 200 yards to the pedestrian bridge. Go right and stay right to the start of the towpath. After passing beneath a bridge, either go right at the next new stone bridge beneath the M4 for Pontypool or continue for Crosskeys. The train stations are Newport, Cwmbran and Pontypool.

Where can you ride?
For nine miles from Newport (Barrack Hill) to Pontypool, via Cwmbran.

What else can you do?
See Newport's dramatic restored Transporter Bridge in the docks, or befriend animals at Cwmbran's Llanyrafon Farm Museum.

Where can you eat?
On the canal at the family-friendly Open Hearth Inn at Sebastopol, two miles south of Pontypool (01435 763752). Just northwest of Pontypool at Pontnewynydd, the Horseshoe Inn benefits from a children's room (01495 762188).

 OS Landranger Map 171

244 Newport to Crosskeys Canal

Why should you go?
To cruise a piece of restored Monmouthshire and Brecon canal, taking in the Fourteen Locks Country Park and the peaks of the Ebbw Valley.

Where is it?
South Wales, the westerly of two canals north out of Newport. The start and parking are at Malpas Road, the A4042, in Newport. From J26 of the M4, take this road south, park in one of the side streets on the right, then follow Malpas Road for 200 yards south to the pedestrian bridge. Go right and stay right to the start of the towpath. After passing beneath a bridge, choose either to go right at the next new stone bridge beneath the M4 for Pontypool, or continue for Crosskeys. Or there's a more countrified start at the picnic site by the Fourteen Locks, just off the B4591, at J27 of the M4. The closest train station is Newport.

Where can you ride?
For up to nine miles, from Newport (Barrack Hill) to Crosskeys, via Risca.

What else can you do?
See Newport to Pontypool Canal (243). Or you can take a carriage ride in the park of stately Tredegar House (signposted from J28 of the M4, 01633 816069). Alternatively, Gothic fantasy awaits at Castell Coch, just off J32 of the M4, five miles north of Cardiff city centre.

Where can you eat?
At a choice of eateries in Newport, Risca and Crosskeys. Or there's the family-friendly pub in Bassaleg on the A468 Caerphilly road, with its large garden and family area, a mile-and-a-half south of the canal where it touches the B4591 near the Fourteen Locks Country Park.

 OS Landranger Map 171

245 Lôn Las Cymru (or The Taff Trail) southern section

Why should you go?
For a choice of pedalling in South Wales on the car-free sections of a renowned 53-mile stretch of trail from the tidal barrage in Cardiff up the Taff Vale to the Brecon Beacons. Only half of the trail is traffic-free (on river paths, rail trails and forest tracks), so note the sections below.

Where is it?
In South Wales between the centre of Cardiff and Brecon. Start at one of the following points: Cardiff College of Music and Drama, Castell Coch, Rhydycar Leisure Centre at Merthyr Tydfil, Pontsticill reservoir, Llanfrynach or Brecon.

Where can you ride?
From Cardiff to Brecon on the signed cycle route via Castell Coch, Pontypridd, Abercynon, Aberfan, Merthyr Tydfil, Pontsticill, Tal-y-Bont on Usk and Llanfrynach. You can easily break up the southerly half. There are plenty of towns on the way, and a railway line with plenty of stops as far as Merthyr Tydfil. One idea

• *Over the green hills: Wales offers truly invigorating cycling through dramatic countryside.*

is to take the train from Cardiff to Merthyr and enjoy the gentle downhill slope on the way back.

The 22 miles north of Merthyr to Brecon tell a different story, as the route enters the Brecon Beacons National Park through forests and beside the Tal-y-Bont reservoir. These 15 miles to Tal-y- Bont on Usk have no facilities and feature steep climbs on the road.

The Taff Trail is the southerly section of the Lôn Las Cymru (Welsh National Cycle Route), which continues from Brecon on to Anglesey. Car-free sections are:
■ Five miles from Cardiff College of Music and Drama on North Road – north of Cardiff Castle on the A470 – to Tongwynlais.
■ Six miles from Castell Coch to Glyntaff Cemetery, southeast of Pontypridd.
■ Nine miles from the Navigation Inn at Abercynon (near the A470/B4275 junction) to Rhydycar Leisure Centre in Merthyr Tydfil.
■ Four miles from Cefn Coed (north of Merthyr Tydfil, just east of the A465/A470 junction) to Ponsticill.

Busy roads to avoid along the way are the A4054 between Glyntaff Cemetery and Abercynon and through Merthyr Tydfil. There's a steep road climb up to Castell Coch which you'll soon be able to by-pass on a low-level alternative. The full-length Lôn Las Cymru (Welsh National Route) continues via Builth Wells, Llanidloes, Machynlleth, Dolgellau and Criccieth to Caernarfon.

Sustrans (0117 9290888) has comprehensive details.

Matthew Roberts

197

Wales

• The 53-mile Taff Trail includes some wonderful stretches of traffic-free forest tracks.

Tim Woodcock

What else can you do?

Visit the amazing Techniquest science discovery centre with its 160 hands-on exhibits at Cardiff Bay Inner Harbour (029 2047 5475). Or tour the Victorian gothic Castell Coch. At Merthyr Tydfil, head for the Ynysfach Engine House Heritage Centre.

Where can you eat?

There's plenty of choice up as far as Merthyr, then a dearth until Tal-y-bont on Usk where the Star Inn welcomes children in the pool room and has a lovely garden (01874 676635).

 OS Landranger Map 160, 161, 170, 171

Where is it?

Northwest of Newport. Park at Sirhowy Park visitor centre, west of Crosskeys off the A467/A4048, J29 of the M4. The nearest station is Hengoed, three miles west of the Wyllie end.

Where can you ride?

For about five miles between Sirhowy Park visitor centre and Wyllie.

What else can you do?

There's little else round here, so just relax on the trails.

Where can you eat?

Pack a picnic, or sample the pubs in Wyllie and Crosskeys.

 OS Landranger Map 171

attraction and a family-friendly pub nearby.

Where is it?

South Wales. Linking Blaenavon (Big Pit) in the north to Newport in the south, NCN46 runs downhill along a railway path and specially-built cycle paths through Abersychan, Pontypool and Cwmbran to link with the canal (243). Your nearest station is Pontypool.

Where can you ride?

For an 11-mile run, from Blaenavon southwards to Pontypool and Cwmbran.

What else can you do?

One of Wales's most popular attractions is the Big Pit at Blaenavon, an ex-colliery with tours of 300ft-deep mineshafts. For safety's sake, children must be aged five or over to join the tour (01495 790311). You should also try the ironworks at Blaenavon and Garn Lakes Country Park nearby.

Where can you eat?

If you haven't packed your own sarnies, you'd do well to head for the family-friendly Horseshoe Inn at Pontnewynydd. It sits two miles south of Abersychan (01495 762188).

 OS Landranger Map 161, 171

JORDANS ALL AGES

246 Sirhowy Country Park

Why should you go?

So you can let the children loose on an old railway line and tracks along the valleysides at Sirhowy Country Park.

JORDANS OVER 8s

247 Pontypool to Blaenavon via Abersychan

Why should you go?

For easy pedalling along an old railway line flanked by high slopes, and with the Big Pit

---

JORDANS OVER 8s

248 Cwm Darran Country Park

Why should you go?

So that you can select your choice of rail trail or mountain bike track through award-winning landscaping in a peaceful country park.

Where is it?

South of Tredegar, South Wales. Cwm Darran Country Park lies on the minor road between the A469 Tredegar road and the A465 Head-of-the-Valleys road. The nearest stations are Bargoed and New Tredegar.

Where can you ride?

For a total of 15 miles on four different tracks. The rail trail runs from Cwm Darran Country Park to Bargoed (four miles). The mountain bike routes are moderate (two miles, following green signs), intermediate (three miles, orange signs) and challenging (six miles, red signs). A route leaflet is available by calling 01443 864312.

What else can you do?

Visit the Ynysfach Engine House Heritage Centre at Merthyr Tydfil, or take a ride on the Brecon Mountain Railway at Pontsticill, two miles north of Merthyr Tydfil. The Big Pit mining museum is at Blaenavon, ten miles to the west.

Where can you eat?

If you haven't packed a picnic, head for the visitor centre.

 OS Landranger Map 171

249 Llanfoist to Govilon rail trail

Why should you go?

Because you and your family are looking for fun on a short and picturesque rail trail that's ideal for smaller children. A number of hillier lanes are also available for older and more energetic kids.

Where is it?

Southwest of Abergavenny. Park in the Cutting (by the Post Office) in Llanfoist. Pick up the rail trail beside the B4246 on the western edge of the village. The nearest station is Abergavenny.

Where can you ride?

For three miles between Llanfoist and Govilon.

What else can you do?

Head for one of South Wales's most popular attractions, the Big Pit mining museum at Blaenavon, four miles to the southwest. See Pontypool to Blaenavon (247) for details.

Where can you eat?

Head into Abergavenny for a choice of cafes.

 OS Landranger Map 161; OS Outdoor Leisure 13 Brecon Beacons

250 Ogmore Valley rail trail

Why should you go?

For easy riding opportunities on an old coal line down the Ogmore Valley.

Where is it?

North of Bridgend, South Wales. There is easy access northward from J36 of the M4. Park at Blackmill on the A4061 near the Fox & Hounds pub. The trail starts on the far side of the river. The best train station is Aberkenfig, north of Bridgend.

Where can you ride?

For about seven miles, from Brynmenyn (north of Bridgend), past Blackmill and Ogmore Vale to Nant y Moel. Starting at Blackmill, it's two miles southward to Brynmenyn and five miles north to Nant y Moel.

What else can you do?

Visit Coity Castle, two miles northwest of Bridgend, or for some history, see the early Christian sculptured stones, including great 'cartwheel' crosses, at Margam Stones Museum (02920 500200). Then again, you may prefer to visit the South Wales Miners Museum, which lies 12 miles west from Nant y Moel on the A4107.

Where can you eat?

There's a limited choice in Blackmill, Ogmore Vale and Nant y Moel.

 OS Landranger Map 170

251 Rhondda Community Forest trail

Why should you go?

Because you're up for the challenge of riding a linear forest route with several steep climbs along the way.

Where is it?

Treorchy, South Wales. The most convenient parking is at Cym-parc west of Treorchy off the A4061 valley road. You can also park at the top of the A4061 pass north of Treherbert.

Where can you ride?

For about 12 miles running from Cwm-parc (west of Treorchy), west along the forest track, then heading northwards to the A4061 pass at Mynydd Beili-glas.

Wales

What else can you do?
The Rhondda Heritage Park lies eight miles south, just before Pontypridd. The South Wales Miners Museum is 12 miles west on the A4107.

Where can you eat?
Pack your own snacks or take your chances in Treorchy.

 OS Landranger Map 170

JORDANS ALL AGES

252 Afan Argoed Countryside Centre

Why should you go?
To take your pick of a number of excellent signposted tracks in the Afan Valley. The routes are rideable in sections, making them suitable for all ages of children.

Where is it?
East of Port Talbot, South Wales. There's parking at the Afan Argoed countryside centre on the A4107 northeast of Port Talbot, off J40 of the M4. The nearest train stations are Maesteg (four miles south of Cymer) and Port Talbot (four miles west of Pontrhydyfen, at the southwestern limit of the trail).

Where can you ride?
Start from the visitor centre at Afan Argoed, and follow the tracks – a mixture of forest and rail trail – which run in both directions on both sides of the valley. It's northeast to Blaen-gwynfi and southwest to Pontrhydyfen, and there are extra spurs off to Efail Fach and Glyncorrwg along the way. The land rises steadily from southwest to northeast, and there's a steep climb crossing from one side of

the valley to the other. A sample route ideal for a strong ten-year-old runs for eight miles between Pontrhydyfen, the Afan Argoed countryside centre, Cymer and Blaengwynfi. Bike hire and a useful Forestry Commission map of the routes are available from the countryside centre (01639 850564).

What else can you do?
Head for the South Wales Miners Museum, it's just up the road from the countryside centre. For a spot of ancient history, visit the Margam Stones Museum in, logically, Margam for examples of early-Christian sculptured stones (02920 500200).

Where can you eat?
Either on site at the countryside centre, or travel five miles to the Old House Inn at Llangynwyd, one of Wales's oldest pubs (01656 733310). It has a huge garden-cum-adventure playground, as well as an excellent restaurant with children's menu. Find it south of Cymer on a minor road off the A4063 heading south out of Maesteg.

 OS Landranger Map 170

JORDANS OVER 8s

253 Neath Canal towpath

Why should you go?
To enjoy a recently restored towpath through the handsome Neath valley. The final section, Clyne-Resolven, should be finished in 2002 to complete 13 miles of unbroken towpath.

Where is it?
Between Neath and Glyn-Neath,

South Wales. For the second section park in the car park at the Resolven basin off the A465 north of Resolven. Parking for section three is in Neath, Tonna or Clyne. Neath is the best station for this option.

Where can you ride?
Currently in three sections: five miles from Briton Ferry to Aberdulais; two miles between Aberdulais and Clyne (rideable but rough); and four miles from Resolven to the B4242 west of Glyn-Neath (ditto). The two miles between Clyne and Resolven will open in 2002 when the aqueduct has been replaced.

What else can you do?
Take a boat trip along the Resolven section or visit the Aberdulais Falls: the famous gorge waterfalls used to drive mills for 300 years and were painted by the artist Turner. It is now the largest electricity generating waterwheel in Europe (contact the National Trust for details, 01639 636674).

Where can you eat?
In season only, try the Ty Banc canalside cafe at Resolven or the Dulais Rock Inn. Out of season, pack your lunch box and find a soft bankside for your backsides.

 OS Landranger Map 160, 170

254 Swansea Valley Canal towpath

Why should you go?
After years of dereliction, the Swansea Valley Canal has been restored. Like other South Wales waterways, it was built to haul coal from the pits to the ports.

Where is it?
In South Wales, between Clydach and Ynysmeudwy. Park at Clydach (on the B4603, north of J45 of the M4). The canal starts at the junction of the Tawe river and Lower Clydach river. In Ynysmeudwy, start at the roundabout by the A4067/B4603 junction. The nearest station is Swansea, which is five miles south of Clydach.

Where can you ride?
For six miles, from Clydach, north of Swansea, to Pontardawe and on to Ynysmeudwy.

What else can you do?
There's a country park beside the canal, and the Glantawe Riverside near Ynysmeudwy, or take a steam train trip on the Swansea Vale railway, and enjoy the seaside at Swansea Bay.

Where can you eat?
There's a small choice in Clydach and Pontardawe.

 OS Landranger Map 160, 170

255 Swansea Bay bike path

Why should you go?
For easy pedalling and views of curving Swansea Bay round to the Mumbles.

Where is it?
South Wales. Start at Swansea marina, the university or the Mumbles. Swansea station is half a mile from the marina.

Where can you ride?
For five miles, from the Swansea end, leaving the Maritime Quarter and heading westward along the front to the university, Blackpill, Oystermouth and the Mumbles. From Blackpill, the wooded Clyne Valley rail trail (256) turns northward and heads towards Gowerton. Get a route leaflet from Swansea Tourist Information (01792 468321).

What else can you do?
Children of all ages will enjoy the arty playground and sound sculpture near Blackpill. The great beaches on the Gower are worth a diversion.

Where can you eat?
At Swansea marina or the Mumbles. There's also a family pub en route on the A4067 near Blackpill. For ice cream head to Verdi on the harbour at the Mumbles.

 OS Landranger Map 159

256 Swansea Bay/ Clyne Valley rail trail

Why should you go?
To experience gentle climbing on a rail trail through Clyne Valley Country Park and along a fabulous seaside route.

Where is it?
South Wales, starting on the A4067 Mumbles road at Blackpill. There's also parking in Gowerton. The nearest train station is Swansea, three miles east of Blackpill.

Where can you ride?
For five miles, from the A4067 at Blackpill, through the entrance to Clyne Valley Country Park and on to Dunvant and Gowerton. A route leaflet is available from Swansea Tourist Information (01792 468321).

What else can you do?
See and sample the Swansea Bay bike path (255) or try out other parts of the Celtic Trail (call 0800 243731 for further details).

Where can you eat?
There are several pubs at Blackpill, the Mumbles, and Gowerton, plus numerous eating options in Swansea.

 OS Landranger Map 159

257 Garwnant Forest trails

Why should you go?
For deep breaths of mountain air on two signposted forest circuits nestling in the Brecon Beacons.

Where is it?
North of Merthyr Tydfil, South Wales. Head for Garwnant Forest visitor centre, on the A470 six miles north of Merthyr Tydfil (the Brecon road). Merthyr Tydfil is the nearest station.

Where can you ride?
For a total of 15 miles, on a five-mile and a ten-mile forest circuit. For a route leaflet, call the visitor centre on 01685 723060.

What else can you do?
Visit the Brecon Mountain

Wales

• Always wear a cycle helmet, no matter where you are riding.

Tim Woodcock

Railway, it's northeast of Merthyr Tydfil.

Where can you eat?
At the visitor centre at the forest, or in Brecon, which caters for holidaymakers.

 OS Landranger Map 160

JORDANS
OVER 8s

258
Brechfa Forest trails

Why should you go?
For trees and fresh air on a choice of three forest routes graded easy, medium and hard.

Where is it?
Northeast of Carmarthen, in west Wales. There are car parks at Abergorlech (on the B4310) and at Byrgwym (three miles southwest of Abergorlech). The nearest station is Llandeilo (ten miles southeast of Abergorlech).

Where can you ride?
For a total of 28 miles, in three separate circuits. It's easy from Abergorlech (eight miles, white signs), medium from Byrgwm

(five miles, green signs) and hard also from Abergorlech (15 miles, red signs). A handy route leaflet is available by calling 01550 720394.

What else can you do?
Jump aboard the Gwili Steam Railway. It's north of Carmarthen on the A484.

Where can you eat?
There's a pub in Abergorlech or, 12 miles to the south of Llanarthne, you'll find the family-friendly Golden Grove Arms, which has a play area and good food.

 OS Landranger Map 146

JORDANS
ALL AGES

259
Elan Valley rail trail

Why should you go?
For easy riding and wide open views on a lovely rail trail in the Elan Valley. The route once served the four Victorian reservoirs and dams that supplied water to the city of Birmingham.

Where is it?
At Rhayader, mid-Wales. Start and park at the Elan Valley visitor centre on the B4518 four miles west from Rhayader.

Where can you ride?
For six miles, as signposted from the start at Caban Coch dam. For a route leaflet, call the Elan Valley visitor centre on 01597 810880.

What else can you do?
With it being far from any other attractions, make the most of the trail's isolation.

Where can you eat?
At the visitor centre.

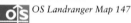 OS Landranger Map 147

JORDANS
ALL AGES

260 Barmouth to Dolgellau rail trail

Why should you go?
For the opportunity to cruise one of the classic rail trails along the beautiful sandy Mawddach Estuary. The trail leads across the long wooden railway bridge over the mouth of the estuary.

Where is it?
In the Mawddach Estuary, mid-Wales, starting at the harbour in Barmouth. There are several car parks on the south side of Barmouth Bridge at Morfa Mawddach Station, and at Penmaenpool (on the A493 west of Dolgellau). Barmouth is the nearest train station.

Where can you ride?
On a six-mile journey which runs from Barmouth Bridge to Penmaenpool.

What else can you do?
Play on the exceptional beaches, climb aboard the narrow gauge

railway or visit the butterfly farm at Fairbourne. Alternatively, there's the great coastal defence of Harlech Castle (12 miles north of Barmouth, 01766 780552) and gadgetry galore at the Machynlleth Centre for Alternative Technology (six miles south of Dolgellau).

Where can you eat?
The Fairbourne Hotel in Fairbourne has a kid's room and garden. It's one mile west of the south end of Barmouth Bridge along the main road (01341 250203). There are also a number of eating options in Barmouth.

 OS Landranger Map 124

JORDANS
OVER 8s

261 Coed y Brenin forest trails

Why should you go?
Because this mountain bike honeypot features an easy trail for families. The main trails – the Red Bull and the Karrimor – attract tens of thousands of visitors each year.

Where is it?
North of Dolgellau, mid-Wales. Park at the visitor centre off the A470, nine miles north of Dolgellau. The nearest train station is Barmouth.

Where can you ride?
On a choice of three routes. The fun/easy seven-mile route follows yellow signs, the sporty/moderate 14-mile Karrimor Trail follows blue signs, and the strenuous 22-mile Red Bull Trail features red signs. Route leaflets are available by calling the visitor centre on 01341 440666.

What else can you do?
Visit Barmouth and Dolgellau.
Where can you eat?
At the cafe on site.

 OS Landranger Map 124

JORDANS
ALL AGES

262 Caernarfon to Bryncir rail trail (Lôn Eifion)

Why should you go?
For easy riding with great views of Caernarfon Bay and Snowdonia.
Where is it?
North Wales. Start at Caernarfon Castle car park, following signs from the harbour for Lôn Eifion and National Cycle Network 8. Go left on to the rail trail after 300m. Bangor's the nearest station.

Where can you ride?
For 12 miles, from Caernarfon via Llanwnda and Penygroes to Bryncir (on the A487). The route is part of Lôn Las Cymru (Cardiff-Holyhead) – the national cross-Wales trail. For a Gwynedd rail trail leaflet, write to the Planning Depart, Gwynedd Council, Caernarfon, Gwynedd LL55 1SH, or call 01286 672255.

What else can you do?
Scramble over Caernarfon Castle, a great 13th-century defence guarding the Menai Strait, or head for Caernarfon Air Museum. The mountains of Snowdonia are just up the road.

Where can you eat?
At Bontnewydd (two miles south of Caernarfon on the A487, 01286 673126), and there's plenty of choice at Caernarfon.

 OS Landranger Map 115, 124

JORDANS
ALL AGES

263 Caernarfon to Y Felinheli rail trail (Lôn Las Menai)

Why should you go?
Because you're looking for a gentle ride on a rail trail to the old slate harbour of Port Dinorwic (Y Felinheli).
Where is it?
North Wales. Start at Victoria Dock in Caernarfon and follow signs for Lôn Las Menai and National Cycle Route 8. The nearest train station is Bangor (ten miles east).

Where can you ride?
It's a four-mile ride which winds between Caernarfon and Y Felinheli. A leaflet detailing the route is available by calling 01286 672255.

What else can you do?
If you're feeling up for more, sample the Caernarfon-Bryncir rail trail (262).

Where can you eat?
There's a choice in Caernarfon and Y Felinheli.

 OS Landranger Map 115

JORDANS
ALL AGES

264 Bangor-Tregarth rail trail (Lôn Las Ogwen or Lôn Bach)

Why should you go?
To explore a nice, easy-riding rail trail which runs inland from the holiday town of Bangor.
Where is it?
North Wales. The start is just off

Wales

Tim Woodcock

the A5122 in Bangor. There's parking at the start and at the finish in Tregarth (four miles south on the B4409). Bangor is the nearest train station.

Where can you ride?

The four-mile route runs from Porth Penryn (Bangor) via Maesgeirchen and Glasinfryn to Tregarth. From Caernarfon, further to the west, it's possible to pick up other rail trails running north and south. A handy leaflet which highlights a number of routes is available by calling 01286 672255.

What else can you do?

Animal attractions on Anglesey include Pill Palas (birds), Plas Coach Garden Zoo, Sea Zoo, Bird World and Foel Farm Park (mostly located along the A4080 from Menai Bridge). Penrhyn Castle has a doll's house museum, model railway and adventure playground. Call 01248 353084 for details.

Where can you eat?

As you'd expect of a holiday resort, Bangor has plenty of choice for hungry visitors.

 OS Landranger Map 115

JORDANS
OVER 8s

265
Gwydyr Forest trails

Why should you go?

Because the mountainous parts of North Wales are a honeypot for off-road bikers, and it's not hard to see why. Gwydyr Forest offers you two great signposted circuits suitable for youngsters with just a little strength and experience.

Where is it?
Betws y Coed, North Wales. Park near the A470/A5 junction on the eastern edge of Snowdonia. The long-stay car parks in the town fill up quickly during the holiday season. The northern trail starts at the car park/toilets on the minor road west off the B5106. For the southern trail, follow the A5 west for half a mile to a starting point soon after the Miners Arms. Your nearest train station is Betws y Coed.

Where can you ride?
Choose from the eight-mile route or the 11-mile alternative, riding anticlockwise for the best signposting. To order the Forestry Commission's map of Gwydyr Forest, call 01492 640578.

What else can you do?
Enjoy the excellent views from Dolwyddelan Castle, built in 1210 to control a strategic pass in Snowdonia. You'll find it on the A470 Blaenau Ffestiniog road, six miles southwest of Betws y Coed. Conwy Valley railway museum (in Betws) and Swallow Falls are also worth a visit (leave Betws on the B5106, then go left immediately out of town. The falls lie two miles on).

Where can you eat?
Betws y Coed offers an excellent choice of eateries. But if they don't appeal, you could head out five miles west of Betws on the A5 to Capel Curig. It's here that you'll find Cobdens Hotel, which offers a children's menu and games, plus a mountain rock face doubling up as a wall in the climber's bar (01690 729243).

 OS Landranger Map 115

JORDAN'S ALL AGES

266 Colwyn Bay to Prestatyn bike path

Why should you go?
To take the family riding for up to 15 miles along a seafront of promenades and beaches.

Where is it?
North Wales. Pick up at any point en route. Nearest train stations are Prestatyn, Abergele and Pensarn, Colwyn Bay and Rhyl.

Where can you ride?
From west to east, heading from Rhos-on-Sea to Colwyn Bay, via Abergele, Rhyl and Prestatyn. Ride it all or select smaller sections to suit. The route is part of National Cycle Route 5 from Bangor to Runcorn (for full details and a map call Sustrans on 0117 9290888 or the Celtic Trail Hotline on 0800 243731).

What else can you do?
You're spoilt for choice. In Llandudno you'll find the Alice in Wonderland Centre (01492 860082). The Welsh Mountain Zoo and Dinosaur World are in Colwyn Bay. Rhyl has Ocean Beach Amusements and the Sealife Centre. Conwy (four miles south of Llandudno) has the magnificent 13th-century fortress and the mile-long town walls with 22 towers (01492 592358). Six miles south of Rhyl is Rhuddlan Castle, a 13th-century fortress with its three-mile sea canal (01745 590777).

Where can you eat?
Take your pick in Colwyn Bay, Rhyl and Prestatyn.

 OS Landranger Map 116

JORDAN'S ALL AGES

267 Llanelli Coastal bike path

Why should you go?
With its rich dose of beach, dune, forest and estuary on this superb piece of cycle engineering, you'd be mad to miss out.

Where is it?
South Wales. One end lies at the castle town of Kidwelly, the other at Llanelli's Wildfowl & Wetland Centre.

Where can you ride?
The full 18-mile route follows the shoreline, at one point along tidal defences on the beach. Ride (west-east) from Kidwelly to the Wildfowl & Wetlands Centre at Llanelli. En route you'll pass through Pembrey Forest, Pembrey, Burry Port, Pwll and the Millennium Coastal Park. At Llanelli the route connects with the Clyne Valley trail to Swansea (256). The route is a popular part of the Celtic Trail (Fishguard to Chepstow). For a map and details call Sustrans on 0117 9290888 or the Celtic Trail Hotline on 0800 243731.

What else can you do?
Children can scamper around 'Watervole City' at the Wildfowl & Wetland reserve at Llanelli, which features a hands-on discovery centre. Call 01554 741087 for details.

Where can you eat?
At the cafe at Pembrey Country Park (just off route) or the Wildfowl & Wetlands Centre at Llanelli.

 OS Landranger Map 159

Choose Jersey!

Why it's the ideal destination for active families…

As invigorating and exhilarating as a day exploring new cycling trails can be, sometimes you can't help but be left wanting more, wishing your adventure would last a little longer.

The solution is simple: pack your bags, grab the kids and transform your next cycling trip into a full-blown family holiday. Though many potential destinations come into the reckoning, one stands head and shoulders above the competition. It's an island where breathtaking scenery surrounds ground-breaking cycling trails,

where beautiful beaches abound and the gastronomy hits heady heights. That island is, unmistakably, Jersey.

5 reasons
to spend a week on the island

1 Beaches

According to the Marine Conservation Society's *Good Beach Guide*, "with 55km of coastline ranging from high cliffs to sweeping bays and bathing waters which rate the highest EC standards, Jersey must count as a prime destination for the discerning beach lover". If sand and sea appeal, it pays to take advantage of Route One of Jersey's excellent 'Round Island Coastal Route'. Connecting most of the island's sandy stretches, Route One makes it easy to visit several beaches in a single day. One of the most dramatic lies to the west of the island, at

St Ouen's Bay, where Atlantic surf pounds a spectacular five-mile sandy stretch. The island's most beautiful beach lies a little further on at tiny Plemont Bay, where the kids can safely explore sandy-bottomed rockpools at low tide. And if it's safe, relaxed, swimming opportunities you're after, cycling further east will bring you to the uncrowded Anneport beach, Grouville Bay and Green Island, a south-facing suntrap with the softest sand on the island. Whichever beach you choose to explore, the coastal route will make your journey quick, easy and highly enjoyable.

2 Eating & drinking

When an island measuring just nine miles by five boasts more than 170 restaurants, cafes and bistros, locating a good place to eat is as simple as it sounds. Although almost every single ethnic option is available, given that you're holidaying on an island, locally caught seafood is highly recommended for being as fresh as it is delicious. Most notable, perhaps, are the Royal Bay oysters – so good they export them to the French. Standards and prices range from the cheap but cheerful to the Michelin-starred budget-busters. When it comes to

• *Sunset over the sea: Jersey boasts more than 55km of stunning coastline.*

drink, the choice is equally abundant. Real ale buffs with a good sense of timing (or sufficient forethought) will delight in CAMRA's annual Real Ale Festival. Throughout the year, however, most pubs stock an excellent range of beers which, thanks to lower tax rates on the island, are much cheaper than on the mainland. Generally, children are welcome in most public bars until 9pm.

3 Countryside

Thanks to its admirable planning laws and Island Plan, much of Jersey's countryside has remained as Mother Nature intended. Vast expanses of the island are comprised of open fields, woodland, cliffs and headland, small country lanes, trees and

• *Jersey's seafood is legendary.*

hedgerows. Such green-friendly initiatives have had a beneficial effect on the wildlife, with numerous rare species (Cetti's Warbler and the Dartford Warbler, for example) making their home on the island. To allow visiting cyclists to make the most of this, riding around the island has been made as simple as possible by the addition of two recent developments. As well as a

96-mile cycling route which takes in coastal and rural paths, Jersey also boasts the 'Green Lanes', a 45-mile network with a speed limit of 15mph, which gives priority to cyclists, walkers and horseriders over cars (see *Making The Most Of Cycling In Jersey*). Additionally, with the exception of St Helier and the arterial roads, most of Jersey's 450 miles of roads are quiet, largely traffic-free country lanes, making them similarly cyclist-friendly.

4 History & heritage

For such a small island, Jersey has an incredibly rich, varied and fascinating history. In painstaking detail, it's a history retold through an endless array of excellent museums, castles and sites of historical interest, each easily

• Most of Jersey's roads are quiet and virtually traffic-free.

reached by bike or on foot. As a mere tip-of-the-iceberg taster, your holiday may include a visit to…

● **La Cotte de St Brelade** Considered to be one of the most important Palaeolithic sites in Europe.

● **Mont Orgueil Castle and Elizabeth Castle** Built to defend the island against foreign invaders.

● **The German Underground Hospital** Created, on Adolf Hitler's orders, to deal with German casualties during WWII.

● **Jersey Museum** Home to an art gallery boasting some 4,000 paintings by Jersey artists or by artists visiting the island.

● **The Maritime Museum** Featuring the 'Shipwrecked' exhibition, including the 18th-century naval sloop 'Havick' as its centrepiece.

● **Hamptonne Country Life Museum** Where you'll find a fascinating taste of life in Jersey's 17th-century farming community.

5 Coastline

Though much of the island's 55km of coastline is rideable – with certain sections including purpose-built cycle routes – negotiating it on foot is often an easier option. However you travel, exploring the coastline will take you to a number of Jersey's most impressive attractions and a dozen exceptional bays.

The North Coast – sloping steeply in places – will bring you to two forts on either side of Bouley Bay and the North Coast Visitor Centre, housed in an old British garrison built during the Napoleonic wars at Greve de Lecq. Along the more open **West Coast** you will pass a collection of German fortifications, three defensive towers and, covering the whole of St Ouen's Bay from the shoreline to the top of the surrounding hills, Les Mielles, a wonderful area of natural beauty also known as Jersey's 'mini national park'.

• Mont Orgueil Castle.

Seymour Tower, built after the Battle of Jersey in 1782, can be found on the rocky **East Coast**, which is especially spectacular at low-tide, when a vast area of rocks, gullies and sand banks is uncovered. You can join in free, guided low-water 'Moon Walks' over the crater-like environment. The area is dominated by the 13th-century Mont Orgueil Castle and La Hougue Bie, one of the finest prehistoric monuments in western Europe.

USEFUL INFORMATION

• Currency
Although Jersey has its own coins and notes, all trade in Jersey is conducted in pounds sterling.
• Holidays & Opening Hours
Jersey has the same public holidays as the UK mainland, with an additional holiday on 9th May to celebrate Liberation Day. The markets and a number of shops are closed on Thursday afternoons, otherwise normal shopping hours apply (9am-5.30pm). During summer months a number of shops are open in the evenings. Public bar opening times are generally 9am-11pm (Monday-Saturday) and Sunday 11am-11pm.

CONTACT NUMBERS

• Jersey Tourism
01534 500777 or visit www.jersey.com
• Jersey Tourism (London Office) 0207 6308787
• Tourist Guides Association
01534 769546

MAIN EVENTS

Time your visit right and you'll be able to sample one of the Jersey's many annual events. Hosting 25 major festivals and 52 events each year – and covering everything from gardening to gastronomy, not to mention celebrations for '2002 Year Of The Cow' – there's truly something for everyone…

• International Air Display
One of Europe's largest free displays of military and civilian aircraft takes place on 12th September.

WHAT ELSE IS ON?
• Walking Festival
Two programmes in the company of qualified ramblers and guides: Spring Tides & Sunsets (21st-28th April) and Autumn Ambles (14th-21st September).
• Jazz Festival
Featuring tributes to Billy Holliday, Bob Crosby and Muggsy Spanier (2nd-5th May).
• International Food Festival
Celebrating its 21st year and offering a taste of the finest local produce and creations of some of the island's top chefs (11th-19th May).
• Battle of Flowers
Look out for two of the largest and most popular events in Jersey's tourism calendar, the Battle of Flowers (8th August) and the Moonlight Parade (9th August).
• Cycling Festival
A guided cycle programme on the island's 96-mile cycle network (6th-11th October). See *Making The Most Of Cycling In Jersey*.
• Jersey Garden Festival
Jersey's celebration of gardening and flowers. Date to be confirmed.
• International Arts Festival
Featuring a sculpture trail, craft fair, poetry readings, live music and street theatre. Date to be confirmed.

For further details and a full list of other festivals and events for 2002, call the Jersey Tourism on 01534 500742.

GETTING THERE

Sailing with **Condor Ferries** takes 12 hours, though a catamaran will have you there in a third of the time – call 0845 3452000 or visit www.condorferries.co.uk for more information. **British Airways** (0845 7733377, www.britishairways.com), **British European** (0870 5676676, www.flybe.com), **British Midlands** (0870 6070555, www.flybmi.com and **CITS** (01534 746181) all fly to Jersey. A return ticket costs from £100. British citizens don't need entry visas, although you should take your passport if you're planning a day trip to France.

Five great rides

Jersey is divided into five distinct cycling routes, each designed to allow cyclists to indulge in the island's geology, countryside, coastal views and inland valleys. All five are well worth exploring at length.

• St Aubin's Bay.

ROUTE A: The West

Why should you go?
Because this route takes in a number of Jersey's most significant landmarks, and you fancy riding the wide open spaces found throughout the island's west coast.

Where is it?
A picturesque circular route to and from St Aubin, taking in St Peter, St Ouen's Bay, Grosnez and Grantez en route.

Where can you ride?
The trail runs for 18 miles, starting and finishing at the Parish Flail in St Aubin. The full route is tracked in the cycling guide available from the Jersey Visitor Service Centre (01534 500777). Bear in mind, however, that the route is steep in places.

What else can you do?
Along the way you'll encounter St Aubin's Harbour, Grosnez Castle and St Ouen's Manor (open Tuesdays only), each of which is well worth exploring for an afternoon.

Where can you eat?
There are various cafes, pubs and restaurants in St Aubin and St Peter, plus facilities at St Peter's Garden Centre, La Forge Bar and the Portinfer Farm Tea Rooms.

MAKING THE MOST OF CYCLING IN JERSEY

Jersey's pioneering 'Green Lanes' and the 96 miles of cycle-friendly tracks make exploring every inch of the island a breeze. But to ensure your family make the most of your visit, it'll pay to follow five simple tips…

1. Hire your bikes when you get there
For around £25 per bike per week, you can save yourself considerable effort and space during your journey by hiring your bike on arrival in Jersey. Bike hire is offered throughout the island from these outlets in the following towns…

St Brelade: Harrington's Garage (01534 41363)
St Helier: Hireride (01534 31995), Holiday Autos & Rides (01534 888700), Jersey Walks (01534 69546), Kingslea Cycle Hire (01534 24777), Zebra Cycles (01534 736556)
St Mary: Jersey Cycle Tours (01534 482898)
St Lawrence: The Hire Shop (01534 873699)

Jersey

• *Liberation Square, St Helier.*

ROUTE B:
West Central

Why should you go?
Because you're looking for an easy-riding route which runs through a large chunk of Jersey's most beautiful countryside, passing through the picturesque Waterworks Valley as you go.

Where is it?
Through Waterworks Valley.
Where can you ride?
For 17 miles in total, between the Mont Félard Hotel at Millbrook in the Parish of St Lawrence and Rue de la Fontaine St Martin. The route gets hilly in places.
What else can you do?
There are numerous attractions en route, including Hamptonne Country Life Museum, the German Underground Hospital and La Mare Vineyards.
Where can you eat?
Stop-off points on this route include most of the visitor attractions, some of the National Trust's properties and several good pubs and cafes.

ROUTE C:
Trinity Lane and Zoo

Why should you go?
To sample some of Jersey's more demanding cycling. The route is extremely steep in places and climbs 149 metres up to the highest point of the island.

Where is it?
Between Vallée des Vaux and Grands Vaux, with numerous picturesque villages in between.

Where can you ride?
From Vallée des Vaux to Grands Vaux is a 15-mile journey.

What else can you do?
Drop in for an afternoon's entertainment at either Pallot's Steam Museum, Jersey Zoo or The Eric Young Orchid Foundation, all of which you'll pass on your journey.

Where can you eat?
Both the Zoo and the Orchid Foundation serve good food and drinks, and there are several decent pubs, cafés and restaurants in both Bonne Nuit Bay and Bouley Bay.

2. Buy the local guide to cycling
The next best thing to slipping a knowledgeable local in your rucksack (and considerably lighter), the *Jersey Cycling Guide* provides you with the essential details you'll need during your visit. Priced £2.50 and available from the Jersey Visitor Service Centre (Liberation Square, St Helier, 01534 500777), the guide outlines the island's five suggested cycle routes (see *Five Great Rides*) and includes maps, suggested itineraries, refreshment stops, attractions and heritage sites to visit en route. Jersey's traditions and history are also included, alongside cycle safety tips, bike hire contacts and emergency repairs advice. A dedicated cycle map, priced £1, is also available from Jersey Tourism.

3. Book a cycle tour
The kind people at Jersey Tourism are determined to make your visit as pleasurable as possible. Not content with producing several visitor guides, they also offer cyclists a variety of free tours accompanied by a qualified and knowledgeable guide. Departing from Jersey Tourism's Visitor Centre at 10am every Monday, Wednesday, Friday and Sunday morning (until the end of September), each tour lasts between two and three hours and is limited to approximately 20 people on a first come, first served basis. All they ask is that you bring your own bikes.

• Jersey Zoo.

Jersey

• Take time to stop and admire the Jersey countryside...

ROUTE D:
North Central

Why should you go?
Because you relish the challenge of one of Jersey's hillier routes, and while you're up on the higher ground, you want to take advantage of the brilliant views you're afforded of Gorey Castle.

Where is it?
St Saviour.

Where can you ride?
This 18.5-mile route starts and finishes at Longueville Manor Hotel in St Saviour.

What else can you do?
Queen's Valley Reservoir is worth exploring, and the excellent Jersey Zoo is a particular favourite with visiting youngsters.

Where can you eat?
The Royal, in St Martin, is a country pub with a good restaurant. Refreshments are available at the Zoo, plus there are several cafes and restaurants in Bonne Nuit Bay, though it's a diversion down and up a steep hill to reach them.

ROUTE E:
East About

Why should you go?
Because this is the fifth and final part of Jersey's cycling set, and you want to be able to say you've cycled them all, don't you? If one-upmanship doesn't drive you on, there's also the chance to cycle through Grouville Marsh, a nature reserve which attracts many migrant birds during the winter months.

Where is it?
At St Clement.

Where can you ride?
On a circular 18-mile route which starts and finishes at St Clement's Recreation Grounds. The few steep sections are worth the effort simply for the view you'll enjoy when you reach the top.

What else can you do?
En route attractions abound on this route, from La Rocque Harbour and Jersey Pottery, to St Catherine's Harbour and historic Samarès Manor.

Where can you eat?
You'll find plenty of choice along the way. Both Grouville Taverne and Pembroke Hotel offer good food, as do the Anne Port Bay Hotel, Jeffrey's Leap Cafe, Archirondel Cafe and Samarès Manor. There's also the option to stop and refuel at the Jersey Pottery and Ransoms Garden Centre.

4. Follow the 'Green Lanes'
In 1994, in an admirable attempt to make cycling as safe and enjoyable as possible for residents and visitors, Jersey introduced its pioneering 'Green Lanes' network, the brainchild of the Constable of St Peter. Running for approximately 45 miles through ten of the island's parishes, these scenic lanes give cyclists (along with walkers and horseriders) priority over cars by virtue of a 15mph speed limit. Winding – via a series of distinctive road-signs – down a variety of scenic inland and coastal routes, the network has rightly attracted attention and praise from all over Europe for putting cyclists before cars.

5. Visit during the Cycle Festival
If you visit the island between 6th-11th of October this year, you may well think you've arrived in cycling heaven. On top of the all-year-round cycling-friendly initiatives the island already offers, you'll also have chance to indulge your-selves in Jersey's inaugural Cycle Festival. Designed to entertain visitors of all ages and cycling abilities, the festival features guided rides through picturesque coun-tryside, stopping off at medieval castles and quiet beaches, before winding down in the evenings with barbecues and a host of sim-ilar social events. For more information call Jersey Tourism on 01534 500777.

...or head to the beach for a picnic.

Pedal

Power.

W. Jordan (Cereals) Ltd., Holme Mills, Biggleswade, Bedfordshire SG18 9JY Tel: (01767) 318222 Fax: (01767) 600695

Discover the world of
Ordnance Survey maps...

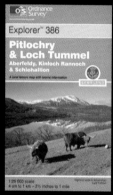  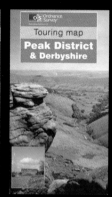 

...your passport to Great Britain

Choosing the right map can help you make the most of your leisure time, and with around 1,000 different titles, there's an Ordnance Survey map for every purpose and every place! Whether you enjoy exploring, outdoor activities or are simply mad about maps, our comprehensive product range, covering the whole of Great Britain, has something to interest you.

OS Landranger maps

Packed full of useful information such as selected places of interest, tourist offices and camping and picnic sites, an OS Landranger map is your passport to both town and country. Covering an area of 40km by 40km (25 miles by 25 miles), it is perfect for planning great days out, whether you are a visitor or a local resident.

Explorer maps

Whether you are looking for adventure, action or inspiration, a highly-detailed Ordnance Survey

Explorer map will point you in the right direction. Ideal for keen walkers, cyclists and hikers, it's your essential companion for outdoor activities.

Road maps

Gear up and go with our regional Road maps or, for a national trip, choose our Great Britain Routeplanner map. Containing all the information you need to plan your route for leisure or business, they will help you to find directions and distances as well as destinations.

Touring Maps

Get set for a summer of fun with Ordnance Survey's range of Touring maps. Simple to use, with clear and easy mapping, they are ideal for anyone needing a helping hand to discover some of Britain's best-loved holiday areas.

Ordnance Survey maps can be ordered online at www.ordnancesurvey.co.uk /leisure or from all good bookshops, outdoor leisure shops and tourist information centres.

Your passport to a place with a view

All you need is a new OS Landranger Map to discover Britain's scenic highways and by-ways.

Whether you want to cycle by the coast or take a short country break, the new-look OS Landranger Map gives you all the information you need.

Ordnance Survey®

Your passport to town and country

For your nearest stockist, ring 08456 050505 or visit www.ordnancesurvey.co.uk

Index of attractions

• *HMS Warrior, Portsmouth Harbour.*

www.britainonview.com

C

• *Stratford-upon-Avon's
Teddy Bear Museum.*

www.britainonview.com

D

• *Heights of Abraham cable car, Matlock Bath.*

www.britainonview.com

• *Slimbridge Wildfowl & Wetland Centre.*

• "Giant Chair" by
Magdalena Jetelova,
in the Forest of Dean.

O

P

• *The Kennet & Avon Canal.*

Q

R